A PRIMER ON POSTMODERNISM

A PRIMER
on
POSTMODERNISM

Stanley J. Grenz

WILLIAM B. EERDMANS PUBLISHING COMPANY
GRAND RAPIDS, MICHIGAN / CAMBRIDGE U.K.

© 1996 Wm. B. Eerdmans Publishing Co.
255 Jefferson Ave. S.E., Grand Rapids, Michigan 49503 /
P.O. Box 163, Cambridge CB3 9PU U.K.

Printed in the United States of America

12 11 10 09 08 07 06   19 18 17 16 15 14 13

Library of Congress Cataloging-in-Publication Data

Grenz, Stanley, 1950-
A primer on postmodernism / Stanley Grenz.
        p.   cm.
Includes bibliographical references and index.
ISBN-10: 0-8028-0864-6 / ISBN-13: 978-0-8028-0864-6 (pbk.: alk. paper)
1. Postmodernism. I. Title.
B831.2.G74   1995
149 — dc20   95-39733
                                          CIP

To Leighton Ford

*a visionary Christian
dedicated to developing leaders
for a postmodern world*

Contents

Preface

"Would you come to Charlotte, North Carolina, October 26-28, 1993, to be one of about a dozen participants in a 'think tank' on ministry to 'baby busters'?" asked Tom Hawkes of Leighton Ford Ministries.

"You've got the wrong person," I protested. "I'm an academician, not a practitioner."

"That's exactly why we want you to be there," came the response. "We practitioners need you to help us understand what postmodernism is all about."

"Postmodernism." This was not exactly a new word in my vocabulary. Indeed, in two of my books I had already raised the question of the shape of evangelical theology in the emerging postmodern context. But the upcoming meeting in Charlotte launched me into a concerted effort to come to understand what — if anything — this term actually means.

The Charlotte experience triggered the idea for a book, a "primer" to assist students, church leaders, youth workers, and even colleagues in understanding the attitude or mind-set that is becoming increasingly prevalent in North America, especially (but not exclusively) on university campuses. Preliminary telephone calls to several publishers (including Jon Pott at Eerdmans Publishing Company) and follow-up discussions at the American Academy of Religion gathering (November 1993) netted keen interest in the project.

Meanwhile came a suggestion from Prof. David Dockery that I present a paper at the Southeastern Regional meeting of the Evangelical Theological Society, scheduled to be held on the campus of the Southern Baptist Theological Seminary in March 1994. The Charlotte experience provided the foundation for an essay, "*Star Trek* and the Next Generation: Postmodernism and the Future of Evangelical Theology."

This essay appeared in our Regent College quarterly journal, *Crux* (30/1 [Mar 1994]), and evoked an astounding response. It has since been reprinted several times, including in the collection of essays from the ETS meeting, *The Challenge of Postmodernism: An Evangelical Engagement* (ed. David S. Dockery [Wheaton, Ill.: BridgePoint, 1995]).

With this preliminary study behind me, I proceeded to immerse myself in postmodernism. I wanted to understand both what the intellectuals of the movement were saying and how pervasive the postmodern ethos is in our culture. An invitation to offer a course at NISET '94, the national training program of InterVarsity Christian Fellowship, provided both a deadline for finishing the initial draft of my findings and a context in which to field test the results. You are now reading a revised version of that material.

This *Primer on Postmodernism* follows a somewhat unusual format. You might view Chapters 1 and 7 as something like bookends. The opening chapter, "*Star Trek* and the Postmodern Generation," presents in embryonic form all the material that is treated in the book as a whole. And the concluding chapter, "The Gospel and the Postmodern Context," offers a condensed response to postmodernism, a preliminary answer to the question "So what?" If postmodernism is unfamiliar to you, you may want to read these bookends first.

In Chapters 2 and 3 I describe the postmodern situation in general, addressing the question, "What is all the noise about anyway?" This section should alert you to the broader intellectual and cultural ethos that increasingly forms the context in which we live and minister today.

The really heady material comes in Chapters 4, 5, and 6. Postmodernism is, in the end, an intellectual develpment, and in this section I survey the intellectual forces that have led many in our society to reject modernity and launch into the uncharted waters of postmodernity. At the apex of this discussion is a presentation of the thought of three major postmodern gurus: Michel Foucault, Jacques Derrida, and Richard Rorty (Chap. 6).

You will note that although the *Primer* is generously documented, the text itself contains no lengthy quotations. When I read, I tend to skip over such materials in books like this one. My primary goal is typically to find out what an *author* says about the topic at hand, not to wade through the cited opinions of others. I'm assuming that if you had wanted to grapple with the writings of such postmodernists as Foucault, Derrida, or Rorty, you would have gone directly to them instead of to this primer. My purpose here is to provide an overview of the primary material and supply basic tools for understanding the topic. I hope that this preliminary discussion will assist and encourage you to read the primary authors later.

In an effort to give you something of the flavor of the work of the major voices in the intellectual discussion, I have sprinkled the *Primer* with quotations from representative works. These quotations are not a part of the body of the text but rather stand alongside it. I hope they will serve to establish a kind of dialogue with the text as you read through them both. And perhaps they will intrigue you enough to make you want to read more in the cited authors' works.

As you read the *Primer*, keep in mind its primary purpose. My goal is to provide a foundational understanding of the postmodern ethos, especially its intellectual orientation. Postmodernism is surely open to serious critique and has been challenged on a number of fronts by a variety of scholars. Christians must not fail in the end to engage postmodernism critically where that is required. At the same time, they must also be open to what postmodernism can teach us positively as a needed corrective to modernity. And in either case, we must first of all thoroughly and fairly understand the emerging intellectual ethos if we are to embody and proclaim the gospel convincingly in the postmodern situation.

I am not in a position to specify precisely how Christians should engage in ministry to the postmodern generation. I am, after all, an academic. I leave to seasoned practitioners — like you — the task of moving from an understanding of, to ministry to, the *Star Trek* generation.

Finally, I wish to acknowledge the support and assistance of many people in the production of this *Primer:* the staff at Carey Theological

College, especially my teaching assistant George Capaque; the people at Eerdmans, especially Jon Pott who encouraged me in this effort and Tim Straayer who shouldered the editing task; but above all students in the Carey/Regent community and in other academic institutions who have participated in my courses, IVCF workers at seminars I have led, and congregants in various churches where I have spoken on this subject, all of whom have listened patiently (and sometimes impatiently) and have helped me hone my own understanding of this complex phenomenon we call "postmodernism." The postmodern ethos explodes the concept of the solitary author, and I acknowledge that each of these persons has played some authorial role in producing this *Primer*.

in omnibus glorificetur Deus
"in everything, may God be glorified"

CHAPTER 1

Star Trek *and the* *Postmodern Generation*

The camera focuses on a futuristic spacecraft against the background of distant galaxies. The narrator's voice proudly recites the guiding dictum: "Space — the final frontier. These are the voyages of the starship *Enterprise*. Its continuing mission — to explore strange new worlds, to seek out new life and new civilizations, to boldly go where no one has gone before."

With these words began each episode of the popular television series *Star Trek: The Next Generation,* which completed its final season in May 1994.

In many ways *The Next Generation* was simply an updated version of the earlier *Star Trek* series, placed in a future era, after the resolution of some of the galactic political difficulties that plagued the universe of the previous space voyagers. Yet, sometime after Jean-Luc Picard's new breed of explorers took over the command of the redesigned *Enterprise* from Captain Kirk's crew, the creators of the series discovered that the world of their audience was in the midst of a subtle paradigm shift: modernity was giving birth to postmodernity. As a result, *The Next Generation* became a reflection — perhaps even a molder — of the worldview of the emerging generation.

The shifts evident in the transition from *Star Trek* to *Star Trek: The Next Generation* reflect a deeper transition occurring in Western society.

1

The Movement from Modernity to Postmodernity

Many social observers agree that the Western world is in the midst of change. In fact, we are apparently experiencing a cultural shift that rivals the innovations that marked the birth of modernity out of the decay of the Middle Ages: we are in the midst of a transition from the modern to the postmodern era.[1] Of course, transitional periods are exceedingly difficult to describe and assess. Nor is it fully evident what will characterize the emerging epoch.[2] Nevertheless, we see signs that monumental changes are engulfing all aspects of contemporary culture.

The term *postmodern* may first have been coined in the 1930s to refer to a major historical transition already under way[3] and as the designation for certain developments in the arts.[4] But postmodernism did not gain widespread attention until the 1970s. First it denoted a new style of architecture. Then it invaded academic circles, originally as a label for theories expounded in university English and philosophy departments. Eventually it surfaced as the description for a broader cultural phenomenon.

Whatever else it might be, as the name suggests, postmodernism signifies the quest to move beyond modernism. Specifically, it involves a rejection of the modern mind-set, but launched under the conditions of modernity. Therefore, to understand postmodern thinking, we must view it in the context of the modern world that gave it birth and against which it is reacting.

The Modern Mind

Many historians place the birth of the modern era at the dawn of the Enlightenment, which followed the Thirty Years' War. The stage, however, was set earlier — in the Renaissance, which elevated humankind to the center of reality. Characteristic of the new outlook was Francis Bacon's vision of humans exercising power over nature by means of the discovery of nature's secrets.

Building on the Renaissance, the Enlightenment elevated the individual self to the center of the world.[5] René Descartes laid the philosophical foundation for the modern edifice with his focus on doubt, which led him to conclude that the existence of the thinking self is the first truth that doubt cannot deny — a principle formulated in his reappropriation of Augustine's dictum *Cogito ergo sum.* Descartes thus defined human nature as a thinking substance and the human person as an autonomous rational subject. Isaac Newton later provided the scientific framework for modernity, picturing the physical world as a machine the laws and regularity of which could be discerned by the human mind. The modern human can appropriately be characterized as Descartes's autonomous, rational substance encountering Newton's mechanistic world.

The Enlightenment Project. The postulates of the thinking self and the mechanistic universe opened the way for the explosion of knowledge under the banner of what Jürgen Habermas called the "Enlightenment project." It became the goal of the human intellectual quest to unlock the secrets of the universe in order to master nature for human benefit and create a better world. This quest led to the modernity characteristic of the twentieth century, which has sought to bring rational management to life in order to improve human existence through technology.[6]

The project of modernity, formulated in the eighteenth century by the Enlightenment *philosophes,* consists of a relentless development of the objectivating sciences, the universalistic bases of morality and law, and autonomous art in accordance with their internal logic but at the same time a release of the cognitive potentials thus accumulated from their esoteric high forms and their utilisation in praxis; that is, in the rational organisation of living conditions and social relations. Proponents of the Enlightenment . . . still held the extravagant expectation that the arts and sciences would further not only the control of the forces of nature but also the understanding of self and world, moral progress, justice in social institutions, and even human happiness.

Jürgen Habermas, "Modernity: An Unfinished Project,"
in *The Post-Modern Reader,* ed. Charles Jencks
(New York: St. Martin's Press, 1992), pp. 162-63.

3

At the intellectual foundation of the Enlightenment project are certain epistemological assumptions. Specifically, the modern mind assumes that knowledge is certain, objective, and good.[7] Moreover, moderns assume that, in principle, knowledge is accessible to the human mind.

The demand for certain knowledge sets the modern inquirer in search of a method of demonstrating the essential correctness of philosophic, scientific, religious, moral, and political doctrines.[8] The Enlightenment method places the many aspects of reality under the scrutiny of reason and assesses it on the basis of that criterion.[9] That is to say that this method exercises an absolute faith in human rational capabilities.

The Enlightenment perspective assumes that knowledge is not only certain (and hence rational) but also objective. The assumption of objectivity leads the modernist to claim access to dispassionate knowledge. Modern knowers profess to be more than merely conditioned participants in the world they observe: they claim to be able to view the world as unconditioned observers — that is, to survey the world from a vantage point outside the flux of history.[10]

The pursuit of dispassionate knowledge divides the scientific project into separate disciplines[11] and gives special status to the specialist, the neutral observer who has gained expertise in a limited field of endeavor.

In addition to assuming that knowledge is certain and objective, Enlightenment thinkers also assume that it is inherently good. The modern scientist, for example, considers it axiomatic that the discovery of knowledge is always good. This assumption of the inherent goodness of knowledge renders the Enlightenment outlook optimistic. It leads to the belief that progress is inevitable, that science, coupled with the power of education, will eventually free us from our vulnerability to nature, as well as from all social bondage.

Enlightenment optimism, together with the focus on reason, elevates on human freedom. Suspect are all beliefs that seem to curtail autonomy or to be based on some external authority rather than reason (and experience). The Enlightenment project understands freedom largely in individual terms. In fact, the modern ideal champions the autonomous self, the self-determining subject who exists outside any tradition or community.[12]

Modernity and Star Trek. Like modern fiction in general, the original *Star Trek* series reflected many aspects of the Enlightenment project and of late modernity. The crew of the *Enterprise* included persons of various nationalities working together for the common benefit of humankind. They were the epitome of the modern universalist anthropology. The message was obvious: we are all human, and we must overcome our differences and join forces in order to complete our mandate, the quest for certain, objective knowledge of the entire universe of which space looms as "the final frontier."

One hero of the old *Star Trek* was Spock. Although he was the only crew member who came from another planet (he was part human, part Vulcan), in his nonhumanness he actually served as a transcendent human ideal. Spock was the ideal Enlightenment man, completely rational and without emotion (or at least able to hold his emotions in check). His dispassionate rationality repeatedly provided the key to solving problems encountered by the crew of the *Enterprise*. In such cases, the writers appear to have been arguing that in the end our problems can be solved by the application of rational expertise.

Postmodernism represents a rejection of the Enlightenment project and the foundational assumptions upon which it was built.

The Postmodern Mind

Modernity has been under attack at least since Friedrich Nietzsche (1844-1900) lobbed the first volley against it late in the nineteenth century, but the full-scale frontal assault did not begin until the 1970s. The immediate intellectual impulse for the dismantling of the Enlightenment project came from the rise of deconstruction as a literary theory, which influenced a new movement in philosophy.

Philosophical Postmodernism. Deconstruction arose as an extension of a theory in literature called "structuralism."

Structuralists argue that language is a social construct and that people develop literary documents — texts — in an attempt to provide structures of meaning that will help them make sense out of the meaninglessness of their experience. Structuralists maintain that literature provides categories that help us to organize and understand our expe-

5

rience of reality. They also contend that all societies and cultures possess a common, invariant structure.[13]

The deconstructionists (or poststructuralists) reject this last tenet of structuralism. Meaning is not inherent in a text itself, they argue, but emerges only as the interpreter enters into dialogue with the text.[14] And because the meaning of a text is dependent on the perspective of the one who enters into dialogue with it, it has as many meanings as it has readers (or readings).

Postmodern philosophers applied the theories of the literary deconstructionists to the world as a whole. Just as a text will be read differently by each reader, they said, so reality will be "read" differently by each knowing self that encounters it. This means that there is no one meaning of the world, no transcendent center to reality as a whole.

On the basis of ideas such as these, the French philosopher Jacques Derrida calls for abandonment of both "onto-theology" (the attempt to set forth ontological descriptions of reality) and the "metaphysics of presence" (the idea that something transcendent is present in reality).[15] Because nothing transcendent inheres in reality, he argues, all that emerges in the knowing process is the perspective of the self who interprets reality.

Michel Foucault adds a moral twist to Derrida's call. Foucault asserts that every interpretation of reality is an assertion of power. Because "knowledge" is always the result of the use of power,[16] to name something is to exercise power and hence to do violence to what is named. Social institutions inevitably engage in violence when they impose their own understanding on the centerless flux of experience, he says. Thus, in contrast to Bacon, who sought knowledge in order to gain power over nature, Foucault claims that every assertion of knowledge is an act of power.

Richard Rorty, in turn, jettisons the classic conception of truth as either the mind or language mirroring nature. Truth is established neither by the correspondence of an assertion with objective reality nor by the internal coherence of the assertions themselves, says Rorty. He argues that we should simply give up the search for truth and be content with interpretation. He proposes replacing classic "systematic philosophy" with "edifying philosophy," which "aims at continuing a conversation rather than at discovering truth."[17]

The work of Derrida, Foucault, and Rorty reflects what seems to have become the central dictum of postmodern philosophy: "All is difference." This view sweeps away the "uni" of the "universe" sought by the Enlightenment project. It abandons the quest for a unified grasp of objective reality. It asserts that the world has no center, only differing viewpoints and perspectives. In fact, even the concept of "world" presupposes an objective unity or a coherent whole that does not exist "out there." In the end, the postmodern world is merely an arena of "duelling texts."

The Postmodern Mood. Although philosophers such as Derrida, Foucault, and Rorty are influential on university campuses, they form only a part of a larger shift in thinking reflected in Western culture. What unifies the otherwise diverse strands of postmodernism is the questioning of the central assumptions of the Enlightenment epistemology.

In the postmodern world, people are no longer convinced that knowledge is inherently good. In eschewing the Enlightenment myth of inevitable progress, postmodernism replaces the optimism of the last century with a gnawing pessimism. Gone is the belief that every day, in every way, we are getting better and better. Members of the emerging generation are no longer confident that humanity will be able to solve the world's great problems or even that their economic situation will surpass that of their parents. They view life on earth as fragile and believe that the continued existence of humankind is dependent on a new attitude of cooperation rather than conquest.

The emphasis on holism among postmoderns is related to their rejection of the second Enlightenment assumption — namely, that truth is certain and hence purely rational. The postmodern mind refuses to limit truth to its rational dimension and thus dethrones the human intellect as the arbiter of truth. There are other valid paths to knowledge besides reason, say the postmoderns, including the emotions and the intuition.

Finally, the postmodern mind no longer accepts the Enlightenment belief that knowledge is objective. Knowledge cannot be merely objective, say the postmoderns, because the universe is not mechanistic and dualistic but rather historical, relational, and personal. The world is not simply an objective given that is "out there," waiting to be discovered and known; reality is relative, indeterminate, and participatory.

7

In rejecting the modern assumption of the objectivity of knowledge, postmoderns also reject the Enlightenment ideal of the dispassionate, autonomous knower. They contend that the work of scientists, like that of any other human beings, is historically and culturally conditioned and that our knowledge is always incomplete.

The postmodern worldview operates with a community-based understanding of truth. It affirms that whatever we accept as truth and even the way we envision truth are dependent on the community in which we participate. Further, and far more radically, the postmodern worldview affirms that this relativity extends beyond our *perceptions* of truth to its essence: there is no absolute truth; rather, truth is relative to the community in which we participate.

On the basis of this assumption, postmodern thinkers have given up the Enlightenment quest for any one universal, supracultural, timeless truth. They focus instead on what is held to be true within a specific community. They maintain that truth consists in the ground rules that facilitate the well-being of the community in which one participates. In keeping with this emphasis, postmodern society tends to be a communal society.

Postmodernism and The Next Generation. The postmodern perspective is reflected in the second *Star Trek* series, *The Next Generation*. The crew of the later *Enterprise* is more diverse than that of the original, including species from other parts of the universe. This change represents the broader universality of postmodernity: humankind is no

---

The post-industrial society . . . is also a "communal" society in which the social unit is the community rather than the individual, and one has to achieve a "social decision" as against, simply, the sum total of individual decisions which, when aggregated, end up as nightmares, on the mode of the individual automobile and collective traffic congestion.

Daniel Bell, "The Coming of the Post-Industrial Society," in *The Post-Modern Reader,* ed. Charles Jencks (New York: St. Martin's Press, 1992), p. 264.

---

longer the only advanced intelligence, for evolution has been operative throughout the cosmos. More importantly, the understanding of the quest for knowledge has changed. Humankind is not capable of completing the mandate alone; nor does the burden of the quest fall to humans alone. The crew of the *Enterprise* symbolizes the "new ecology" of humankind in partnership with the universe. Their mission is no longer to boldly go "where no *man* has gone before" but "where no *one* has gone before."

In *The Next Generation*, Spock is replaced by Data, an android. In a sense, Data is a more fully realized version of the rational thinker than Spock, capable of superhuman intellectual feats. Nevertheless, despite his seemingly perfect intellect, he is not the transcendent human ideal that Spock embodies, because he is a machine. Unlike Spock, he desires not only to understand what it means to be human but in fact to become human. He believes he is somehow incomplete because he lacks such things as a sense of humor, emotion, and the ability to dream (and, indeed, he feels that he has become more complete when he later discovers that his maker programmed a capacity to dream into his circuitry.)

Although Data often provides valuable assistance in dealing with problems, he is only one of several who contribute to finding solutions. In addition to the "master of rationality," the *Enterprise* crew includes persons skilled in the affective and intuitive dimensions of human life. Especially prominent is Counselor Troi, a woman gifted with the ability to perceive the hidden feelings of others.[18]

The new voyages of the *Enterprise* lead its variegated crew into a postmodern universe. In this new world, time is no longer simply linear, appearance is not necessarily reality, and the rational is not always to be trusted.

In contrast to the older series, which in typical modern fashion generally ignores questions of God and religious belief, the postmodern world of *The Next Generation* shows interest in the supernatural, embodied, for example, in the strange character "Q." Yet its picture of the divine is not simply that of traditional Christian theology. Although possessing the classical divine attributes of omniscience and omnipotence, the godlike being "Q" is morally ambiguous, displaying both benevolence and a bent toward cynicism and self-gratification.

Postmodernity and Evangelical Christianity

As George Marsden correctly concludes, in some sense evangelicalism — with its focus on scientific thinking, the empirical approach, and common sense — is a child of early modernity.[19] But our society is in the throes of a monumental transition, moving from modernity to postmodernity. The emerging generation has been nurtured in a context shaped less by commitment to the Enlightenment project embodied in *Star Trek* than by the postmodern vision of Rorty and *Star Trek: The Next Generation.*

The transition from the modern era to the postmodern era poses a grave challenge to the church in its mission to its own next generation. Confronted by this new context, we dare not fall into the trap of wistfully longing for a return to the early modernity that gave evangelicalism its birth, for we are called to minister not to the past but to the contemporary context, and our contemporary context is influenced by postmodern ideas.

Postmodernism poses certain dangers. Nevertheless, it would be ironic — indeed, it would be tragic — if evangelicals ended up as the last defenders of the now dying modernity. To reach people in the new postmodern context, we must set ourselves to the task of deciphering the implications of postmodernism for the gospel.

Imbued with the vision of God's program for the world, we must claim the new postmodern context for Christ by embodying the Christian faith in ways that the new generation can understand. In short, under the banner of the cross, we must "boldly go where no one has gone before."

CHAPTER 2

The Postmodern Ethos

Postmodernism was born in St. Louis, Missouri, on July 15, 1972, at 3:32 P.M.

When it was originally built, the Pruitt-Igoe housing project in St. Louis was hailed as a landmark of modern architecture. More importantly, it stood as the epitome of modernity itself in its goal of employing technology to create a utopian society for the benefit of all. But its unimpressed inhabitants vandalized the buildings. Government planners put a lot of effort into attempts to renovate the project. But finally, having sacrificed millions of dollars to the project, the government planners gave up. On that fateful afternoon in mid-July 1972, the building was razed with dynamite. According to Charles Jencks, who has been hailed as the "single most influential proponent of architectural postmodernism,"[1] this event symbolizes the death of modernity and birth of postmodernity.[2]

Our society is in the throes of a cultural shift of immense proportions. Like the Pruitt-Igoe housing project, the edifice that housed thought and culture in the modern era is crumbling. As modernity dies around us, we appear to be entering a new epoch — postmodernity.

The postmodern phenomenon encompasses many dimensions of contemporary society. At the core of them all, however, is an intellectual mood or outlook, an "ism" — "postmodernism."

Scholars disagree among themselves as to what postmodernism involves, but they have have reached a consensus on one point: this phenomenon marks the end of a single, universal worldview. The postmodern ethos resists unified, all-encompassing, and universally valid explanations. It replaces these with a respect for difference and a celebration of the local and particular at the expense of the universal.[3] Postmodernism likewise entails a rejection of the emphasis on rational discovery through the scientific method, which provided the intellectual foundation for the modern attempt to construct a better world. At its foundation, then, the postmodern outlook is anti-modern.

But the adjective *postmodern* describes more than an intellectual mood. The postmodern rejection of the focus on rationality characteristic of the modern era finds expression in various dimensions of contemporary society. In recent years, the postmodern mind-set has been reflected in many of the traditional vehicles of cultural expression, including architecture, art, and theater. In addition, postmodernism has increasingly become embodied in the broader society. We can detect a shift away from the modern toward the postmodern in pop culture ranging from disjunctive music videos to the new *Star Trek* series and even in the day-to-day aspects of contemporary life, such as the new quest for spirituality in the marketplace and the juxtaposing of different styles in the clothes many people wear.

Postmodernism refers to an intellectual mood and an array of cultural expressions that call into question the ideals, principles, and values that lay at the heart of the modern mind-set. *Postmodernity*, in turn, refers to an emerging epoch, the era in which we are living, the time when the postmodern outlook increasingly shapes our society. Postmodernity is the era in which postmodern ideas, attitudes, and values reign — when postmodernism molds culture. It is the era of the postmodern society.

Our goal in this chapter is to look more closely at the broader postmodern phenomenon and understand something of the ethos of postmodernity. What characterizes the cultural expressions and the broader day-to-day dimensions of the world of the "next generation"? What evidence is there that a new intellectual mind-set is shaping life in our society?

The Postmodern Phenomenon

Postmodernism refers to the intellectual mood and cultural expressions that are becoming increasingly dominant in contemporary society. We are apparently moving into a new cultural epoch, postmodernity, but we must pinpoint in greater detail what the postmodern phenomenon entails.

The Postmodern Consciousness

The early evidences of the basic ethos of postmodernism have been largely negative. This ethos flows from a radical rejection of the Enlightenment mind-set that gave rise to modernity. We can find traces of the postmodern ethos everywhere in our society. Above all, however, it pervades the consciousness of the emerging generation, and it constitutes a radical break with the assumptions of the past.

The postmodern consciousness has abandoned the Enlightenment belief in inevitable progress. Postmoderns have not sustained the optimism that characterized previous generations. To the contrary, they evidence a gnawing pessimism. For the first time in recent history, the emerging generation does not share the conviction of their parents that the world is becoming a better place in which to live. From widening holes in the ozone layer to teen-on-teen violence, they see our problems mounting. And they are no longer convinced that human ingenuity will solve these enormous problems or that their living standard will be higher than that of their parents.

The postmodern generation is also convinced that life on the earth is fragile. They believe that the Enlightenment model of the human conquest of nature, which dates to Francis Bacon, must quickly give way to a new attitude of cooperation with the earth. They believe that the survival of humankind is now at stake.

In addition to its dark pessimism, the postmodern consciousness operates with a view of truth different from what previous generations espoused.

The modern understanding linked truth with rationality and made reason and logical argumentation the sole arbiters of right belief. Postmoderns question the concept of universal truth discovered and proved through rational endeavors. They are unwilling to allow the human intellect to serve as the sole determiner of what we should believe. Postmoderns look beyond reason to nonrational ways of knowing, conferring heightened status on the emotions and intuition.

The quest for a cooperative model and an appreciation of nonrational dimensions of truth lend a holistic dimension to the postmodern consciousness. Postmodern holism entails a rejection of the Enlightenment ideal of the dispassionate, autonomous, rational individual. Postmoderns do not seek to be wholly self-directed individuals but rather "whole" persons.

Postmodern holism entails an integration of all the dimensions of personal life — affective and intuitive as well as cognitive. Wholeness also entails a consciousness of the indelible and delicate connection to what lies beyond ourselves, in which our personal existence is embedded and from which it is nurtured. This wider realm includes "nature" (the ecosystem), of course. But in addition it involves the community of humans in which we participate. Postmoderns are keenly conscious of the importance of community, of the social dimension of existence. And the postmodern conception of wholeness also extends to the religious or spiritual aspect of life. Indeed, postmoderns affirm that personal existence may transpire within the context of a divine reality.

The conviction that each person is embedded in a particular human community leads to a corporate understanding of truth. Postmoderns believe that not only our specific beliefs but also our understanding of truth itself is rooted in the community in which we participate. They reject the Enlightenment quest for universal, supracultural, timeless truth in favor of searching out truth as the expression of a specific community. They believe that truth consists in the ground rules that facilitate personal well-being in community and the well-being of the community as a whole.

In this sense, then, postmodern truth is relative to the community in which a person participates. And since there are many human communities, there are necessarily many different truths. Most postmoderns make the leap of believing that this plurality of truths can exist alongside one another. The postmodern consciousness, therefore, entails a radical kind of relativism and pluralism.

Of course, relativism and pluralism are not new. But the post modern variety differs from the older forms. The relativistic pluralism of late modernity was highly individualistic; it elevated personal taste and personal choice as the be-all and end-all. Its maxims were "To each his/her own" and "Everyone has a right to his/her own opinion."

The postmodern consciousness, in contrast, focuses on the group. Postmoderns live in self-contained social groups, each of which has its own language, beliefs, and values. As a result, postmodern relativistic pluralism seeks to give place to the "local" nature of truth. Beliefs are held to be true within the context of the communities that espouse them.

The postmodern understanding of truth leads postmoderns to be less concerned than their forebears to think systematically or logically. Just as some people feel comfortable mixing elements of what traditionally has been considered incompatible clothing styles, postmoderns feel comfortable mixing elements of what have traditionally been considered incompatible belief systems. For example, a postmodern Christian may affirm both the classic doctrines of the church and such traditionally non-Christian ideas as reincarnation.

Nor are postmoderns necessarily concerned to prove themselves "right" and others "wrong." They believe that beliefs are ultimately a matter of social context, and hence they are likely to conclude, "What is right for us might not be right for you," and "What is wrong in our context might in your context be acceptable or even preferable."

When did this postmodern consciousness, with its pessimism, holism, communitarianism, and relativistic pluralism, arise?

The Birth of Postmodernity

In a sense, postmodernity has undergone a long incubation period. Although scholars disagree as to who originally coined the term,[4] there is a general consensus that it likely first appeared sometime in the 1930s.[5]

One leading proponent of postmodernism, Charles Jencks, claims that the genesis of the concept lies in the work of the Spanish writer Federico de Onis. In his *Antologia de la poesia espanola e hispanoamer-*

icana (1934) de Onis apparently introduced the term to describe a reaction within modernism.[6]

More often cited as the first use of the epithet is its appearance in Arnold Toynbee's monumental multivolume *Study of History*.[7] Toynbee was convinced that a new historical epoch had begun, although he apparently changed his mind as to whether it was inaugurated by World War I or had emerged already in the 1870s.[8]

In Toynbee's analysis, the postmodern era is marked by the end of Western dominance and the decline of individualism, capitalism, and Christianity. He argues that the transition occurred as Western civilization drifted into irrationality and relativism. When this occurred, according to Toynbee, power shifted from the West to non-Western cultures and a new pluralist world culture.

Although the term was coined in the 1930s, postmodernism as a cultural phenomenon did not gain momentum until three or four decades later. It appeared first on the fringes of society. During the 1960s, the mood that would characterize postmodernism became attractive to artists, architects, and thinkers who were seeking to offer radical alternatives to the dominant modern culture. Even theologians got in the act, as William Hamilton and Thomas J. J. Altizer invoked the ghost of Nietzsche to proclaim the death of God.[9] These varied developments led "culture watcher" Leslie Fiedler in 1965 to affixed the label "postmodern" to the radical counterculture of the day.[10]

During the 1970s, the postmodern challenge to modernity infiltrated further into mainstream culture. By mid-decade it produced one of its most articulate defenders, Ihab Hassan, acclaimed as the "most consistent promoter of the idea of the 'postmodern turn.'"[11] This self-proclaimed spokesperson for postmodernism tied the phenomenon to experimentalism in the arts and ultratechnology in architecture.[12]

But the postmodern ethos was rapidly expanding beyond these two realms. University professors in various humanities departments began to speak about postmodernism, some even becoming infatuated with postmodern ideas.

Eventually, the adoption of the new ethos became so widespread that the designation "postmodern" crystallized as the overarching label for a diverse social and cultural phenomenon. The postmodern storm swept through various aspects of culture and several academic disciplines, most notably influencing literature, architecture, film, and philosophy.[13]

In the 1980s, the move from fringe to mainstream came to completion. Increasingly, the postmodern mood invaded pop culture and even the day-to-day world of the larger society. Postmodern ideas became not only acceptable but popular: it was "cool" to be postmodern. Consequently, culture critics could speak of the "unbearable lightness of being postmodern."[14] When postmodernism became an accepted part of the culture, postmodernity was born.

The Progenitor of Postmodernity

Between 1960 and 1990 postmodernism emerged as a cultural phenomenon. But why? How can we account for the meteoric rise of this ethos in our society? Many observers link the transition to changes that occurred in society during the second half of the twentieth century. No factor, however, looms more significant than the arrival of the information era. In fact, the spread of postmodernism parallels and has been dependent on the transition to an information society.[15]

Many historians label the modern era "the industrial age," because the period was dominated by manufacturing. Focusing as it did on the production of goods, modernity produced the industrial society, the symbol of which was the factory. The postmodern era, in contrast, focuses on the production of information. We are witnessing a transition from an industrial society to an information society, the symbol of which is the computer.

Job statistics offer clear evidence that we are experiencing a shift from an industrial society to an information society. In the modern era, the vast majority of nonagricultural employment opportunities centered in the manufacturing sector of the economy and involved the production of goods. By the late 1970s, however, only 13 percent of American workers were involved in the manufacture of goods, whereas a full 60 percent were engaged in the "manufacture" of information.[16] As fewer and fewer workers are needed to stand at the assembly line, training for careers related to information — whether as a data processor or a consultant — has become almost essential.

17

The information society has produced a whole new class of persons. The proletariat has given place to the "cognitariat."[17] And for business, the emergence of the postmodern society has meant a shift from the modern technique of centralized control to the new model of "networking." Hierarchical structures have been replaced by a more decentralized, participatory form of decision making.

The information age has not only altered the work we do but brought the world together in a manner never before possible. The information society functions on the basis of an organized communication network that spans the globe. The efficiency of this integrated system is astounding. In the past, information could spread no faster than human beings could travel. But now information can transverse the globe at the speed of light. More important than the modern ability to travel around the world relatively quickly and painlessly is the postmodern capability to gain information from almost anywhere on earth almost instantaneously.

As a consequence of the global communication system, we now have at our fingertips access to knowledge of events throughout the world. In this sense, we do indeed inhabit a global village.

The advent of the global village has produced seemingly self-contradictory effects. The mass culture and global economy that the age of information is creating are uniting the world into what one droll observer has called "McWorld."[18] But at the same time that the planet is coming together on one level, it is falling apart on another. The advent of postmodernity has fostered simultaneously both a global consciousness and the erosion of national consciousness.

Nationalism has diminished in the wake of a movement toward "retribalization," toward increased loyalty to a more local context. This impulse is found not only in the countries of Africa but also in such unlikely places as Canada, which is repeatedly plagued by threats of secession by the largely French-speaking province of Quebec and by feelings of alienation among its Western provinces. People are increasingly following the new dictum: "Think globally, act locally."

The advent of the postindustrial information society as the successor to the modern industrial society provides the foundation for the postmodern ethos.[19] Life within the global village imbues its citizens with a vivid awareness of the cultural diversity of our planet — an awareness that seems to be encouraging us to adopt a new pluralist mind-set. This new mind-set embraces more than just tolerance for other practices and viewpoints: it affirms and celebrates diversity. The celebration of cultural diversity, in turn, demands a new style — eclecticism — the style of postmodernity.

The information society has also witnessed a shift from mass production to segmented production. The repetitive manufacture of identical objects has given way to the fast-changing production of many different objects. We are moving away from the mass culture of modernity, which offered a few styles that changed with the seasons, toward a fragmented "taste culture," which offers an almost endless variety of styles. High school students, who once defined themselves in terms of a relatively few social categories, such as jocks and nerds, now think in terms of as many as a dozen different categories, reflecting differing tastes and styles.

The Uncentered Realm of Postmodernism

These characteristics indicate that in an important sense the postmodern ethos is centerlessness. No clear shared focus unites the diverse and divergent elements of postmodern society into a single whole. There are no longer any common standards to which people can appeal in their efforts to measure, judge, or value ideas, opinions, or lifestyle choices. Gone as well are old allegiances to a common source of authority and a commonly regarded and respected wielder of legitimate power.

As the center dissolves, our society is increasingly becoming a

---

The postmodern condition . . . manifests itself in the multiplication of centres of power and activity and the dissolution of every kind of totalizing narrative which claims to govern the whole complex field of social activity and representation.

Steven Connor, *Postmodernist Culture*
(Oxford: Basil Blackwell, 1989), p. 9.

---

conglomerate of societies. These smaller social units have little in common apart from geographic proximity.

The postmodern philosopher Michel Foucault offers a name for this centerless postmodern universe: "heterotopia."[20] Foucault's designation underlines the monumental shift away from modernity that we are witnessing. The Enlightenment belief in inevitable progress provided the motivation for the utopian vision of modernity. The architects of modernity sought to design the one perfect human society in which peace, justice, and love would reign — utopia. Postmoderns no longer dream of utopia. In its place they can offer only the incommensurable diversity of the postmodern heterotopia, the "multiverse" that has replaced the universe of the modern quest.

Postmodernism as a Cultural Phenomenon

The loss of centeredness introduced by the postmodern ethos has become one of the chief characteristics of our contemporary situation. It is perhaps most evident in the cultural life of our society.[21] The arts have undergone a profound transition as we have moved from modernity to postmodernity.

The Postmodern Celebration of Diversity

The central hallmark of postmodern cultural expression is pluralism. In celebration of this pluralism, postmodern artists deliberately juxtapose seemingly contradictory styles derived from immensely different sources. This technique not only serves to celebrate diversity but also offers a means to express a subtle rejection of the dominance of rationality in a playful or ironic manner. Postmodern cultural works are often "double-coded," carrying meaning on two levels. Many postmodern artists have employed features of older styles specifically in order to reject or ridicule certain aspects of modernity.

One widely used juxtaposing technique is the *collage*, which offers the artist a natural means of bringing together incompatible source materials. At the same time, by allowing for obvious confiscation, quotation, or

Post-Modernism is fundamentally the eclectic mixture of any tradition with that of the immediate past; it is both the continuation of Modernism and its transcendence. Its best works are characteristically doubly-coded and ironic, making a feature of the wide choice, conflict and discontinuity of traditions, because the heterogeneity most clearly captures our pluralism.

Charles Jencks, *What Is Post-Modernism?* 3d ed.
(New York: St. Martin's Press, 1989), p. 7.

repetition of existing images, the collage heightens the postmodern critique of the myth of the single, creating author. A related juxtaposing tactic is *bricolage,* the reconfiguration of various traditional objects (typically elements from previous stages in the tradition of the artistic medium) in order to achieve some contemporary purpose or make an ironic statement.

The postmodern artist's use of diverse styles means that postmodern works often reflect an eclecticism that draws from many historical eras. Purists consider this sort of juxtaposition abominable, on the grounds that it violates the integrity of historical styles for the sake of making an impression in the present. These critics fault the postmodern form of expression for moving beyond history to a flat present without depth or extension, in which styles and histories circulate interchangeably.[22] They find postmodernism lacking in originality and crassly devoid of style.

But there is a deeper principle operative in postmodern cultural expressions. The intent of postmodern works is not necessarily tastelessness. Rather, postmoderns often seek to undermine the concept of the powerful originating author. They attempt to destroy what they see as the modernist ideology of style, replacing it with a culture of multiple styles. To achieve this end, many postmodern artists confront their audience with a multiplicity of styles, a seemingly discordant polyphony of decontextualized voices. This technique — lifting elements of style from their original historical context — is what their critics denounce as the dislocation and flattening of history.[23]

Regardless of the opinions of these critics, however, postmodernism is exerting a powerful influence on contemporary Western culture.

21

The juxtaposition of styles, with an accompanying emphasis of diversity and deemphasis of rationality, has become a hallmark of our society and is evident in a wide range of contemporary cultural expressions.

Postmodern Architecture

In architecture, as in other aspects of culture, modernism dominated until the 1970s. Modernist architects throughout the West developed what came to be known as the International Style. As an expression of the wider modernist ethos, this architectural movement was guided by faith in human rationality and the hope of constructing a human utopia.

Imbued with modern utopianism, architects constructed buildings according to the principle of unity. Frank Lloyd Wright set the pace for many others when he claimed that the modern edifice should be an organic entity. He declared that a building should be "one great thing" instead of a "quarrelling collection" of many "little things."[24] Each building should express one unified, essential meaning.

The modern commitment to the principle of unity produced an architecture characterized by what Charles Jencks calls "univalence." Modern buildings display simple, essential forms typified by the nearly universal pattern of glass-and-steel boxes. Architects attain simplicity of form by allowing one theme to dominate the construction, which they usually achieve by a device known as "repetition." At the same time, by their approximation to geometrical perfection, modern buildings exemplify a type of otherworldliness.

As it developed, the central stream of modern architecture became a universalizing movement. It promoted the program of industrialization and demoted the variety characteristic of local expression. As a consequence, the expansion of modern architecture often destroyed the existing urban fabric. It virtually decimated everything that stood in the way of the bulldozer, the chief tool of the modern quest for "progress."[25]

Some modernist architects were not satisfied to limit the modern vision to their own discipline. They believed that architecture should become the visible expression of a new unity of art, science, and industry.

22

Together let us desire, conceive, and create the new structure of the future, which will embrace architecture and sculpture and painting in one unity and which will one day rise toward heaven from the hands of a million workers like the crystal symbol of a new faith.

> Walter Gropius, "Programme of the staatliches Bauhaus in Weimar" (1919), in *Programmes and Manifestoes on Twentieth-Century Architecture*, ed. Ulrich Conrads, trans. Michael Bullock (London: Lund Humphries, 1970), p. 25.

Postmodern architecture emerged in response to certain tendencies in modernist architecture. Instead of the modern ideal of univalence, postmoderns celebrate "multivalence." Postmodern architects reject as too austere the modernist requirement that buildings be designed to reflect an absolute unity. Their works, in contrast, purposely explore and display incompatibilities of style, form, and texture.

The rejection of modern architecture is evident in several features of the postmodern reaction. For example, in response to the modernist contempt for anything unessential or superfluous, postmodern buildings give place to ornamentation. Further, where modernist architects sought to demonstrate an absolute break with the past by rigorously purging from their designs any relics of earlier eras, postmodernist architects retrieve historical styles and techniques.

Lying behind the postmodern rejection of modernist architecture is a deeper principle. Postmoderns claim that all architecture is inherently symbolic. All buildings, including modern structures, speak a kind of language. In their quest for pure functionality, many modernist architects sought to banish this dimension. But after the modern scalpel has cut away everything that does not conform to the utility principle, postmoderns claim, all that is left is the technique of building. Eliminated is the artistic dimension that allows a structure to represent an imaginary world or to convey a story. Postmoderns complain that none of the architectural wonders of the past, such as the great cathedrals, which point to another realm, could have been built during the reign of modernism.

A building itself has the power, by having been built right or wrong or mute or noisy, to be what it wants to be, to say what it wants to say, which starts us looking at buildings for what they are saying rather than just accepting their pure existence in the Corbusian manner.

Charles Moore, in *Conversations with Architects*, ed. John Cook and Heinrich Klotz (New York: Praeger, 1973), p. 243.

Through such devices as the addition of ornamentation, postmoderns are attempting to restore what they call the "fictional" element to architecture. They want to rescue the discipline from its captivity to pure utility and reinstitute its role in creating "inventive places."[26]

But the postmodern critique of modernist architecture is even more extensive. Postmoderns challenge modernism's claims to universality and its assertions of transhistorical value. They argue that, contrary to the assertions of the modernists, their archictectual accomplishments were less expressions of reason or logic than they were articulations of a language of power. Modern buildings derive their language from the industrial forms and materials of the modern era and the industrial system they served.[27] These forms and materials give expression to the brave new world of science and technology.[28]

Postmodernists want to abandon this language of power to which modernist architects are seemingly oblivious. They want to move away from what they see as the dehumanizing uniformity of an architecture that speaks the language of standardized mass production. In its place, postmoderns seek to explore new hybrid languages that incorporate the postmodern concepts of diversity and pluralism.

Postmodern Art

Postmodern architecture was born out of a rejection of the principles of the predominant modernist architecture of the twentieth century.

24

Postmodernism has made its presence felt in the world of art in a similar manner.

Modernist architecture seeks to rid itself of all remnants of preceding styles. Art theorists such as Clement Greenberg define modernist art in similar terms.[29] Modernism becomes what it is by engaging in self-criticism in order to purge itself of what it is not; modern artists engage in this sort of self-criticism in order to render their art "pure."[30] Thus, the expression of modernism in art, like its expression in architecture, follows the univalence impulse. One of the great virtues for modernist artists, then, is stylistic integrity.

Postmodernist art, in contrast, moves from an awareness of the connectedness between what it acknowledges as its own and what it excludes. For this reason, it embraces stylistic diversity, or "multivalence." It chooses "impurity" rather than the "purity" of modernism.

Many postmodern artists conjoin diversity with the typically postmodern technique of juxtaposition. As we have already noted, one of their favorite forms of composition is the collage. In fact, Jacques Derrida, who has been called "the 'Aristotle' of montage," considers the collage to be the primary form of postmodern discourse.[31] A collage naturally draws the viewer into the production of its meaning, and the inherent "heterogeneity" of the collage ensures that the meaning it elicits can be neither univocal nor stable. It continually invites the viewer to find new meaning in its juxtaposition of images.

Pressed to its limits, artistic juxtaposition becomes what is some-

---

At root Post-Modern art is neither exclusionary nor reductive but synthetic, freely enlisting the full range of conditions, experiences, and knowledge beyond the object. Far from seeking a single and complete experience, the Post-Modern object strives toward an encyclopedic condition, allowing a myriad of access points, an infinitude of interpretive responses.

Howard Fox, "Avant-Garde in the Eighties," in *The Post-Avant-Garde: Painting in the Eighties*, ed. Charles Jencks (London: Academy Editions, 1987), pp. 29-30.

times termed *pastiche*. The goal of this tactic, which has been employed in both high-culture and pop-culture contexts (e.g., MTV videos), is to barrage the viewer with incongruous, even clashing images that call into question any sense of objective meaning. The disjointed, unharmonious design of pastiche with its gaudy color schemes, discordant typography, and the like, has moved beyond the world of avant-garde art into the everyday realm of book jackets, magazine covers, and mass advertising.

Postmodern artists don't view stylistic diversity merely as a means to grab attention. The attraction is deeper than that. It's part of a more general postmodern attitude, a desire to challenge the power of modernity as invested in institutions and canonical traditions. Postmodern artists seek to challenge the modernist focus on the stylistic integrity of the individual work and undermine what they see as the modernist "cult" of the individual artist. They seek ways of purposely denying the singleness of works of art. Through methods such as obvious confiscation, quotation, excerption, accumulation, and repetition of already existing images, they attack the "fiction" of the creating subject.[32]

An example of this radical postmodern critique can be found in the work of the photographic artist Sherrie Levine. For one exhibition, Levine rephotographed well-known artistic photographs of Walker Evans and Edward Weston and presented them as her own. Her act of art piracy was so obvious that she could not be charged with simple plagiarism. Her goal was not to fool anyone into believing that someone else's work was her own but rather to call into question the idea of a distinction between an "original work" and its public reproduction.[33]

Postmodern Theater

In a sense, the theater is perhaps the most appropriate artistic venue for the expression of the postmodern rejection of modernism. The modernist movement saw a work of art as transcending time, as expressing timeless ideals. The postmodern ethos, in contrast, celebrates transience — and transience is inherent in performance.[34] Postmoderns view life, like the story told on the stage, as an assemblage of intersecting narratives. That being the case, what better way to depict transience and

26

performance than through the cultural medium that is intrinsically dependent on these two features.

Despite this close connection, obviously not every theatrical production is an expression of the postmodern ethos. Many scholars date postmodern theater to the upsurge of performance art during the 1960s.[35] Its roots lie further back, however, in the work of the French writer Antonin Artaud in the 1930s.

Artaud challenged artists — especially dramatists — to become protesters who would destroy what he considered to be the idolatry of classical art. He advocated replacing the traditional stage and the production of theatrical masterpieces with a "theater of cruelty." He called for the abandonment of the older script-centered style and an exploration of the language intrinsic to theater, which includes light, color, movement, gesture, and space.[36] In addition, Artaud advocated transcending the distinctions between actors and observers and drawing the audience into the dramatic experience. It was Artaud's intent to force the audience to confront the primal reality of life that lies beyond all social convention.[37]

In the 1960s, aspects of Artaud's dream began to become a reality. As theorists rethought the nature of theatrical expression, they called for the freeing of performance from its subservience to what they saw as the repressive power of the traditional authorities.

Some of the new theorists concluded that this repressive power was exercised by the underlying script or text.[38] To solve the problem, they eliminated the script and made each performance immediate and unique. Once performed, each work would truly disappear forever.[39]

Other theorists attributed the repressive power to the director.[40] They sought to solve the problem by emphasizing improvisation and group authorship. And, moving against all classical conventions, they celebrated the resulting loss of the concept of the theatrical work as a unified production.

Postmodern theatrical performance builds on these earlier experiments. It sets in opposition different constituents of performance, such as sound, light, music, language, setting, and movement. In this manner, postmodern theater displays a specific theory of performance — an "aesthetics of absence" in contrast to the older "aesthetics of presence."[41] The aesthetics of absence rejects the idea that a performance ought to

27

> The stage will no longer operate as the repetition of a *present,* will no longer *re*-present a present that would exist elsewhere and prior to it, a present whose plenitude would be older than it, absent from it, and rightfully capable of doing without it: the being-present-to-itself of the absolute Logos, the living present of God.
>
> Jacques Derrida, *Writing and Difference,* trans. Alan Bass
> (Chicago: University of Chicago Press, 1978), p. 237.

evidence a sense of underlying, permanent truth. It maintains that the sense of presence that the performance evokes can be no more than an "empty presence." In keeping with the postmodern ethos generally, the meaning of the performance can be only transient, dependent on the situation or context in which it occurs.

Postmodern Fiction

The influence of the postmodern ethos on literature is particularly difficult to assess. Literary critics continue to debate exactly what it is that distinguishes postmodern fiction from its predecessors. Nevertheless, this style of writing reflects the central characteristics evidenced in the other artistic genres we have surveyed.[42]

Following the general postmodern style, postmodern fiction employs the tactic of juxtaposing. Some postmodern authors have brought together traditional forms in displaced ways in order to provide ironic treatments of otherwise perennial themes.[43] Others have juxtaposed the real and the fictitious.

This juxtaposition may involve the characters themselves. Some postmodern author-narrators draw attention to the fictitiousness of the characters and their actions at one point and present the same characters as participants in a kind of history at another point, thereby evoking from the reader the same sort of moral or emotional response evoked by traditional realistic fiction.

Some postmodern authors juxtapose the real and the fictitious by interjecting themselves into the work. They may even discuss the problems and processes involved in the act of narration. Through this paradoxical device, the author blurs the distinction between the real and the fictional. The tactic also underlines the close connection between author and fictional work. Insofar as the fiction is the vehicle through which the author speaks, the author's voice is no longer separable from the fictional story.

Postmodern fiction repeatedly juxtaposes two or more pure, autonomous worlds. When this occurs, the characters who inhabit the literature are often confused as to which world they are in and uncertain about how they should act in this "close encounter."

As is the case in the use of this postmodern technique in other genres, juxtaposition is used in literature with a specific, antimodernist purpose. The goal of the modernist writer was to gain a handle on the meaning of a complex but nevertheless singular reality. Postmoderns, in contrast, raise questions about how radically different realities can coexist and interpenetrate.

Like other postmodern cultural expressions, postmodern literary works focus on contingency and temporality, implicitly denying the modern ideal of an atemporal, universal truth.[44] Postmodern fiction also heightens the focus on temporality in order to dislodge the reader from his or her attempt to view the world from a vantage point outside time. Postmodern authors want to leave the reader naked in a world devoid of eternal essences that are unaffected by the flow of time and the contingencies of temporal context.[45]

And need one say that the more nakedly the author appears to reveal himself in such texts, the more inescapable it becomes, paradoxically, that the author as a *voice* is only a function of his own fiction, a rhetorical construct, not a privileged authority but an object of interpretation?

David Lodge, "Mimesis and Diegesis in Modern Fiction,"
in *The Post-Modern Reader*, ed. Charles Jencks
(New York: St. Martin's Press, 1992), pp. 194-95.

Postmodern authors sometimes achieve the same effect by incorporating language that breaks closed thought structures or calls into question the standard canons of reason as a means of denying that any discourse is ultimately capable of presenting an account of the real.[46]

Perhaps the best representative of modernist fiction was the detective story. Fictional works such as the adventures of Sherlock Holmes take the reader on a quest to uncover the hidden truth that lies beneath the perplexing surface of reality. Despite what appears to be an insufficient number of clues, master detectives always manage to solve the mystery in the end. They will often then almost condescendingly show the audience (represented by some awed observer in the text, such as Dr. Watson in the Holmes mysteries) how the application of human powers of observation and reason to the facts of the situation lead inevitably and logically to the correct conclusion. In this manner, the seemingly disjointed narrative becomes a unified whole.

One typically postmodern fictional form is the spy novel.[47] Although set in the context of the contemporary "real" world, this type of narrative in fact juxtaposes two radically different worlds. The most obvious is the realm of appearance, which seems to reflect the real but often turns out to be an illusion. Operative beneath and within the realm of appearance is a second realm, which is somewhat sinister and yet generally more authentic than the "real" world.

By juxtaposing these two realms, the story holds the reader in a continual state of uncertainty. Is anyone truly who he or she appears to be? What is actually real and true, and what is deception and danger?

The spy story leads us to raise the same questions about our own world. Are we also living between two juxtaposed realms? Are people and events around us truly what they appear to be?

Science fiction is a less subtle postmodern genre.[48] It more obviously presents a rejection of the modern quest. Typically, science fiction stories are less interested in uncovering timeless truth than in exploring otherness. They bring other worlds or other realities into collision in order to highlight the disparities between them.

Science fiction leads us to ask the central philosophical questions about our world: What is reality? What is possible? What forces are actually at work?

Postmodernism as a Phenomenon in Popular Culture

Most of us have likely had our our most direct contact with postmodernism through science fiction and spy stories, for these have penetrated deeply into the popular culture of our day. But through our immersion in our world, we are constantly and often unconsciously exposed to — even bombarded with — the postmodern ethos.

In a sense, exposure to the postmodern ethos through popular culture is itself characteristically postmodern. The refusal to set "high art" above "pop" culture is a defining feature of postmodernity.[49] Postmodernism is unique among avant-garde movements in that it appeals not to an artistic elite but to all those engaged in the activities of daily life through popular culture and the mass media.

To this end, postmodern works often display another type of double coding. They speak a language and use elements that are accessible to nonprofessionals as well as professional artists and architects. In this manner, postmodern expressions bring the professional and the popular realms together.[50]

Filmmaking as the Foundation for Postmodern Culture

Certain technological developments have facilitated postmodernism's penetration into the most influential dimensions of popular culture. One of the most significant of these is the development of the film industry.

Filmmaking technology fits the postmodern ethos in that its products — films — give the illusion of being what they are not. The film may appear to be a unified narrative presented by a specific group of performers, but in fact it is a technological artifact assembled by a variety of specialists from a range of materials and with a range of techniques that are seldom evident in the film itself. In this sense, the unity of a film is largely an illusion.

For example, a film is different from a theatrical production in that it is almost never the record of a single performance by a group of actors. What the viewer sees as a continuous, unified performance is actually a kind of residue that emerges from a sequence of events — the making of the film — that was disjointed in both time and space.

31

The scenes themselves participate in the "hoax." What appears to be a continuous narrative moving from start to finish is actually a compilation of events filmed at various times and in various locations. Indeed, the sequence in which the scenes appear in the film seldom reflects the order in which they were filmed. What unity there is in the film is imposed by the editor, who assembles the footage into the finished product.

Nor are the characters necessarily represented by the same actors throughout the film. Filmmakers have long employed stunt doubles in the filming of hazardous scenes, for example. And new technologies make possible the editing of individual frames of the film to insert duplicate images of an actor, actors from old films into new productions, and even wholly computer-generated images.

In the end, the film we view is the product of technology. Different teams use photography and other methods to assemble an accumulation of materials that the editor then combines (with the help of other techniques to preserve the illusion) to produce what seems to the viewer to be a unified whole. But, in contrast to a theatrical production, a film derives its unity from technology rather than from the contribution of the human actors.[51]

Because the unity of a film lies in the techniques of the filmmaking process rather than in the narrative as such, filmmakers have considerable freedom to fracture and manipulate the story in various ways. They are able, for instance, to juxtapose scenes depicting incompatible topics and themes drawn from footage shot at spatially or temporally separated locations without compromising the unity of the whole.

Postmodern filmmakers delight in collapsing space and time into an eternal here-and-now. Their efforts in this regard are facilitated by the growing body of previously produced film on which they can draw in various ways to augment fresh footage. Thus we see Humphrey Bogart in scenes of *The Last Action Hero* and Groucho Marx in a Diet Pepsi commercial. New technology promises to make possible even more disjunctive mergers of the "real world" with other realities, along the lines of the juxtaposition of cartoon and human characters in the box office hit *Who Framed Roger Rabbit?*

The ability to juxtapose diverse pieces of footage into what for the viewer becomes a unified whole gives the filmmaker a unique opportunity to blur distinctions between "truth" and "fiction," "reality" and "fantasy." Postmodern filmmakers have exploited these capabilities to express the postmodern ethos. For example, postmodern films treat the purely fictitious and fantastic with the same seriousness as the real (e.g., in *Groundhog Day*). They endow a purely fictional story with the air of a documentary (e.g., in *The Gods Must Be Crazy*). They intermix bits of the historical record with speculation and pass the whole off as historically accurate (e.g., in *JFK*). And they use filmmaking techniques to juxtapose totally incongruent worlds inhabited by characters unsure of which is truly real (e.g., in *Blue Velvet*).[52]

Living in a postmodern society means inhabiting a film-like world — a realm in which truth and fiction merge. We look at the world in the same way we look at films, suspicious that what we see around us may in fact be illusion. Despite a film's disjunctions, however, the viewer can at least be certain that it expresses something about the minds that produced it; the filmmaker provides an often unattended center to the world the film creates. Looking at the world, on the other hand, post-moderns are no longer confident that any Mind lies behind it.

Television and the Dissemination of Postmodern Culture

Filmmaking technology may have provided the foundation for post-modern pop culture, but television proved a more efficient vehicle for disseminating the postmodern ethos throughout society.

Viewed from one perspective, television is merely the most effective means to date for transmitting "film" from its creators to the public. Much of television programming simply consists of broadcasting what a multitude of filmmakers produce in a variety of formats ranging from the short commercial to the miniseries. Television is a medium through which film invades the day-to-day lives of millions of people, and in this sense it can be viewed simply as an extension of the film industry.

But beyond its connection with film, television displays characteristics uniquely its own. There are ways in which television is more flexible than film. A film is a static finished product. Television can go beyond this to offer live broadcasting. The television camera can give viewers a picture of events as they are happening almost anywhere in the world.

This ability to provide the viewer with a live picture of an event leads many people to believe that television presents actual events in themselves — without interpretation, editing, or commentary. For this reason, television has quickly become the "real world" of postmodern culture, and television reporting has emerged as the new test for being real. Many viewers don't think something is really important unless it shows up on CNN, *Sixty Minutes,* or a made-for-TV miniseries. Anything not submitted to the "ontological test" of being aired on television is relegated to the periphery of life in contemporary society.[53]

Television has the ability both to offer live broadcasting of the "facts" happening in our world and to disseminate the products of the filmmaker's creativity. This double ability endows television with a unique power. It has the ability to juxtapose "truth" (what the public perceives as actual event) with "fiction" (what the public perceives as never having actually happened in the "real" world) in ways that film cannot. And, indeed, contemporary television performs this feat incessantly. It happens, for example, every time a live telecast is interrupted for "a word from our sponsor."

Television exceeds the capacity of film to realize the postmodern ethos in another sense as well. As a matter of course, commercial television broadcasting presents the viewer with an ongoing variety of incompatible images. A typical evening newscast, for example, will bombard the viewer with a series of unrelated images in quick succession — a war in a remote country, a murder closer to home, a sound bite from a political speech, the latest on a sex scandal, a new scientific discovery, highlights from a sporting event. This collage is interspersed with advertisements for better batteries, better soap, better cereal, and better vacations. By giving all these varied images — news stories and commercials alike — roughly equal treatment, the broadcast leaves the impression that they are all of roughly equal importance.[54]

The news broadcast is followed by a plethora of prime-time programs that seek to attract and hold an audience by focusing on action, scandal, violence, and sex. The evening's sitcoms and dramas seem to be invested with the same weight as the earlier news stories. In this manner, television blurs the line between truth and fiction, between the truly earth-shattering and the trivial.

And as though a single channel's programming did not supply the viewer with enough discordant images, contemporary television offers the viewer dozens — soon to be hundreds — of different channels. Cable and direct satellite broadcasts supply an incredible variety of viewing options, and, armed with remote control, a viewer can shuttle through the wasteland perpetually in search of something interesting — a news update, a boxing match, a financial report, an old movie, a weather forecast, a stand-up comedian, a documentary, an infomercial, or anything from the vast sea of sitcoms, cop shows, westerns, soap operas, medical dramas, and other reruns of more than four decades of network programming.

By offering its collage of images, television unintentionally juxtaposes the irreconcilable. But in addition, it obliterates spatial and temporal distinctions. It merges the past and the present, the distant and the local, bringing all together into one perpetual here-and-now — the "present" of the television viewer. In this manner, television intrinsically displays what some critics see as two central characteristics of postmodern texts: it effaces the boundary between past and present, and it locates the viewer in a perpetual present.[55]

Many social observers speak of television as representing the postmodern psychological and cultural condition. It presents a multitude of images that are readily detached from their reference to reality, images that circulate and interact in a ceaseless, centerless flow.[56]

And film and television have been joined by a newer and increasingly popular conduit of information — the personal computer.

The advent of "the screen" — whether the movie, the television, or the computer screen — epitomizes the postmodern blurring of the traditional contrast between the subjective self and the objective world. The screen is not merely an external object that we look at. What happens on the screen is neither wholly "out there" (merely on the screen), nor wholly in us; rather, it seems to occur in some space between the two.[57] The screen brings us into its world just as it enters into ours. As what happens on the screen becomes an extension of ourselves, we become an extension of it. The screen thus becomes an embodied form of our psychic worlds.

Living in the postmodern era means inhabiting a world created by the juxtaposition of diverse images. The world of the screen blurs undifferentiated images into a fragmented present, and postmoderns

35

> The disappearing ego [is] the victory sign of postmodernism. . . . The self is transformed into an empty screen of an exhausted, but hyper-technical culture.
>
> Arthur Kroker, Marilouise Kroker, and David Cook, "Panic Alphabet," in *Panic Encyclopedia: The Definitive Guide to the Postmodern Scene* (Montreal: New World Perspectives, 1989), p. 16.

who are wedded to this world remain unsure that it is anything more than a blur of images.

Other Expressions of Postmodernism in Pop Culture

Film may have made postmodern popular culture possible, and television may have disseminated that culture, but rock music is probably the most representative form of postmodern pop culture.[58] The lyrics of many rock songs reflect postmodern themes, but the connection between rock music and postmodern pop culture runs deeper. Rock music embodies a central hallmark of postmodernity: its dual focus on the global and the local.

Contemporary rock music now enjoys a global audience, endowing it with world-unifying capabilities. We need only remind ourselves of the international following that allows popular rock figures to embark on highly profitable "world tours." At the same time, though, rock music retains a local flavor. In the offerings of the big stars and the small-town bands alike, rock reflects a plurality of styles borrowed from local and ethnic musical forms.

Equally significant as an embodiment of the postmodern ethos is the connection to electronic production that rock music shares with television and filmmaking. A crucial dimension of the rock culture is the live performances of its most popular stars. But today's "live" experience no longer takes the traditional form of an intimate concert in which the performer seeks to communicate directly with audience. Far more often it consists of what some observers call "manufactured mass closeness."[59]

Today's rock concert is typically a mass event, involving audiences numbering in the tens of thousands. Most fans in attendance are simply too far away to see the performers on the stage clearly. Even so, they still manage to "experience" the event. The performance is brought to them through the use of enormous video screens that relay closeups of the performer throughout the location. This technique both abolishes and re-emphasizes the actual distance between performer and audience. Jubilant fans feel close to their hero despite the fact that the performer's presence is artificial, mediated by a screen. Technology transforms the intimacy of a "live performance" into a mass gathering of fans who watch "live" videos together while being bombarded with special effects.

Technology also blurs the distinction between the original performance and its reproduction. It breaks down the distinction between the "live" and the reproduced dimensions of the musical experience. In fact, the performance is no longer a separate reality lying behind the particular context in which it occurs. Rather, it is a blend of what the performers do and a technological reproduction of their actions. The performance is enmeshed in the technology that delivers it to the audience.

Perhaps more subtle than the interplay between postmodernism and rock music is the presence of the postmodern ethos in contemporary clothing styles. Postmodern fashions reveal the same tendencies found in other pop cultural expressions. We see it in the popularity of clothes that prominently display trademarks and product labels, for example, a feature that blurs the distinction between fashion and advertising.

Above all, the postmodern outlook is evident in what is called "bricolage." In pointed defiance of the traditional attempt to coordinate individual pieces of clothing in a unified look, the postmodern style intentionally juxtaposes incompatible or heterogeneous elements, such as garments and accessories from each of the preceding four decades.

As in other expressions of postmodernism, the juxtaposition of traditionally incompatible fashion elements is not merely random. It may be calculated to produce an ironic effect or to parody modern fashion norms or perhaps the modern fashion industry as a whole.[60]

The pop culture of our day reflects the centerless pluralism of postmodernity and gives expression to the antirationalism of postmodernism. As evidenced in the clothes they wear and the music they

> From rock music to tourism to television and even education, adver-
> tising imperatives and consumer demand are no longer for goods, but
> for experiences.
>
> Steven Connor, *Postmodernist Culture*
> (Oxford: Basil Blackwell, 1989), p. 154.

listen to, postmoderns are no longer convinced that their world has a center or that human reason can perceive any logical structure in the external universe. They live in a world in which the distinction between truth and fiction has evaporated. Consequently, they become collectors of experiences, repositories of transitory, fleeting images produced and fostered by the diversity of media forms endemic in postmodern society.

Postmodernism assumes various forms. It is embodied in certain attitudes and expressions that touch the day-to-day lives of a broad diversity of people in contemporary society. Such expressions range from fashions to television and include such pervasive aspects of popular culture as music and film. Postmodernism is likewise incarnated in a variety of cultural expressions, including architecture, art, and literature. But postmodernism is above all an intellectual outlook.

Postmodernism rejects the very idea of the solitary scholar born of the Enlightenment. Postmoderns denounce the pretense of those who claim to view the world from a transcendent vantage point from which they are able to speak imperiously to and on behalf of all humankind. Postmoderns have replaced this Enlightenment ideal with the belief that all claims to truth — and ultimately even truth itself — are socially conditioned.

CHAPTER 3

The Postmodern
World View

Postmodernity may have been born in St. Louis on a July afternoon in 1972, but another seven years passed before postmodernism became a fixture on the intellectual landscape.

In 1979 the Conseil des Universites of the government of Quebec (Canada) requested a report on "knowledge in the most highly devel oped societies." For this task, they turned to Jean-Francois Lyotard, a French philosopher from the Institute Polytechnique de Philosophie of the Universite de Paris in Vincennes, France. His response came in the form of a short, occasional piece bearing the unpretentious title *The Postmodern Condition: A Report on Knowledge*.

The publication of *The Postmodern Condition* put postmodernism on the intellectual map.[1] The book did not so much initiate the discussion as describe in an accessible manner the revolution in outlook that lay beneath the cultural phenomenon occurring throughout the Western world and the theoretical and philosophical basis of the postmodern view.[2]

But what is the intellectual outlook that undergirds the new mood in Western culture and society? Viewed from the perspective of its intellectual agenda, postmodernism marks a new way of viewing reality. It is a revolution both in our understanding of knowledge and in our view of science.

Postmodernism and Knowledge

As we have already seen, postmodernism defies definitive description. Whatever else it may be, however, it involves a radical rejection of the modern intellectual outlook. It is a revolution in knowledge. More specifically, the postmodern era spells the end of the "universe" — the end of the all-encompassing worldview.

In a sense, postmoderns have no worldview. A denial of the reality of a unified world as the object of our perception is at the heart of postmodernism. Postmoderns reject the possibility of constructing a single correct worldview and are content simply to speak of many views and, by extension, many worlds.

By replacing the modern worldview with a multiplicity of views and worlds, the postmodern era has in effect replaced knowledge with interpretation.

Postmodernism as the End of the "World"

The loss of the modern worldview marks the end of the objective world of the Enlightenment project.

Foundational to the modern outlook is the assumption of an objective world around us. The modern worldview assumes that reality is ordered and that human reason is capable of discerning this order as it is manifested in the laws of nature. The Enlightenment project is based on the presumption that the path to human fulfillment lies primarily in discovering and utilizing these laws for the benefit of humankind.

Postmodernism rejects the understanding of our knowledge of the world that stands at the foundation of the Enlightenment project and modernity. Specifically, the postmodern era has abandoned the notion of an objective world.

This abandonment of the concept of the objective world is a result of the postmodern rejection of a realist understanding of knowledge and truth in favor of a nonrealist understanding.[3] That is to say, we have moved from an *objectivist* to a *constructionist* outlook.[4]

In most of our day-to-day living we operate with an objectivist understanding of the world, knowledge, and truth. In fact, we accept this "common sense" view of the world as self evident. We assume that the world is objectively real, that it displays an order inherent to itself and independent of human activity. Most of us assume that the human mind is capable of more or less accurately mirroring this external, nonhuman reality; most of us also assume that language, as a product of the human mind, provides an adequate means of declaring to ourselves and to others what the world is like.

In making these objectivist assumptions, we are operating with what is called the correspondence theory of truth. According to this theory, assertions are either true or false, and we can determine whether they are true or false by comparing them with the world. If you say, "There is an apple pie in the refrigerator," I need only look in the refrigerator to determine whether the statement is true. Operating on objectivist assumptions, the realist defines truth as the correspondence between our assertions and the objective world about which they are made.

The objectivist understanding generally works well in day-to-day life. But Enlightenment realists do not stop there: they universalize this approach into a general theory of truth. They assert at least in theory that the human mind can grasp reality as a whole and hence that we can devise a true and complete description of the way the world actually is. These theorists extend the limits of the "reality" that they believe we can grasp to include not just the everyday objects around us but the entire realm of nature as explored by the natural sciences. They maintain that we can attain sure knowledge in all realms of human inquiry, including history, which they define as the study of humankind as the center of the cosmos.

Postmodern thinkers no longer find this grand realist ideal tenable.[3] They reject the fundamental assumption on which it is based — namely, that we live in a world consisting of physical objects that are easily identifiable by their inherent properties. They argue that we do not simply encounter a world that is "out there" but rather that we construct the world using concepts we bring to it. They contend that we have no fixed vantage point beyond our own structuring of the world from which to gain a purely objective view of whatever reality may be out there.

The Enlightenment realist view also assumes that a simple, one-to-one relationship exists between the bits of language we use to describe the world and the bits of the world we seek to know. Twentieth-century linguists argue that this is a faulty assumption. We do not simply match bits of language to bits of the world, they say, nor does any given language provide an accurate "map" of the world. Languages are human social conventions that map the world in a variety of ways, depending on the context in which we are speaking.

Ludwig Wittgenstein suggested that all words ("linguistic signifiers") are embedded in "language games." Each linguistic "game" is defined by a system of rules that govern the way words are used within that context. In this sense, language resembles a game such as chess, which has rules that determine how the game pieces can be moved.[6] An important implication of this view is that our various language games color and alter the way we experience our world.

Considerations such as these lead postmodern thinkers to abandon the realist view in favor of a nonrealist or constructivist view. Constructivists emphasize the role of language in providing access to the world. They contend that what we call the "real world" is actually an ever-changing social creation. Ours is a "symbolic" world, a social reality that we construct through our common language. We say that snow is white, the sky is blue, and grass is green because we have chosen our categories in this way. But, because our social context is always changing, meanings — and, as a consequence, the world as we see it through language — are constantly shifting as well.

Another factor has also contributed to the jettisoning of the objectivist understanding. The Enlightenment position retained credibility as long as people in the West assumed that theirs was the most advanced and civilized culture in the world. Moderns simply assumed that all of humankind would eventually come to appreciate and strive to attain the benefits of the Western ideal. In the postmodern era, however, this dream is no longer credible: it has fallen victim to the phenomenon that many observers call "globalization."[7] Today people in the West are confronted with a variety of cultures, each of which prizes its own beliefs and its own picture of the world.

Our globalized, pluralistic situation has subverted the Enlightenment vision. Postmoderns contend that we can no longer reasonably hold out the prospect of discovering the one, universal symbolic world that unites humanity at a level deeper than that of our apparent differences. Instead, they say, we must come to grips with the realization that we inhabit a globe consisting of "multiple realities." Different groups of people construct different "stories" about the world they encounter. These different languages, in turn, facilitate different ways of experiencing life. As a result, people do not merely espouse different political opinions and religious beliefs; they actually live in different worlds with respect to basic matters of personal identity, time, and space.

The postmodern understanding of knowledge, therefore, is built on two foundational assumptions: (1) postmoderns view all explanations of reality as constructions that are useful but not objectively true, and (2) postmoderns deny that we have the ability to step outside our constructions of reality.[8]

As a result, the postmodern outlook constitutes an attack on realism in the name of reason. Because we cannot view the world apart from the structures we bring to it, the argument goes, we cannot measure our theories and propositions in comparison to an objective, external world.[9] To the contrary, the theories we devise create the different worlds we inhabit.[10]

On the strength of this kind of argumentation, postmodernism has risen out of the alleged ruins of a theory that undergirded the entire modern project.[11] Postmoderns have adopted a pluralistic view of knowledge. Having rejected the notion of a single objective world as such and, indeed, any other single basis on which to judge the validity of thought and knowledge,[12] they have demonstrated a willingness to allow competing and seemingly conflicting constructions to exist side by side.[13] The point at issue for them is not "Is the proposition or theory correct?" but rather "What does it do?"[14] or "What is its outcome?"

Certain postmodern scholars see themselves as the harbingers of the demise of realism. They see it as their task to bring to light the ways in which concepts that people generally assume to be commonsense or universal are in fact cultural constructions. If language really does construct meaning (as opposed to revealing an objective meaning already present in the world), then the work of the scholar is to take apart ("deconstruct") this meaning-constructing process. By deconstructing influential concepts, perhaps we can break their control over our thoughts and actions.[15]

The postmodern outlook likewise demands a "post-pedagogical classroom." No longer is teaching merely the transmission of a discipline or knowledge that lies prior to the educational experience; rather, it should encompass the active production of (as well as the deconstruction of) meaning.[16]

Postmodernism as the End of the "Metanarrative"

At the heart of the Enlightenment project is the desire to explore the world (including humanity) as it exists in itself apart from this human exploratory activity. The modern explorer describes the world by appeal to universal "laws" or principles that govern action, assuming that the compilation of these laws constitutes knowledge of the world.

The architects of modernity believed that they were building a new society on the foundation of universal rationality alone. Their goal was to move beyond wars and conflicts, which they believed to be the inevitable result of the myths and religious dogmas of premodern peoples. The modern outlook assumes the Enlightenment program of discovery is purely objective, free of the premodern dependency on myths and stories to explain the world. The moderns believed that they were able to see the world as it really is. Postmodernism says that this was an illusion.

The postmodern rejection of this Enlightenment hubris developed out of changing perceptions in a variety of areas. As the twentieth century unfolded, anthropologists became increasingly aware of the foundational importance of myths in human society. Some scholars argued that myths are more than just stories that primitive cultures tell; in fact, they embody the central core of a culture's values and beliefs and are in that sense fundamentally religious.[17] Their research led them to the conclusion that each society is bound together by a system of myths, that these myths sustain social relations within the society and form the basis of its claim to legitimacy.[18]

Postmodern thinkers speak of these systems of legitimizing myths as "narratives" (or "metanarratives"). They contend that a narrative exercises a force apart from argumentation and proof[19] and, in fact, that it provides the principal means by which every community legitimates itself.

The modern outlook claims to have replaced myths with rational postulates, but postmodern thinkers assert that the Enlightenment project is itself dependent on an appeal to narrative. The scientific method that gave birth to modernity, they say, was born out of an interpretation of the Christian narrative, which speaks of a rational God who is the creator of, and sovereign over, the universe. The modern era viewed itself as the embodiment of a narrative of progress — a myth that legitimated technological invention and economic development as the means of creating a better world for all human beings. For a time, this story was challenged by a variant — the Marxist narrative of an inevitable revolution that would lead to the utopia of international socialism. But at no point, say the postmoderns, did moderns ever really free themselves from the directive force of myth.

According to postmoderns such as Lyotard, the decline of modernity was not the result of a failure of nerve, of an inability to sustain faith in rational postulates rather than myths. Rather, it occurred because the grand narratives that legitimated modern society have been losing their power.[20] This situation is scarcely unique. In fact, history can be viewed as a series of transitions from one defining myth to another; older narratives inevitably wane and are replaced by newer ones.

What makes our condition "postmodern" is not only that people no longer cling to the myths of modernity. The postmodern outlook entails the end of the appeal to any central legitimating myth whatsoever. Not only have all the reigning master narratives lost their credibility, but the idea of a grand narrative is itself no longer credible. We have not only become aware of a plurality of conflicting legitimating stories but have moved into the age of the demise of the metanarrative.[21] The postmodern era is a period in which everything is "delegitimized." Consequently, the postmodern outlook demands an attack on any claimant to universality — it demands, in fact, a "war on totality."[22]

The demise of the grand narrative means that we no longer search for the one system of myths that can unite human beings into one people or the globe into one "world." Although they have divested themselves of any metanarrative, postmoderns are still left with local narratives. Each of us experiences a world within the context of the societies in which we live, and postmoderns continue to construct mod-

45

I will use the term *modern* to designate any science that legitimates itself with reference to a metadiscourse of this kind making an explicit appeal to some grand narrative, such as the dialectics of Spirit, the hermeneutics of meaning, the emancipation of the rational or working subject, or the creation of wealth. For example, the rule of consensus between the sender and addressee of a statement with truth-value is deemed acceptable if it is cast in terms of a possible unanimity between rational minds: this is the Enlightenment narrative, in which the hero of knowledge works toward a good ethico-political end — universal peace. . . .

Simplifying to the extreme, I define *postmodern* as incredulity toward metanarratives.

Jean-Francois Lyotard, *The Postmodern Condition: A Report on Knowledge*, trans. Geoff Bennington and Brian Massumi (Minneapolis: University of Minnesota Press, 1984), pp. xxiii-iv.

els (or "paradigms") to illumine their experience in such contexts. Because they perceive life itself as drama or narrative, their major concerns revolve around the process of fabricating stories that can define personal identity and give purpose and shape to social existence.[23] Postmoderns continue to reject the modernist illusion — they deny that modernist models represent reality — but as a practical matter, they grant that these models still serve as "useful fictions" in everyday life.

Postmodernism as the End of Science

Lyotard defines the postmodern condition as the end of the grand narrative. As we have seen, his observation carries important implications for all aspects of human society and for our understanding of knowledge. But Lyotard's chief concern is with that dimension which has exerted a more significant formative influence than any other in the modern era — the scientific enterprise. Postmodernism, he says, marks the end of science.

Modern science arose in part out of a desire to dispel from the realm of knowledge the "prescientific" beliefs, myths, and stories that primitive peoples use to speak about the world. At the heart of the scientific method is the undermining of any appeal to such narratives in order to legitimate knowledge. Postmodernism marks the end of this attempt.

According to the postmodern appraisal, science cannot achieve its goal of expelling myth from the realm of knowledge. In fact, science must inevitably turn to the very endeavor it seeks to explode — narrative — in order to legitimize its own enterprise.[24]

Lyotard suggests that since the 1700s, two major narratives have served this legitimizing purpose. Both of these embody the idea of progress toward a goal, and each provides a unifying foundation for the different disciplines that it brings together under the rubric of *science*.

The first, a political myth legitimates science by appeal to liberty. All peoples have a right to scientific knowledge, the myth asserts, but they are hindered in attaining it by priests and tyrants. Through science, humanity rises up in freedom and dignity to emancipate itself by assaulting the bastions of ignorance and oppression.

The second narrative is philosophical. Here the subject engaging in the quest for knowledge is not humanity but knowledge itself (or "the spirit" or "life"). This narrative asserts that the scientific enterprise is legitimate because it facilitates the growth of knowledge. It also affirms that the various scientific disciplines all contribute to the gradual evolution of knowledge.[25]

Both legitimizing narratives of the "advance of science" provide a framework for organizing other, "local" narratives. Modern interpreters orient the stories of new scientific discoveries or the biographies of the heroes of the tradition around these metanarratives. The local narratives receive their meaning from the way they echo and confirm the grand narratives of scientific progress. The progress of science unites these smaller, divergent stories into a single unified history.

According to Lyotard's analysis, however, the age of unified inquiry has come to a close. Since the Second World War, the grand narratives of scientific progress have lost their credibility.[26] As a result, the appeal to science as an organizing and unifying category is weakening. Specifically, the notion of a single scientific enterprise subdivided into well-defined parallel disciplines is being replaced by the notion of a cluster of ill-defined and constantly shifting areas of inquiry. Each of these specialties boasts its own "language game" (method or procedure of inquiry) and conducts its work without recourse to a universal scientific "metalanguage" that links the sciences and provides an external court of appeal as well as a set of authoritative methodological principles.[27]

The splintering of science has altered the goal of research. Scholars no longer legitimate their work through appeals to their participation in the quest for scientific knowledge. Their goal is now "performativity" rather than "truth." Financial backers fund research not in order to promote the emancipation of humanity or to extend knowledge but to augment their own power.[28] The question is no longer "Is it true?" but "What use is it?" And the question of usefulness means either "Is it salable?" or, in the context of the focus on power, "Is it efficient?"[29]

While acknowledging the potential problems associated with the loss of the scientific metanarrative, postmodern thinkers do not bemoan the situation this loss has introduced. Lyotard welcomes a world in which multiple incompatible language games flourish alongside one another. He rejoices that we are no longer ruled by the modern concern that all discussion lead toward consensus. He pointedly concedes that he has given up the quest to reconcile the differing language games.[30]

Post-modernism signals the death of such 'metanarratives' whose secretly terroristic function is to ground and legitimate the illusion of a 'universal' human history. We are now in the process of awakening from the nightmare of modernity, with its manipulative reason and fetish of the totality, into the laid-back pluralism of the post-modern, that heterogeneous range of life-styles and language games which has renounced the nostalgic urge to totalise and legitimate itself. . . . Science and philosophy must jettison their grandiose metaphysical claims and view themselves more modestly as just another set of narratives.

Terry Eagleton, "Awakening from Modernity,"
Times Literary Supplement, 20 February 1987, p. 194.

In his estimation, the postmodern condition is beneficial because it heightens our ability to cope with our pluralistic situation. It assists us in the task of living with differences and tolerating things that cannot be brought together into a single whole.[31] But, more importantly, he anticipates that the postmodern era will be a time of great invention. According to Lyotard, the postmodern condition fosters invention because invention is always born of dissension, not consensus.[32]

The heralds of postmodernity consistently join Lyotard in celebrating the glorious event of the death of the modern age.

The Postmodern Scientific Revolution

The postmodern era was born out of the loss of the modern idea of the "universe." Postmoderns no longer accept the validity of the vision of a single integral world. In connection with this, the postmodern intellectual ethos resists explanations that are held to be all-encompassing and universally valid. Postmoderns are inclined to prize difference over uniformity and to respect the local and particular more than the universal.[33] For this reason, postmodern thinkers do not regret the loss of science as a unifying enterprise. Postmodernism may spell the end of the "world," of "metanarratives," and of "science," but it marks the beginning of a revolution in knowledge.

The postmodern outlook has another connection to science as well. In a sense, the postmodern view is the outworking of certain developments in twentieth-century science. Recent discoveries have revolutionized the way scientists — especially physicists — view the world and the nature of scientific inquiry. Altogether these developments have undermined our confidence in an objective order and in knowable absolutes.[34]

The New View of the Physical World

Modernity was born out of an intellectual revolution. The specifically scientific dimension of that revolution was sparked by Galileo (1564-1642) and reached its climax with Newton (1642-1727).

49

Galileo's innovation consisted in his attempt to interpret the world from a strictly quantitative point of view. Experimentation that yields quantifiable results (i.e., numbers rather than nonnumerical qualities) became the central technique of the emerging scientific enterprise. The focus on numerical measurements gave scientists the sense that they were practitioners in a field of inquiry that produces exact and unambiguous knowledge. Organized into equations, such knowledge gives expression to laws or patterns within nature itself and therefore can be used to predict other "natural" occurrences.

The impulse that Galileo and Newton provided led modern thinkers to reject the organic view of the world that dominated the ancient understanding and to replace it with a mechanistic understanding.

The mechanistic outlook reduces reality to a set of basic elements or elementary particles and forces (e.g., electromagnetism and gravity). Each elementary particle embodies an essence that determines its nature and value; each is what it is apart from other particles. These autonomous particles come together to form various kinds of natural "machines." Finally, the mechanistic view suggests that these elements interact with each other mechanically — in a sense, that they push each other around — but that these interactions do not affect the inner natures of the particles.[35]

Armed with the mechanistic model, modern scientists busied themselves with the task of unlocking the mysteries of the universe. And on the basis of this model, which appeared to offer an unassailable view of the world, the modern scientific enterprise celebrated discovery after discovery. As a result, science commanded near-universal respect in the modern society, and modern people looked to the scientist for the answers to life and for guidance along the pathway toward the betterment of the human situation.

In the midst of its greatest technological triumphs, however, certain foundational aspects of the modern scientific worldview were shaken from within. The most devastating internal challenge came from physics, the discipline that had provided its firmest foundation. Discoveries in the early twentieth century called into question the modern assumption that the universe displays an internally consistent order that the human mind can easily come to understand and picture. And the mechanistic model that earlier had appeared to be beyond question came under increasing fire as evidence increasingly suggested that there is much about the universe that is virtually indescribable and even unimaginable.

At the beginning of the twentieth century, Max Planck declared that on the atomic level, energy comes in distinct "packets" (quanta) rather than in a steady flow. Albert Einstein, in turn, noted that light is not only a wave but also a shower of individual packets of energy (photons). Niels Bohr related these phenomena to the behavior of electrons. Electrons do not orbit atomic nuclei at random distances. Rather, they sit in specific orbits that are multiples of a fundamental quantum of energy. In addition, they "jump" from one orbit to another as energy is applied to the atom or as they give up that energy. Then Louis de Broglie proved that all matter — including the electron — has both particle and wavelike properties. Quantum theory was born, and our view of the world has not been the same since.[36]

Paralleling the development of quantum theory was another important series of discoveries that we cumulatively refer to as "relativity theory." By means of his "special theory of relativity," Einstein undermined the seemingly commonsense notion that space and time are absolute.[37] He disproved the centuries-old belief that length and time can be measured against absolute standards by showing that a rocket traveling at high speeds will shrink slightly in comparison to its earthbound counterparts and that a clock on that rocket will run more slowly.[38] This theory also implies that matter and energy are not independent constants but are reciprocally related; the one can be changed into the other according to his famous equation, $E = mc^2$.

Einstein's "general theory of relativity" is equally far-reaching, though not as well known in wider society. This theory postulates the mind-boggling idea that gravity is essentially a curvature of the space-time continuum.[39]

Like relativity theory, quantum physics reveals some startling features of the universe that undermine both the modern mechanistic model of the world and the modern assumption of scientific certitude. For example, there are no commonsense models that help us reconcile the dual nature of matter and energy — the fact that they sometimes act like waves and sometimes act like particles, depending on the way we examine them. Likewise, the familiar image of an electron orbiting an atomic nucleus like a planet orbiting the sun has proved wholly inadequate to characterize what really goes on at the subatomic level. Physics in this environment is not nearly so mechanical and clear-cut. Evidence indicates that subatomic particles do not necessarily move in a continuous manner, for instance: they are able to travel from point A to point B without passing through each of the points in between. And in his now-famous Uncertainty Principle, Werner Heisenberg notes that we can determine with certainty either the position of a subatomic particle or its momentum, but we cannot determine both these characteristics for any given particle at any given time. Certainty simply evaporates at the subatomic level, leaving us with little more than probabilities and paradoxes.

Newer theories overthrow the idea of a "substantial" universe altogether. The universe is not composed of individual particles possessing specific essences within themselves, say the new physicists; elementary particles are actually far more dependent on their context — their relationships to one another — than the mechanistic model anticipates. In fact, at its most fundamental level, physical reality does not seem to be composed of independently existing particles at all but of dynamic relations.[40]

Quantum theory also demands that we acknowledge the limitations of scientific inquiry. The modern scientific enterprise is built on the assumption that the scientist approaches the universe as a neutral observer. The world is an object that the scientist probes. Contemporary physics, however, has effectively exploded this understanding.

Adherence to a set of procedures accepted by the scientific community may ensure *relative* objectivity on the part of an observer, but no experimental protocol can produce a *purely* objective, uninvolved observation. In observations performed at the subatomic level, it is easier to see the operation of the general principle that the scientist's act of observation itself affects the object of his or her investigation, because the techniques of observation are so large and clumsy and the observed phenomena so delicate and ephemeral. But the point rings true in other sorts of observations as well: we cannot neatly separate the observed object from the observing subject.[41] This overturns the modern assumption that "facts" are present in nature independent of some particular observer. Postmoderns insist that we are not spectators who approach the world but rather participants in what we seek to know.[42]

Recent developments place another limitation on the scientific enterprise as well. Modern science is erected on the assumption that the universe is open, at least in principle, to full and complete description, that when nature is subjected to the scrutiny of detached, impersonal scientific observation of the facts, it yields objective knowledge about its deepest secrets.

When Heisenberg formulated his Uncertainty Principle in 1927, however, he established that there is an essential indeterminacy about all phenomena that no kind or amount of observation can overcome. In a sense, he established the point that the universe is ultimately an unfathomable mystery.[43] David Bohm has proposed an intriguing alternative to Heisenberg's principle known as "quantum potential" — the notion that all particles are linked together in a huge interconnected web that enables each of them to know instantaneously what the others are doing.[44] In either case, however, the realm of today's physicist is no longer the simple world of independent particles depicted by the mechanistic model.

Developments in physics since the advent of relativity theory and quantum physics have come at an overwhelming rate. The list of identified subatomic particles has grown. Black holes have been discovered. The Big Bang has been plotted in minute detail. And physicists tell us we live on the curved surface of an expanding universe.

The new discoveries have led contemporary scientists to an increasing awareness of the complexity of the universe. In fact, some scholars speak of the advent of a third scientific revolution characterized by a new "physics of complexity." The "explosion of complexity" is laying to rest the assumption that we can gain unambiguous knowledge of the universe.[45] The emerging consensus is that ours is a relative and participatory world.

The complex world of the new physics is vastly different from the simple, static, objective universe of Galileo and Newton. It is not so much a creation as a creating.[46] And the universe is not a existing entity that *has* a history; rather, it *is* a history.

The New View of the Nature of Scientific Inquiry

The changing understanding of the world has triggered a shift in our understanding of what knowledge is and how we come to know. Science no longer looms as a haven of objectivity in the sea of cultural relativity. Not even scientific discourse stands outside participation in the world we seek to understand. In fact, the sciences constitute additional examples of the language games Ludwig Wittgenstein spoke about.

Like all human discourse, the scientific enterprise is a form of human linguistic activity (a game). It is not merely a neutral means for discovering the nature of reality. Instead, like other types of language, scientific discourse is directed at the achievement of certain ends. There simply are no culturally neutral facts.[47]

But the postmodern exposing of the myth of science goes a step farther. The modern scientific enterprise operated on the assumption that science progresses in a logical manner. The scientist observes the world, offers a hypothesis about how the world functions, and then devises an experiment to substantiate or disprove the hypothesis. The outcome provides the foundation for the next cycle of observation, hypothesis formulation, and experimentation. Philosophers of science now challenge this understanding of the linear conception of the rise of scientific knowledge. Many voices have been involved in this development, but perhaps the most important — and controversial — seminal statement is Thomas S. Kuhn's *The Structure of Scientific Revolutions* (1962).[48]

Kuhn pioneered a new analysis of how science develops. He argues that foundational shifts in theory are not simply logical modifications or reinterpretations of past knowledge. Nor do scientists simply add one fact to another in a mechanistic, objective sort of way. Rather, science is a dynamic historical phenomenon. Shifts in theory come as radical transformations in the way scientists view the world. Scientists lurch ahead from time to time in sudden creative bursts that Kuhn calls "paradigm shifts."

According to Kuhn, a *paradigm* is a social construction of reality. The term refers to "the entire constellation of beliefs, values, techniques, and so on shared by the members of a given community."[49] More specifically, it is a belief system that prevails in a given scientific community at a given time in history. Kuhn also uses the term more narrowly in reference to some particularly important element within this constellation of beliefs that is useful in helping to explain the puzzles posed by the scientific community.

While possessing great interpretive power, no belief system or puzzle-solution is ever able to explain all the data. Researchers keep coming across anomalies or findings that the prevailing theory cannot explain. The anomalies compound. Then someone proposes a new explanatory system that more successfully accounts for the anomalies, and eventually this new system replaces the old one. This transition from one explanatory system to another constitutes a scientific revolution.

The work of Kuhn and others has resulted in an increased recognition that the foundations of scientific discourse — and hence scientific "truth" — are ultimately social. Science is not merely the neutral observation of data, as the modern outlook assumes.[50] Nor does science

---

Examining the record of past research from the vantage of contemporary historiography, the historian of science may be tempted to exclaim that when paradigms change, the world itself changes with them. Led by a new paradigm, scientists adopt new instruments and look in new places. Even more important, during revolutions scientists see new and different things when looking with familiar instruments in places they have looked before. It is rather as if the professional community had been suddenly transported to another planet where familiar objects are seen in a different light and are joined by unfamiliar ones as well. Of course, nothing of quite that sort does occur: there is no geographical transplantation; outside the laboratory everyday affairs usually continue as before. Nevertheless, paradigm changes do cause scientists to see the world or their research-engagement differently. In so far as their only recourse to that world is through what they see and do, we may want to say that after a revolution scientists are responding to a different world.

Thomas S. Kuhn, *The Structure of Scientific Revolutions*, 2nd ed. rev. (Chicago: University of Chicago Press, 1970), p. 111.

---

lead us to definitive statements about the world as an objective reality "out there." In fact, one recent theory, the Duheim-Quine thesis, denies that an experiment can test a theoretical prediction in any final way, because the test itself depends on the validity of the various theories that support the experiment.[51] Every experiment ultimately rests on a network of theories, opinions, ideas, words, and traditions — that is to say, on culture or the community in which it transpires.[52]

According to the new understanding, scientific knowledge is not a compilation of objective universal truths but a collection of research traditions borne by particular communities of inquirers. And its discourse — its language game — is largely unintelligible outside the lived practice of such communities.[53]

But Kuhn adds yet another important twist. Paradigms constitute not just the scientific enterprise, he argues, but also the world of the scientist.[54] The reigning paradigm determines what scientists see when they look at the world. Specific paradigms influence even the operations and measurements that scientists choose in conducting experiments.[55]

Postmodernism takes this aspect of paradigmatic beliefs seriously. It affirms that the world is not a given, an object "out there" that encounters us and that we can gain knowledge about. On the contrary, it affirms that through language we create our world and that there are as many differing worlds as world-creating languages.

This plurality of worlds marks the postmodern ~~world~~ view.

CHAPTER 4

The Rise of the Modern World

One day a little-known German philosophy professor who was already well into midlife and well beyond the midpoint in his career picked up a volume by the British skeptic David Hume. The effect of Hume's treatise was traumatic. As its reader, Immanuel Kant, later recounted, it aroused him from his "dogmatic slumber." Kant set himself to find a path beyond the philosophical cul-de-sac that Hume had exposed. His efforts proved fruitful. In response, Kant wrote what has been perhaps the most monumental and influential philosophical work since the Middle Ages, his *Critique of Pure Reason* (1781). Its publication set in place the last plank in the platform of modernity.

Whatever it may eventually become, postmodernism began as a reaction to the modern worldview and the Enlightenment project that is so integral to it. For this reason, if we are to understand the postmodern agenda, we must look at the rise of the modern mentality to which contemporary thinkers are so vehemently responding.

The Renaissance Foundation for Modernity

Most historians suggest that the modern era was born when the Enlightenment brought new hope to war-ravaged Europe. However, the machinery that would deliver the great cultural shift was set in motion long before the Peace of Westphalia brought an end to the devastation of the Thirty Years' War in 1648. A century earlier, Renaissance thinkers had already elevated humankind to the center of reality, proposed the principles that anchored the scientific method, and unleashed the forces that would undercut the political and cultural dominance of the Roman Catholic Church.

Renaissance is a French term meaning "rebirth" or "revival," and the historical period of that name was in a sense both: it involved a rebirth of the classical spirit exemplified in the ancient Greek and Roman civilization, and it brought a revival in learning after the so-called "dark ages."

Renaissance thinkers were humanists in that they adhered to the human values presented in the classical writings. In addition, the return to the classics included a rejection of the Aristotelianism of the Middle Ages in favor of Platonism and even mysticism. Above all, however, these intellectuals rekindled an interest in the workings of the world around them, thereby establishing the foundation for the modern scientific enterprise.

In many ways the quintessential Renaissance thinker was the English philosopher and scientist Francis Bacon (1561-1626). While a product of the Renaissance, Bacon also stood at the beginning of the Age of Reason. In a sense, therefore, he marks the transition from the Renaissance to the Enlightenment.

Bacon did not place mathematics at the center of natural knowledge as did the Enlightenment thinkers who came after him.[1] Nevertheless, he has been hailed as one of the first modern scientists. In keeping with the emerging scientific method, Bacon emphasized experimentation.

In many ways Bacon anticipated the Enlightenment project that would characterize modernity. He was convinced that the scientific method would not only lead to individual discoveries but also show the interrelations of the sciences themselves, thereby bringing them into a unified whole. To this end, Bacon placed at the foundation of the sciences a body of truths he called "first philosophy," which consisted of the laws of reasoning and the axioms shared by the various sciences.[2] In his posthumously published book *The New Atlantis,* Bacon described the ideal society. Above all, in this society people would look to science as providing the key to happiness.

It was not only for a way of understanding the universe that Bacon looked to the fledgling scientific enterprise, however. He believed that it also held the promise of providing a means of ruling over nature. He viewed truth and utility as two sides of a single coin, and he maintained that the aim of science should be to endow humans with power. This explains his famous dictum, "Knowledge is power." Knowledge mediates power over our circumstances, said Bacon; it offers the ability to alter our circumstances to conform to our desires. He thus taught that learning is for action, and action forms the justification for knowledge.[3]

This understanding led Bacon to envision humans discovering nature's secrets in order to exercise power over nature. He anticipated the enterprise of harnessing the scientific method as the means of altering our environment for our benefit.

Bacon's vision laid the foundation for the modern technological society. But Western technology has expanded far beyond what Bacon himself ever envisioned. When he suggested that the pursuit of knowledge is justified by the utility of its results, he had in mind the power to alter our *physical* circumstances. He was advocating the pursuit of what we might call *technical* knowledge. However, Bacon's late-modern successors sought to devise laws pertaining to *human* behavior and action. In so doing, they pursued *behavioral* knowledge, which promises the power to alter the actions of human beings in accordance with our goals. Bacon inaugurated an alliance between the researcher and the "technologist of nature," but his successors inaugurated an alliance between the researcher and the "technologist of society."[4]

The modern program that emerged from the work of Bacon and others has come under the sharp scrutiny of postmodern thinkers. Michel Foucault, for example, alerts us to the dark side of Bacon's vision. He asserts that when the researcher acts as the ally of the technologist of society, knowledge is transformed into the exercise of power over others in the form of violence against others. Foucault concurs with Bacon's assertion that knowledge is power, but he maintains that its power is the power of violence.

Modernity and the Enlightenment

The Renaissance laid the foundation for the modern mentality, but it did not erect the superstructure of modernity. The Renaissance cosmology elevated humankind to the center of the universe, but it did not establish the individual ego as the self-determining center of the world. Renaissance theorists pioneered the scientific method, but they did not reconstruct the pursuit of knowledge in accordance with the scientific vision. The Renaissance spirit undercut the authority of the church, but it did not enthrone the authority of reason.

Modernity was born only after a lengthy gestation period. Perhaps we could say that the Renaissance was a grandmother of modernity, and the Enlightenment was its true mother.

The Period of the Enlightenment

The explosive era in Western intellectual history from about 1650 to 1800 is commonly referred to as the Enlightenment or the Age of Reason. It is typically difficult to secure any sort of scholarly consensus about the specific starting and ending points of intellectual eras. Still, a number of historians have associated the beginning of the Enlightenment with the Peace of Westphalia in 1648 that ended the Thirty Years' War and the publication of Kant's *Critique of Pure Reason* in 1781. The former event provided a social and political context that fostered the elevation of reason and the denigration of religion in human affairs. The latter event marked both the culmination of and an effective challenge to many of the presuppositions characteristic of the Age of Reason. Especially important were the focus on the powers of human reason and the emphasis on sense experience.

The Enlightenment lasted barely two centuries; yet during this relatively brief period a new cosmology managed to displace the one that had reigned in Western civilization since the time of Augustine. The Age of Reason inaugurated the modern era, which only now seems to be in its twilight stage.

From Augustine to the Reformation, the intellectual aspects of Western civilization were dominated by theologians and theological

60

considerations. Although differing in the details, Christian theologians all agreed that reality was an ordered whole. God stood at the apex, followed by the angelic hosts; humans found their place "a little lower than the heavenly beings" (Ps. 8:5) but above the rest of the created order. The sovereign creator God had predestined certain humans — the elect — to salvation. Repeatedly and sporadically — but supremely in Jesus Christ — God entered the realm of human affairs from a lofty position above the world in order to effect this salvation. And medieval theologians affirmed that God continues to be operative in human lives, directing the flow of history and, more significantly, operating through the church, especially through the imparted grace connected with ecclesiastical activities. The great gothic cathedrals that dominated the medieval cities and villages bore witness to the centrality of Christian theology in Western society.

The Enlightenment permanently and radically disrupted the theological worldview created in the Middle Ages and honed by the Reformation. A new cosmology replaced the older hierarchical ordering of reality, and a new enterprise displaced the theological craft as the arbiter of truth.

The Enlightenment Anthropology

The Enlightenment had profound and lasting effect on the development of modern Western culture. Building on the Renaissance, it signaled the victory of a fundamental change in outlook that marked a final break with the medieval mentality and paved the way for the modern era.[5] Central to this changed outlook was the development of a paradoxical understanding of the human person.

The Age of Reason brought an enhanced status to humans and an elevated estimation of human capabilities. It replaced God with humanity on center stage in history. Medieval and Reformation theology viewed people as important largely insofar as they fit into the story of God's activity in history. Enlightenment thinkers tended to reverse the equation and gauge the importance of God according to his value for the human story.[6] In this manner, the Age of Reason dislodged God from the lofty position in the heavens to which the gothic cathedrals had pointed and brought him into the world of human affairs.

In addition to elevating humanity's status in the cosmos, Enlightenment thinkers formulated an exalted understanding of the human potential. They attributed greater intellectual and moral abilities to humans than had premodern theologians, whether Catholic or Protestant.

We find evidence of the Enlightenment appraisal of human potential in the central role that its proponents accord to human reason in the knowing process. In the premodern era, divine revelation functioned as the final arbiter of truth. The task of human reason, in turn, was to seek to understand the truth given through revelation. A maxim commonly attributed to Anselm governed the quest for knowledge: "I believe in order that I may understand." In keeping with this principle, reason sought to demonstrate the rightness of revealed truths and to reconcile experience with the understanding of the cosmic drama taught by the Christian faith.[7]

Enlightenment thinkers began to appeal to human reason rather than externally imposed revelation as the final arbiter of truth. In fact, they appealed to reason in order to determine what constitutes revelation. We could characterize the resulting mind-set by turning Anselm's thesis on its head: "I believe what I can understand." Proponents of the Age of Reason contended that people should no longer blindly accept the "superstitions" proclaimed by external authorities, such as the Bible or the church. Instead, they should dispassionately employ reason to systematize the data of sensory experience and follow reason wherever it would lead.[8]

Thinkers during the Age of Reason evidenced an equally exalted appraisal of our human moral capabilities. The Enlightenment emphasized morality rather than dogma, and Enlightenment intellectuals declared that the powers of human reason could both discover and foster conformity to the natural moral law, which God had written within each heart.

In addition to elevating the human position in the cosmos and articulating an exalted sense of human potential, the Enlightenment pictured the human person quite differently than medieval theology had. Building on ideas set forth in the Renaissance, it rejected the medieval ideal of the static, contemplative soul in favor of a vision of humanity as creative and appropriately discontented, yearning to transform the environment. Enlightenment thinkers viewed the human person as a restless wanderer engaged in an unending adventure. They viewed time not in terms of the eternal circling of the heavenly bodies, as medieval cosmology had, but rather as an onrushing and forward-moving stream.[9]

The Enlightenment elevation of humankind extracted a heavy price, however. In fact, the new outlook simultaneously exalted and demoted humanity. In contrast to the medieval and Reformation cosmology, the Enlightenment view no longer understood the world as a cosmos in which humans enjoy a special status. Rather, the new science of the Age of Reason pictured the universe as a giant machine in which humans were but a small part. Human beings managed to stop thinking of themselves as creatures subservient to God, but in doing so they also dethroned themselves from their lofty position near the pinnacle of creation, exercising authority as stewards over the rest of the created order.

The Foundation of the Enlightenment Outlook

The monumental shift in outlook that occurred during the Enlightenment did not happen in a vacuum. Rather, it came as the outgrowth of various social, political, and intellectual factors that led up to and transpired during this traumatic era in human history.

A series of military conflicts, commonly lumped together as the Thirty Years' War, had devastated Europe in the early seventeenth century. In the eyes of many intellectuals, the doctrinal disputes that divided Christians into competing confessional camps lay behind the armed conflicts that had ravaged the continent. Their disgust with confessional wars led these thinkers to question the validity of doctrine itself. Doctrinal commitments, they argued, only serve to divide people.

In addition to the religious quarrels of the century, the intellectual pathway was opened for the critical spirit of the age by two interrelated revolutions. One occurred in philosophy, the other in science.

The Revolution in Philosophy. Above all, the Enlightenment was the product of a philosophical revolution. Although its roots lay earlier in the discussions of the medieval theologians, the revolution was inaugurated by René Descartes (1596-1650), who is often referred to as the father of modern philosophy.[10]

63

Descartes's intent was to devise a method of investigation that could facilitate the discovery of those truths that were absolutely certain. He was strongly influenced in this effort by the growing importance of mathematics during this period. The ascendancy of the mathematical model in the Renaissance was a part of the new emphasis on the quantitative rather than the qualitative dimensions of reality, which had become evident in the work of such individuals as Johannes Kepler (1571-1630) and Galileo (1564-1642).

Descartes typified the emerging Age of Reason. Like most of the great thinkers of the period, he attempted to introduce the rigor of mathematical demonstration into all fields of knowledge.[11] His elevation of mathematical knowledge was not arbitrary: he believed that because the truths of mathematics arise from the nature of reason itself, they are more certain than knowledge derived from empirical observation, which may be faulty.

In his pursuit of certain knowledge, Descartes began with doubt. Unlike certain empiricists of the next century, Descartes managed to avoid falling into skepticism. He proposed to doubt everything, but he reached the conclusion that there is at least one thing that no thinking subject can doubt — namely, the subject's own existence. This conclusion is neatly expressed in the well-known adage of Cartesian philosophy (which Descartes actually borrowed from Augustine), *Cogito ergo sum* — "I think, therefore I am." A thoroughgoing commitment to doubt had to Descartes's satisfaction yielded an unquestionable certainty and thus a foundation on which to build a secure rational structure.

Descartes's philosophical method led to a new conception of the human person. Descartes himself ended by defining the human being as thinking substance and the human person as an autonomous rational subject.

The fact that Augustine provided Descartes with *Cogito ergo sum* demonstrates that Descartes did not discover subjectivity. The chief importance of his contribution lies in his emphasis on personal experience and personal knowledge, on knowledge arising from the individual's unique point of view.

In establishing the centrality of the human mind in this manner, Descartes set the agenda for philosophy for the next three hundred years.[12] Modern philosophers accepted the Cartesian method of begin-

I had noticed for a long time that in practice it is sometimes necessary to follow opinions which we know to be very uncertain, just as though they were indubitable . . . ; but inasmuch as I desired to devote myself wholly to the search for truth, I thought that I should take a course precisely contrary, and reject as absolutely false anything of which I could have the least doubt, in order to see whether anything would be left after this procedure which could be called wholly certain. Thus, as our senses deceive us at times, I was ready to suppose that nothing was at all the way our senses represented them to be. As there are men who make mistakes in reasoning even on the simplest topics in geometry, I judged that I was as liable to error as any other, and rejected as false all the reasoning which I had previously accepted as valid demonstration. Finally, as the same percepts which we have when awake may come to us when asleep without their being true, I decided to suppose that nothing that had ever entered my mind was more real than the illusions of my dreams. But I soon noticed that while I thus wished to think everything false, it was necessarily true that I who thought so was something. Since this truth, *I think, therefore I am,* [*or exist,*] was so firm and assured that all the most extravagant suppositions of the sceptics were unable to shake it, I judged that I could safely accept it as the first principle of the philosophy I was seeking.

René Descartes, *Discourse on the Method,* part 4, trans. Laurence J. Lafleur (Indianapolis: Bobbs-Merrill, 1960), p. 24.

ning with doubt and insisting that every belief be considered false until proven true, and they devoted their energies to solving the ensuing "egocentric predicament": How do we come to know — and how do we know that we know — a world "outside" our experience?[13]

Descartes exercised immense influence on all subsequent thinking.[14] Throughout the modern era, intellectuals in many disciplines have turned to the reasoning subject rather than divine revelation as the starting point for knowledge and reflection. Even modern theologians felt constrained to build on the foundation of rationalistic philosophy. They, too, accepted the primacy of reason advocated by Descartes. In fact, in the Enlightenment climate, the only alternative to such rationalism entailed a denial that reason by itself is able to yield knowledge of eternal realities.[15] But to make such a denial, one had to stand against the new intellectual flood engulfing the Western world with its emphasis on the voice of reason within rather than the voice of God from above. In the end, modern theologians ended up following Descartes's lead rather than trying to swim against the surge generated by the Age of Reason.

The Scientific Revolution. The Enlightenment was the product of revolution and the driving force toward additional revolution not only in philosophy but also in science. Its arrival marked a radical departure from the worldview of the Middle Ages. Central to the new thinking was a change in cosmology ushered in by the assertion of Copernicus that the earth is not the center of the universe. This and subsequent discoveries gradually undermined the medieval model of the cosmos as a three-story structure in which heaven was spatially above the earth and hell beneath it.

Perhaps even more foundational to the scientific revolution inaugurated in the Enlightenment was a change in the prevailing way of thinking and talking about the physical world. This change was marked by a shift from qualitative to quantitative terminology. Medieval science, following Aristotle, focused on "natural principles." Every object was believed to follow a "natural" tendency to fulfill its own inner purpose. Thinkers in the Age of Reason, however, dismissed the medieval talk of "natural tendencies" and "inner purpose" as mere metaphysical speculation.

In the Enlightenment, the earlier emphasis on final causes (the *telos* or purpose of objects) gave way to the mathematical, quantifying view of the scientific enterprise pioneered by Galileo over a century earlier. The new study of natural phenomena focused on applying analytical techniques to produce quantifiable results. The new tools of research included precise methods of measurement and a dependence on mathematical logic. In turning to this method, Enlightenment investigators narrowed their focus of interest — and hence began to treat as real — only those aspects of the universe that are measurable.[16]

Over time, Enlightenment thinkers began to apply the new method to all disciplines of knowledge. Not only the natural sciences, but also the human sciences — politics, ethics, metaphysics, and even philosophy and

---

Nature and Nature's laws lay hid in night:
God said, Let Newton be! and all was Light.

Alexander Pope, epitaph intended for Sir Isaac Newton.

---

theology — came under scientific scrutiny. In this way all fields of the human endeavor became, in effect, branches of natural science.

The high-water mark of this revolution in science came in the work of Isaac Newton (1642-1727). Newton's universe was a grand, orderly machine. Its movements could be known, because they followed certain observable laws. Newton's own goal was to explain the workings of this universe. He set out to show that the properties and behavior of every particle could be determined, at least in principle, by relatively few fundamental laws.

Newton's goal in seeking to describe the universe was not simply academic. He believed that by charting the regularities of the universe, science enhanced our sense of the greatness of God. As a Christian, he affirmed that "the heavens declare the glory of God," but he wanted to discover how. Hence, Newton's scientific enterprise served a theological end.

Both Descartes and Newton sought to use the power of reason to enhance a theological agenda. However, the revolutions in philosophy and science they engendered resulted in a new view of the world and of our place in it that has not always been sympathetic to the Christian faith. The modern world turned out to be Newton's mechanistic universe populated by Descartes's autonomous, rational substance. In such a world, theology was forced to give place to the natural sciences, and the central role formerly enjoyed by the theologian became the prerogative of the natural scientist.

Enlightenment Principles

These revolutions in philosophy and science sought to elevate reason over "superstition." As a result, the epoch was appropriately designated the Age of Reason. Reason replaced revelation as the arbiter of truth. It shared the stage with several other principles, forming a unified whole at the center of the Enlightenment mind-set. Significant among these principles are "autonomy," "nature," "harmony," and "progress."[17] But among these, reason remained the first principle of the Enlightenment.

The Age of Reason placed great emphasis on human rational capabilities, but in the Enlightenment understanding, *reason* comprised more than just a human faculty. The concept recalled the ancient Greco-Roman Stoic assertion that a fundamental order and structure lies within all of reality and is evidenced in the workings of the human mind. Enlightenment theorists assumed that a correspondence between the structure of the world and the structure of the human mind enables the mind to discern the structure inherent in the external world.

The Enlightenment principle of reason, therefore, presumed a human ability to gain cognition of the foundational order of the whole universe. It was their belief in the objective rationality of the universe that gave the intellectuals of the Age of Reason confidence that the laws of nature are intelligible and that the world is capable of being transformed and subdued by human activity. It was likewise their commitment to the consonance of the rational world and the workings of the human mind that made the exercise of critical reason so important to the Enlightenment thinkers.

Closely related to the principle of reason for representatives of the Age of Reason was the principle of *nature*. Enlightenment intellectuals emphasized what is grounded in or arises from "the very nature of things." They postulated that the universe is an orderly realm governed by the laws of nature. *Nature* and *natural law* became watchwords in the intellectual quest during the Age of Reason.

Enlightenment thinkers accorded a central place in their cosmology to God. They asserted that the working of the grand Designer of nature was responsible for the orderliness found in "the very nature of things." Operating on this belief, they sought to comprehend the laws of God by investigating the "book of nature," which lay open for all to read. The universal availability of these "natural laws" transformed nature into the common court of appeal, the arbiter of all quarrels. And it became the goal of the intellectual endeavor to bring all of human life into conformity with the laws of nature as discovered by reason.

Elevation of the principles of reason and nature led to elevation of the third principle of the Enlightenment mind-set — *autonomy.* During the Age of Reason, autonomous human reason dethroned the reverence for external authority as an arbiter of truth that had characterized the medieval and Reformation period. People were increasingly disinclined to rely solely on the dictates of ancient authorities. In many cases, simple appeals to the Bible, the teaching office of the church, or Christian dogma were no longer sufficient to bring about compliance in belief or conduct. Individuals became increasingly bold in testing all such external claims to authority.

The principle of autonomy did not give license to lawlessness, however. To the contrary, the principle of autonomy presupposed the presence in the world of a universal natural law that all humans could come to know through the power of reason. Rather than opening the door to lawlessness, autonomy demanded that each person discover and follow the universal natural law. Personal employment of reason lay at the heart of the Enlightenment emphasis on autonomy. Each person was supposed to follow the path toward the discovery of the natural law by using his or her personal endowment of reason and conscience, and it was assumed that doing so would produce a well-ordered life.

The fourth principle of the Age of Reason was *harmony.* Enlightenment thinkers assumed that the universe has an overarching order, that it is inherently reasonable and orderly. Some believed that this inherently orderliness ensured that, despite the apparent selfish and independent activity of each person or thing in the universe, the whole

---

Tutelage is man's inability to make use of his understanding without direction from another. Self-incurred is this tutelage when its cause lies not in lack of reason but in lack of resolution and courage to use it without direction from another. . . . . "Have courage to use your own reason" — that is the motto of enlightenment.

Immanuel Kant, *What Is Enlightenment?* in *"Foundations of the Metaphysics of Morals" and "What Is Enlightenment?"* (New York: Liberal Arts Press, 1959), p. 85.

---

would turn out most adequately. Some extrapolated from their belief in the inherent harmony of the world to a belief that all truth is part of a single, harmonious whole. These thinkers focused on philosophical method as a means of discovering truth. They believed that the application of the one true method to the hitherto disjointed and seemingly contradictory disciplines of human knowledge would cleanse them of their irrational elements and bring them together into the one true, unified body of knowledge.

Here again, Enlightenment thinkers managed to avoid the antinomian impulse. They viewed harmony not merely as a characteristic of the realm of nature but as a type of ethical principle that should govern human action. They believed that humans ought to act in accordance with the overarching harmony of the whole of reality.

Enlightenment anthropology neatly integrated humankind into the harmony of the cosmos, in part by emphasizing the inherent potential of the human individual and by deemphasizing the traditional Christian emphasis on human depravity. Enlightenment ethicists stepped away from the belief that all human beings are born in sin and naturally inclined to evil. They embraced instead the assertion of John Locke (1632-1704) that the human mind begins as a blank slate. Beginning with the notion that this initially pliable mind could be shaped by divinely created nature, they concluded that the employment of reason could bring human life into harmony with the universal natural order.[18]

Finally, the Enlightenment was an era of belief in *progress*. Building on the work of Descartes and others, thinkers in the Age of Reason were convinced that because the universe was both orderly and knowable, the use of the proper methods could lead to true knowledge. Armed

The eighteenth century is perhaps the last period in the history of Western Europe when human omniscience was thought to be an attainable goal.

Isaiah Berlin, *The Age of Enlightenment*
(Boston: Houghton Mifflin, 1956), p. 14.

with this belief, philosophers, theologians, and scientists alike set forth to construct systems that would approximate truth.

But the attainment of knowledge was not merely an end in itself. According to the Enlightenment mind-set, knowledge of nature's laws has practical significance. The discovery and application of these laws offered the promise of making humans happy, rational, and free. The scientific method could change the world by providing ways to apply nature's laws to the problems of personal and social life. Enlightenment thinkers were convinced that such change was just around the corner.

The belief in progress arose as well from the Enlightenment reading of history. Historians in the Age of Reason painted the Middle Ages as an era of superstition and barbarism. But they were confident that humankind was now emerging out of that era. The progress they noted in their own time led Enlightenment thinkers to ooze with optimism for the future. Despite the ebb and flow of history, they were convinced that in a larger sense the world historical process was directed upward and forward. They looked to the future with hope, certain that they were on the boundary of a new and glorious "promised land."[19] If humans could learn to live in the light of the laws of nature, Enlightenment thinkers confidently asserted, then the utopia would dawn. The Age of Reason was truly one of the most hopeful episodes in human history.[20]

Enlightenment Religion

The Enlightenment era challenged traditional viewpoints and reformulated thinking in every area of Western society, including religious belief. The Age of Reason marked the end of the dominance of the church in Western culture. The implications for Christian faith and theology were immense.

The new scientific mentality of the era inaugurated a changed understanding of the nature of religion. Increasingly scientists and theologians alike differentiated two types of religion — *natural* and *revealed*. Natural religion involved a set of foundational truths (typically believed to include the existence of God and a body of universally acknowledged moral laws) to which all human beings were presumed to have access through the exercise of reason. Revealed religion, on the

71

other hand, involved the set of specifically Christian doctrines that had been derived from the Bible and taught by the church over time.

As the Age of Reason unfolded, revealed religion increasingly came under attack, and natural religion increasingly gained the status of true religion. In the end, among Enlightenment intellectuals natural religion or the "religion of reason" replaced the focus on dogma and doctrine that had characterized the Middle Ages and the Reformation period.

The British empiricist John Locke helped pave the way for the ascendancy of natural religion over revealed religion. He set forth the revolutionary thesis that, once divested of its dogmatic baggage, Christianity was the most reasonable form of religion. On the basis of Locke's work, Enlightenment thinkers constructed a theological alternative to orthodoxy that came to be known as *deism*. The theologians of deism sought to reduce religion to its most basic elements, which they believed to be universal and therefore reasonable.[21]

Because natural religion is reasonable, the deists added, it is truer than any expressions of religion still constrained by belief in the supernatural — Christianity included.[22] They dismissed various dogmas that the church had traditionally attributed to divine revelation as unfit to serve as the standard for religious truth. They evaluated all such doctrines using the criteria of the religion of reason. The result was a bare minimum of dogmas, among which most deists included the existence of God (the First Cause or Creator of the universe), the immortality of the soul, and some kind of postmortem retribution for sin and blessing for virtue.[23]

The minimizing of doctrine cohered with the deists' understanding of the nature of religion. They viewed religion not as a system of belief but as a system for structuring ethical behavior. The chief role of religion, they maintained, is to provide a divine sanction for morality.[24]

While the deists were shifting the focus away from dogma, the Enlightenment theorists were setting forth an exalted appraisal of the human capacity to attain religious truth. The new outlook that emerged from their efforts reduced — even eliminated — the need for revealed religion. They were satisfied with the idea of a benevolent Creator who had written the crucial religious truths in the great book of nature and left it open for all to read.

Some proponents of Enlightenment natural religion grew harshly critical of traditional Christianity, charging that it was a corruption of the religion of reason.[25] Some also attacked the central pillars of the Christian apologetic of the day — the appeal to fulfilled prophecy[26] and to miracles.[27] And some characterized ecclesiastical authorities as perpetrators of ignorance and superstition.

Other voices of the Age of Reason simply equated the two belief systems. They asserted that in its purest form Christianity is merely a restatement of the truths of natural religion as known by reason.

Of course, proponents of traditional Christianity also made a case for their position. Some sought to accommodate Enlightenment thought by arguing that revealed religion is a necessary supplement to the religion of reason.[28] Others argued that Christianity is one historic stage in an ongoing process that will climax in the coming of the perfect, universal religion in the future.

Regardless of how Enlightenment thinkers viewed Christianity, however, they all endowed the religion of reason with canonical status and emphasized "nature" and "nature's God" at the expense of the God of the Bible. In focusing on the God of nature, the Enlightenment outlook bound the deity closely to nature and human reason — so closely that the supernatural was submerged in the natural. This move paved the way for the discarding of God in late modernity.

Modernity and the Kantian Revolution

As the 1700s drew to a close, the Enlightenment appeared to be running out of steam, especially in England. The religion of reason, once hailed as the replacement for divided Christianity, was losing adherents to both skepticism and religious relativism.[29] Its former supporters had concluded that reason alone is ultimately unable to answer the basic questions about God, morality, and the meaning of life.

These trends were evident in the field of philosophy as well. David Hume (1711-76) notably embraced skepticism, for example, and other philosophers likewise reached the conclusion that the empirical method demanded by the Enlightenment focus on a mathematical model of science could never lead to true and certain knowledge. In the end, the enlightened individual mind had produced nothing more than modern skeptical rationalism.

Although the Enlightenment itself had come to an end, Western society continued to bear its mark. No subsequent intellectual trends could remain aloof from the developments of that epoch in the history of the West. There was no going back to a mind-set that predated the phenomenal changes that had washed up on the intellectual shore of Europe. But was there a way forward? Or would the Enlightenment project itself be dashed on the shoals of skepticism?

By the time Hume and others were burying the Age of Reason, the legacy of Western thought had been transferred to Germany. Hume's writings awakened the creative genius of a man who was to become the greatest philosopher of modernity, Immanuel Kant (1724-1804).

Kant's life was outwardly uneventful. He was born, studied, taught, and died in the same place — the East Prussian port city of Königsberg (now Kalingrad, Russia). He never married or traveled. His schedule was so regimented that the women of the town are said to have set their watches by his daily afternoon walk.

Not until he was 57 years old did Kant produce a major work. Yet the book he published that year, *The Critique of Pure Reason*, rocked the philosophical world. It initiated an intellectual tidal wave the effects of which are still felt.

Chronologically and intellectually, Kant stands at the end of the Age of Reason. Yet his keen reformulation of the ideals of the Age of Reason breathed new life into the Enlightenment project and gave it the shape that would mark the modern era.

Kant's Philosophy

Kant set into motion what he saw as a "Copernican Revolution" in philosophy. The great Polish astronomer Nicolas Copernicus (1473-1543) had defied the wisdom of his day. Against the prevailing assumption that the earth was the center of the solar system, he argued that the planets revolve around the sun. In a similar manner, Kant elevated the mind to the center of the human knowing process (epistemology). He theorized that we can experience the world around us only because of the active participation of the mind.

The Context: Hume's Skepticism. The background to Kant's revolution lay in a grave problem of epistemology bequeathed by empiricism, the philosophical movement that came to characterize the Age of Reason in Britain. Central to the empiricist understanding of the process of knowing was what might be called "the passive mind."

In his *Essay concerning Human Understanding* John Locke rejected a central thesis of Cartesian philosophy — namely, that all human beings are born with a set of innate ideas. Locke argued to the contrary that the mind begins as a *tabula rasa,* a blank slate, and that it is totally passive in the knowing process. Through the senses, the mind simply receives "impressions" from the external world, which it uses to formulate ideas.

At first glance the empiricist theory appears to be obviously true. It seems to reflect our common, day-to-day experience. Yet this theory of knowing eventually led to the skepticism of David Hume, who showed its inadequacy as a explanation of human cognition. The empirical method, he argued, is unable to give us knowledge of certain features of reality we take for granted. All we know are our perceptions, Hume declared. But these do not provide a sufficient foundation for many of our most commonplace concepts.

According to Hume, one such unsupportable concept is *causality.* We continually gain perceptions of the coincidence of the sequence of events. From these perceptions we induce the relationship of causality. But we do not actually experience causality itself.

For example, during a game of billiards we see the cue ball make contact with a colored ball, which in turn moves into a pocket. From this perception we conclude that the cue ball *caused* the colored ball to roll away. But we have no direct perception of the cause-and-effect relationship itself.

Hume cited *substance* as a second concept that lacks empirical support. He argued that we readily experience a series of impressions (size, color, etc.), but we do not experience actual substances. Our imagination attributes these impressions to objects, said Hume, but we have no actual knowledge of substances as existing in the world. The identity of external objects (and likewise of causality) is not found "out there." It is merely the result of a habit of the mind.

Hume's epistemological skepticism had important consequences not only for epistemology in general but also for Enlightenment religion. It called into question the reigning religion of deism, which was built on the edifice of empiricism. Hume showed that the arguments for the reasonableness of natural religion are not as certain as their proponents had believed.

For example, Hume undercut the foundations of the cosmological argument, which states that the reality of the world demands the existence of a Creator as its first cause. Indeed, if we have no actual experience of causation, then how can the cosmological argument, which assumes just such an experience, be valid? In the same way, Hume argued that the doctrine of the immortality of the soul cannot survive the demise of the concept of substance. And he argued that the injustice and evil of the present undercut the case for a future realm of retributive justice based on the goodness of the Creator.[30]

Kant's Response: The Active Mind. Kant found Hume's radical skepticism challenging — challenging enough to awaken him from his "dogmatic slumber." Kant's probing of the problem led him to agree with Hume's cautious assessment of the human epistemological process. But, unlike his British predecessor, Kant believed that this limitation did not demand a skeptical rejection of all metaphysical concepts, such as God, the soul, and freedom.

In the *Critique of Pure Reason* (1781) Kant sought to set metaphysics on firmer footing. To this end, he proposed a bold hypothesis: the mind is *active* in the knowing process. We do not derive knowledge of the external world from sense experience alone, he argued. The senses merely furnish "raw data," which the mind then systematizes. This process of organizing sensations (i.e., "knowledge"), he added, is made possible by certain formal concepts present in the mind. These concepts act as a type of grid or filter providing the parameters that make knowing possible.[31]

Among the various formal concepts that Kant explored, he found two to be foundational: space and time. He maintained that space and time are not properties that inhere in things but are rather parts of the ordering that the mind imposes on the world it encounters. The objects that we perceive may not actually exist "in space and time," he said, but we have no means of knowing the external world of sense experience apart from employing these two concepts.

His hypothesis that the mind is active in the epistemological process led Kant to posit a distinction between objects present in the experience of the human knower ("phenomena") and objects lying beyond experience ("noumena"). Generally Kant uses "noumenon" to refer to an object as it exists apart from any relation to a knowing subject — what he called the "thing-in-itself." Sometimes, however, he uses "noumenon" to refer to an object that we simply lack the needed apparatus to detect.

In either case, Kant was forthright in declaring that we have no sense experience — and hence no direct knowledge — of noumena. All we truly "know" are phenomena, objects as they are present in our experience. We can gain no knowledge of things-in-themselves, at least not through sense experience and use of the scientific method.

Practical Reason. Like Hume's epistemology, Kant's theory of knowing placed strict limits on the ability of thinkers to argue from sense experience to transcendent realities (e.g., God, the immortal soul, human freedom). No reality that lies beyond space and time can be known through the scientific enterprise, because science is based on sense experience.

It was not Kant's intention to support the religious skepticism of Hume, however. He wanted to approach metaphysical postulates from a more secure direction. To that end, he argued that such postulates belong to another domain of human reason — reason in its "practical" aspect. And he placed this aspect in relationship to the moral dimension of human existence.

According to Kant, the human person is not only a creature capable of sense experience but also a moral being. Our relation to the world is not limited to scientific knowledge. Rather, life is a stage on which humans act; it is a realm of moral value. Kant established the moral nature of existence by appeal to what he saw as the universal

---

I have therefore found it necessary to deny *knowledge,* in order to make room for *faith.*

Immanuel Kant, *Critique of Pure Reason,* trans. Norman Kemp Smith
(New York: St. Martin's Press, 1929), p. 29.

Act as if the maxim of thy action were to become by thy will a Universal Law of Nature.

Immanuel Kant, *Fundamental Principles of the Metaphysic of Morals,* trans. Thomas K. Abbott (Indianapolis: Bobbs-Merrill, 1949), p. 38.

---

human moral experience: a sense of moral conditionedness or "ought-ness." Human beings are cognizant of a "pressure" placed on them to make choices that can only be described in terms of morality, he declared.

Like the theoretical aspect, this practical or moral dimension of human existence is fundamentally rational, Kant argued. He was convinced that certain rational principles control all valid moral judgments, just as other rational principles lie at the foundation of all theoretical or sense-based knowledge. Consequently, he held that the goal of the moral dimension of human life is to become as rational as possible.

Kant spoke of this rationally moral way of living as "duty." He argued that the way of duty culminates in a supreme principle of morality — his famous *categorical imperative.* According to Kant, the moral life consists in acting in accordance with principles that we would wish all persons to follow. For example, if we are tempted to lie, we need only ask, "Would I want others to be dishonest?"

The categorical imperative requires that we take stock of the fundamental considerations that ought to motivate our actions as rational beings and test to see if they should be universalized. Kant's ethical method thus focuses less on specific actions and more on the motivating considerations underlying action.[32]

Kant and the "Transcendental Pretense"

Kant believed that his Copernican revolution provided a way forward through the wreckage of the Enlightenment. His solution to the problems Hume had posed marked the completion of the Enlightenment construction of the modern human person. Kant's elevation of the active

78

mind as the definitive agent both in the process of knowing and in the life of duty encouraged subsequent philosophers to focus their interest on the individual self. The centrality of the autonomous self, in turn, laid the foundation for the modern engagement in the Enlightenment project and in fact became the chief identifying characteristic of the emerging modern era.

Kant thus provided the foundation for the final emergence of modernism as a cultural phenomenon. And his work marked the inauguration of modernity in its fullness, the era characterized by a focus on intense self-reflection. Kant was the first philosopher to scrutinize so thoroughly the nature and limitations of reason itself. In succeeding centuries, representatives of other forms of cultural activity have been equally anxious to subject their areas of interest to exhaustive internal critiques.[33]

But Kant's Copernican revolution exacted a price. The elevation of the autonomous self to the center of the philosophical agenda gave birth to the "transcendental pretense" of modernity.[34] Beginning with Kant's philosophy, the Western mind-set has exalted and universalized the thinking self. This new focus opened the way for the modern Western attempt to complete the Enlightenment project.

The exalted sense of the importance of the self arose from the subtle shift Kant introduced into Descartes's proposal. In the Kantian system, the Cartesian self became not just the focus of philosophical attention but the entire subject matter of philosophy. Rather than viewing the self as one of several entities in the world, Kant envisioned the thinking self in a sense "creating" the world — that is, the world of its own knowledge. The focus of philosophical reflection ever since has been this world-creating self.

The universalizing of the self readily followed. Underlying Kant's philosophy was the presumption that in all essential matters every person everywhere is the same. When Kant's self reflected on itself, it came to know not only itself but *all* selves, as well as the structure of any and every possible self.

The transcendental pretense evident in Kant's philosophy helped produce "the white philosopher's burden." Kant's presumption that all selves resemble each other led some philosophers to conclude that they should be able to construct a universal human nature. Even thinkers (like Kant) who never left their hometowns should be able to make authoritative pronouncements on human nature and morality. They should be able to assess the conduct and practices of societies around the globe, determining which were "civilized" and which were "barbaric."[35] And they should on this basis have the authority and even the duty to instruct those whom they concluded were "savages" for the sake of the advancement of true civilization.

The transcendental pretense assumes that the workings of one's own mind and the mores of one's own culture reflect what is universally rational and therefore what is universally human. Critics contend that this assumption is simply unwarranted and that it can lead to arrogant and aggressive efforts to prove what it assumes. They contend that the history of the modern era is strewn with instances in which the transcendental pretense has led Westerners to claim that reason itself confirms that they possess the only legitimate set of morals, the only legitimated form of government, and the only true belief structure.[36]

Kant's philosophy provided the intellectual foundation for another dimension of modernity as well — the shift to radical individualism. In a sense, his epistemological proposal is a more intricate and sophisticated version of the Enlightenment elevation of reason. Like his forebears, Kant was confident that through observation, experiment, and careful reflection, human beings could discover the truth of the world. That being the case, he believed that the burden of discovering truth is ultimately a private matter, that the knowing process is fundamentally a relationship between the autonomous knowing self and the world waiting to be known through the creative power of the active mind.

In the same way, Kant viewed morality as a relationship between the autonomous active agent and the universal law, which the self can know through practical reason. He accorded little significance to any role played by human communities, whether in the form of providing social customs, traditions of value, or moral education. Kant's world consists simply of the individual and the universal. His philosophy sets forth the self coming to know — and to harness — the universal.[37]

Thinkers such as Descartes, Newton, and Kant provided the intellectual foundation for the modern era that was born in the late 1600s, flowered in the 1700s and 1800s, and is apparently now entering its final stage.

The modern, post-Enlightenment mind assumes that knowledge is certain, objective, and good. It presupposes that the rational, dispassionate self can obtain such knowledge. It presupposes that the knowing self peers at the mechanistic world as a neutral observer armed with the scientific method. The modern knower engages in the knowing process believing that knowledge inevitably leads to progress and that science coupled with education will free humankind from our vulnerability to nature and all forms of social bondage.

The ideals of the thinking self knowing itself and of the mechanistic universe opened the way for the modern explosion of knowledge under the banner of the Enlightenment project. From Francis Bacon to the present, the goal of the human intellectual quest has been to unlock the secrets of the universe in order to master nature for human benefit and create a better world. This Enlightenment quest, in turn, produced the modern technological society of the twentieth century. At the heart of this society is the desire to rationally manage life, on the assumption that scientific advancement and technology provide the means to improving the quality of human life.[38]

Whatever else postmodernism may be, it embodies a rejection of the Enlightenment project, the modern technological ideal, and the philosophical assumptions upon which modernism was built.

CHAPTER 5

The Prelude to Postmodernism

After a ten-year solitary sojourn in the mountains, forty-year-old Zarathustra decided the time had come to return to human society. He arrived at a town that bordered the forest. As he entered the village, the returning hermit noticed that the townspeople had gathered in the marketplace. To this group Zarathustra preached the death of God and the coming of the Superhuman (*Übermensch*).

The publication of *Thus Spake Zarathustra* (1883), Friedrich Nietzsche's fanciful account of the teachings of this legendary figure, spelled the beginning of the end of modernity and the inauguration of the gestation period of postmodernity.

Postmodernism entails a radical rejection of the Enlightenment project and the modern technological ideal along with the philosophical assumptions lying behind them. Devotees of the Enlightenment project seek to uncover a central unity underlying the seemingly disjointed flux of all experience. For the source of this unity, modern thinkers look to human culture, universal history, or nature — but above all they begin with the human person, the self.

Postmodernism is marked by a rejection of this enterprise. Postmoderns conclude that all attempts to describe an objective, unifying center — a single real world — behind the flux of experience are doomed; in the end they produce only fictions, creations of the human mind. In detaching human explanation from the notion of an underlying objective world, the postmodern critique of modernism cuts us off from *things* and leaves us only *words*.[1] It also cuts us off from the Enlightenment ideal of the human *self*.

The modern world was not built in a day, of course, and neither was the postmodern rejection of modernity. It was preceded by certain intellectual developments that challenged the underpinnings of the modern mentality. These earlier volleys prepared the way for the full-scale frontal assault against the fortress of modernity launched in the late twentieth century.

In this chapter we will survey the philosophical developments that prepared the way for postmodernism. In particular, we will look at ways in which the concept of the self that was foundational for the modern era — the concept that the Enlightenment tradition from Descartes to Kant had so carefully crafted — came to be completely undermined.

The Questioning of the Enlightenment

The modern era grew out of an intellectual revolution that challenged the assumptions of medieval philosophy and science. Modernity began to unravel when a similar revolution challenged the explanatory power of modern categories.

The intellectual revolution that eventually led to the demise of the Enlightenment project began already in the nineteenth century with certain developments in European philosophy. The modern outlook proved to be highly resilient in the face of the early threat. In fact, in many ways it reached its full maturity and cultural influence only in the twentieth century. Despite its tenacity, however, in the waning decades of our century, modernism has clearly begun to collapse under the torrent of new modes of thinking that have bombarded it.

Challenges to the Enlightenment Self

In many ways René Descartes and Immanuel Kant can be said to have written the first and last chapters of the story of Enlightenment philosophy. The Cartesian dictum introduced the principal character — the self as a thinking substance. The problems that arose from this vision of the self, culminating in the skepticism of Hume, were finally resolved by Kant's postulate of the active mind and affirmation of transcendental categories as the foundation for knowledge, which elevated the autonomous self to the center of the intellectual agenda.

The work of these two philosophers set the parameters that defined the modern enterprise. No subsequent thinkers could escape the long shadow they cast. They seemed to have left the self firmly entrenched in the intellectual landscape. But not all of their followers were completely satisfied with the legacy they inherited from these two philosophical giants.

The Critique of the Cartesian Thinking Self. Since its inception, Cartesian philosophy has enjoyed lasting importance in the Western intellectual tradition.[2] With the arrival of the Romantic movement in the nineteenth century, however, critics began to take a closer look at the reigning Cartesian philosophy. From that point until the present, Descartes's act of grounding philosophy in the thinking self has been subjected to sustained criticism.

Attacks on Descartes's philosophical foundation have tended to focus on several perceived difficulties. For one thing, critics charge that Descartes's reasoning inevitably leads to a problematic dualism of material and nonmaterial substances, even in the context of the Cartesian view of the human person. In setting out to establish a philosophy grounded in propositions that could not be doubted, Descartes begins with the concept of the self as a thinking substance. The "I" whose existence he cannot doubt is the conscious self, the subject of mental acts. But by focusing on the thinking self, Descartes relegates the body to a sphere outside of and apart from the thinking subject. Critics charge that this split between "myself" and "my body" is inconsistent with our experience of a unity between the mind and the body.[3]

Critics also charge that Descartes does not provide adequate grounding for his assertion that the thinking self has an objective existence. Appealing to what Edith Wyschogrod terms the principle of "parsimony,"[4] Gilbert Ryle offers the classical expression of this criticism using the example of Oxford University. He notes that people regularly speak of the university as though it were an entity distinct from its constituent colleges. But there is no such separate entity, says Ryle; the term *Oxford University* simply provides us with a convenient way of talking about a particular conglomerate of schools.

In the same way, say the critics, the thinking self is not an actual entity existing apart from or beyond our thoughts, doubts, and wishes. It is simply a useful descriptive term. On the basis of this argument, Ryle encourages us to reject the idea of the thinking substance as an extant entity. The Cartesian self, he argues, is nothing more than a "ghost in the machine."[5]

But the feature of Cartesianism that has received the most criticism is its inherent subject-object dualism. If the self is a thinking subject, then the self necessarily perceives every other kind of thing as an object. The resultant distinction between subject and object endows the subject with greater importance than the object. It sets the knowing subject apart from and above the world, which is the object of the self's knowledge.

The twentieth-century philosopher Martin Heidegger offers the most telling critique of this emphasis on the human being as a thinking subject, arguing that Descartes and Kant directed all modern philosophy down an illegitimate and destructive path.[6] Heidegger contends that the human being is not primarily a thinking self, a subject that engages in cognitive acts; rather, we are above all else beings-in-the-world, enmeshed in social networks.

Although Heidegger's analysis has become common parlance in our day, in the nineteenth century most post-Kantians had not yet come to his radical rejection of the self. They struggled with the question of how to overcome the subject-object dualism Descartes precipitated. And in contrast to proponents of the late modern and postmodern rejection of the self, Kant's disciples — often known as the German idealists — looked to the self for the solution to this knotty philosophical problem.

The Critique of the Noumenal: Johann Fichte. Related to the criticism of the Cartesian legacy is a substantial body of criticism directed at the other pillar of modern philosophy, Immanuel Kant. The critique of Kant began already among the generation of thinkers who immediately succeeded him.

Perhaps the quintessential example of an early post-Kantian is Johann Gottlieb Fichte (1762-1814). Kant set the stage, defined the terms, and determined the rules with which Fichte operated. Yet, having accepted the form and content of Kantian philosophy, Fichte was enabled to explode it from the inside.[7] It was not his intent to eliminate Kant's transcendental self but rather to expose the Kantian "fiction" of an objective world existing in its own right beyond the self.

According to Fichte, the task of philosophy is to explain how we can possibly experience objects that appear in space and time and seem to be governed by natural laws. At the heart of his answer lies a presupposition that we participate in a moral realm (which Kant referred to as the realm of "practical reason") — or, more specifically, that we exercise free will. In his *Science of Knowledge* (1794), Fichte asserts that as acting, willing agents we are independent of the objects of our sense experience. In this assertion he reveals his sympathies as a "transcendental idealist": he affirms that the knowing self creates and determines the objects that constitute its own external world. The purpose of this creative act is to provide a field or context for one's endeavors (i.e., for one's moral conduct). Hence, the realm that Kant claims to know through "pure" reason (the world of sense perception) Fichte claims to produce through the exercise of "practical" reason.

Fichte's work marks a bold thrust beyond his mentor. While elevating the active mind in the knowing process, Kant nevertheless presumed a noumenal realm of actual entities independent of the knowing self. He speaks of "things-in-themselves," which he believes are not knowable through sense perception but which are nevertheless real. In essence, Fichte dismisses the notion of the "thing-in-itself." He maintains that the notion of a noumenal realm of objects lying beyond the grasp of the knowing subject no longer carries any philosophical significance.

Fichte admits that ordinary experience suggests that an objective world — a "not-self" — exists independently of us. On this level, the "not-self" does stand apart from the self. But on a deeper level, says Fichte, it has its source in the self. Specifically, the source of the "not-self" — and, ultimately, the source of individual human selves as well — lies in the primordial activity that Fichte designates as the "absolute self."[8]

In this manner, Fichte manages to sustain Kant's commitment to the concept of the transcendental self. The concept of the "absolute self" accounts for the existence of the finite self and its counterpart, the seemingly objective world of the non-self. But by ejecting from his world the "thing-in-itself," Fichte cuts Kant's one remaining link to an absolutely external reality.

Eliminating the noumenal realm opened the way for an additional step beyond Kant that Fichte himself may have taken — namely, the creation of what some philosophers refer to as "alternative conceptual frameworks." Kant applies the concept of human freedom to the realm of ethical action alone. Fichte applies it to what he considers the more important realm of thought or the play of the imagination. This sort of freedom is important because it holds the potential of liberating us from a single way of understanding the world. It opens up the possibility of describing objects using multiple sets of concepts or "conceptual frameworks."[9] Operating with differing conceptual frameworks would in effect allow us to create different worlds for ourselves.

The Rejection of the Enlightenment: Friedrich Nietzsche

Post-Kantian philosophers in the modern era questioned the exalted Cartesian-Kantian view of the knowing self and the capabilities that the Enlightenment understanding fostered, but in the end they did not reject the Enlightenment itself. Instead, they tended to raise their voices within the context that Descartes and Kant had created.

The distinction of hurling the first volley against the Enlightenment structure itself and thereby blazing the way for what eventually became the postmodern assault fell to Friedrich Nietzsche (1844-1900). He, if anyone, deserves the accolade "patron saint of postmodern philosophy."[10] Although he spoke with many different voices, Nietzsche consistently showed himself to be a foe of modernity.[11]

Nietzsche was born on October 15, 1844, into a strongly religious family; his father and both grandfathers were Lutheran pastors. Although intensely pious as a boy, Nietzsche abandoned his faith during his late teens. After studying classical philology at the universities of Bonn and Leipzig, he was called to a professorship at the University of Basel in 1869. On the basis of this call, the Leipzig faculty conferred on him a doctoral degree without his having written a dissertation. The following year, at the age of twenty-five, Nietzsche was promoted to a full professorship in classical philology.

Throughout his life Nietzsche was plagued by various disorders. In 1879 he left Basel and spent the next ten years largely in solitude in Italy and Switzerland. Finally, his health problems culminated in an irreversible breakdown in 1889. Its onset was marked when he collapsed on a street in Turin. After an eleven-year struggle with mental illness, Nietzsche died on August 25, 1900 — as the nineteenth century was giving birth to the twentieth.

Before he died, though, Nietzsche formulated most of the themes that would be essential to the development of the postmodern intellectual climate. Above all, he established the course of philosophy toward postmodernism with his thoroughgoing rejection of Enlightenment principles.

The Demise of the Enlightenment Concept of Truth. Lying at the foundation of Nietzsche's attack on modernism is his rejection of the Enlightenment concept of truth.

In Nietzsche's view, the world is made up of fragments that are totally different from one another. In constructing concepts, however, we overlook the fact that no two things or occurrences are exactly the same. Consequently, rather than mediating genuine knowledge, our conceptualizing robs reality of its multiplicity and destroys the original richness and vitality of human experience.

As an example, Nietzsche considers the relationship of our concept "leaf" to real leaves.[12] Although all leaves may share certain characteristics, each leaf differs from every other leaf. We can form the concept "leaf" only by overlooking these differences. Nietzsche held that the concept "leaf" is thus a falsification of the reality of leaves. The term introduces into the world of objects the form of "leaf," which in fact we do not find there, and it also robs reality of those qualities that differentiate individual leaves from one another.

This problem is compounded by the fact that we not only construct individual concepts but combine them in a "great edifice of ideas" in our efforts to comprehend the world.[13] This structure, says Nietzsche, is actually an illusion. It merely repeats on a higher and more complex level the falsification present in each individual concept. Rather than being inherent in the real world, constructs such as the "laws of nature" are in fact human impositions upon the world, which in its individuality and creativity transcends our intellectual constructions.

Nietzsche is not merely repeating what Kant had said a century earlier. Kant argued that the self constructs knowledge by means of transcendental categories derived from the mind, which he assumed to be structurally the same in all persons. He believed that this sameness of structure — this shared human nature — provides the foundation for universal human knowledge and that our imposition of categories on the flux of experience constitutes a positive ordering of reality.

Nietzsche, in contrast, calls into question the entire enterprise of rationalistic human knowledge. He claims that what we view as "knowledge" is a purely human creation, on the grounds that the process of fabricating reality is an arbitrary and individual matter. Our construction of categories constitutes a displacement or disarranging *(Verstellung)* of the world. Rejecting Kant's grand theoretical comprehension of reality, Nietzsche argues that what we commonly accept as human knowledge is in fact merely a self-contained set of illusions. He essentially viewed "truth" as a function of the language we employ and hence believed that truth "exists" only within specific linguistic contexts.[14]

In one sense, we can place Nietzsche in the company of the Romantic philosophers who preceded him. Like Fichte, the Romantics grappled with the question of how to overcome the Enlightenment subject/object dualism. As post-Kantian idealists, they looked to the self rather than the flux of diverse sensations and experiences for the means to organize the world. When the self organizes the world, it actually organizes its own experiences. Consequently, the Romantic philosophers concluded that the result is identical with the self. They maintained that through this world-organizing activity, the self actually discovers itself and in the process overcomes the subject-object distinction.

Romantics such as Friedrich Schelling (1775-1854) found in the artist's experience of creating a work of art an illuminating example of this dynamic. In the creative act of molding the unformed medium, artists discover what form the medium has in their own minds. In a similar manner, he asserted, the aesthetic intuition of the human "artistic" self gives unity and meaning to the world and overcomes the subject-object dualism.[15] Schelling proceeded to characterize all human knowledge as an aesthetic phenomenon.

Although standing with the Romantic philosophers in their focus on aesthetics, Nietzsche also differs radically from them. His predecessors believed that art could bring subject and object together in a supreme moment of aesthetic insight. Nietzsche denies the possibility of such a fusion. He insists that artistic expression, like intellectual conceptualizing, is not a vehicle of truth but a flight from the truth.[16] Indeed, he contends that the aesthetic dimension is as much a realm of illusion as the intellectual dimension.

This makes Nietzsche a nihilist. In the end he contends that we have no access to reality whatsoever. In fact, he claims that there is no "true world." Everything is a "perspectival appearance" the origin of which lies within us. We live in a constructed world that comes from our own perspective.[17] Rather than a vehicle for conceptualizing truth, language is an expression of an innate human talent for aesthetic creation. But our grand abstractions turn out to be metaphors in disguise, "fictions" that we author. Although we are constrained to recount it, says Nietzsche, this artistic fiction has nothing to do with a "real world" that supposedly exists outside ourselves.[18] In short, he characterizes truth as a kind of error without which a certain species of life — humankind — could not live.[19]

According to Nietzsche, our world is a work of art that is continually being created and recreated. But nothing lies either "behind" or "beyond" this web of illusion.[20] The whole elaborate "work of art" is in a sense self-creating: in some way, it gives birth to itself.[21]

What, then, is truth? A mobile army of metaphors, metonyms, and anthropomorphisms — in short a sum of human relations, which have been enhanced, transposed, and embellished poetically and rhetorically, and which after long use seem firm, canonical, and obligatory to a people; truths are illusions of which one has forgotten that this is what they are; metaphors which are worn out and without sensuous power; coins which have lost their pictures and now matter only as metal, no longer as coins.

Friedrich Nietzsche, "On Truth and Lie in an Extra-Moral Sense," in *The Portable Nietzsche*, ed. and trans. Walter Kaufmann (New York: Penguin Books, 1976), pp. 46-47.

Nietzsche's assertion that the world is aesthetically self-creating was a far-reaching innovation. He has been hailed as the founder of what developed into the "aesthetic metacritique" of that understanding of truth which views "the work of art," "the text," or "language" as providing the grounds for truth's own possibility.[22] This critique, which Nietzsche whispered softly within the pages of his literary corpus, would eventually be shouted from the rooftops by his postmodern heirs.

The Rejection of the Enlightenment Concept of Values. The Western philosophical tradition from the ancient Greeks through the Enlightenment was built on an "objectivist" understanding of values. It was assumed that values were not merely a product of the human intellect but that they were are embedded in a reality that transcends us. It was assumed not that we *create* truth and value but that we *discover* them. Enlightenment thinkers believed that the pathway to this discovery came through autonomous reason and philosophical inquiry.

Nietzsche's writings constitute a sustained attack on this view. He launched a philosophical effort to "unmask" what he saw as the Enlightenment illusion. He argued that our understanding of truth and value derives not from our ability to pierce the veil into the transcendent realm but from the immediacy of the "will to power."[23]

Nietzsche grounds his attack in his famous assertion of "the death of God." He used this arresting phrase to capture his sense that Western civilization was no longer influenced by the Christian tradition as it once had been. Belief in God, in the Christian story, and especially in divine rewards and punishments for human behavior had lost the power they had once exercised, said Nietzsche, and no comparable beliefs had emerged to take their place. The only thing remaining in the relative vacuum left by the death of God was a body of primitive instincts aimed at self-preservation and self-promotion, chief among them being what Nietzsche referred to as the "will to power" (the desire to perfect and transcend the self through the exercise of personal creative power rather than dependence on anything external).[24] In short, Nietzsche announced that Western culture had separated itself from the transcendent.

Nietzsche perceived the radical consequences of this phenomenon. In fact, he has been hailed as the first person to recognize the profound implications of the death of God.[25] For one thing, he saw that value can no longer be grounded in appeals to a realm beyond the human mind (i.e., to God). He asserted that nothing undergirds human values except the will of the person who holds them. Things have value in our world only to the extent that we give them value.[26]

At the foundation of Nietzsche's concept of the "will to power" is his suggestion that the cardinal instinct of all living things is the desire to "discharge" their strength.[27] In connection with this, the "will to power" constitutes the primary motive of human behavior. We desire to bring all our capabilities to perfect fruition. We desire to be creative rather than merely creaturely.[28]

As an extension of this human motivation, the "will to power" refers to the pragmatic use of language, values, and moral systems for personal or social advancement. Motivated by the will to power, we devise metaphysical concepts — conceptions of "truth" — that advance the cause of a certain species or people.

Nietzsche's postmodern heirs draw heavily from this social aspect of the will to power and its related understanding of knowledge, which we might call "perspectivism." As we have already noted above, Nietzsche claims that there is no truth as such but only relative truths for a certain sort of creature or a certain society. Because all knowledge is a matter of perspective, knowledge is really interpretation — and all interpretations are lies.

These are primarily matters of epistemology, and specifically of the relationship between language and truth. Because Nietzsche was most concerned with morality — how we should live — he predictably viewed the epistemological situation in terms of its moral overtones. He charged his culture with having transformed the duty to be truthful into "the obligation to lie according to a fixed convention, to lie herd-like in a style obligatory for all."[29] And he complained that the herd-like stampede of Enlightenment theorists toward reason had implications in the realm of ethics as well as that of epistemology.

Nietzsche faults philosophical moralists for seeking to avoid the conclusion that morality, like intellectual knowledge, is merely local custom or an expression of undependable sentiments. He attacks these thinkers — and Christian theologians in particular — for improperly claiming that their own moral beliefs are rational, universal, and axiomatic. Like the democratic values of the moralists, he says, the Christian values of humility and self-abnegation are but the expressions of a "slave morality" that is rooted in resentment and the desire for revenge.

According to Nietzsche, this universalization of beliefs is dangerous. He maintains that the slave morality underlying both democracy and Christianity has been the bane of European culture and that its propagation only serves to limit those who have the greatest abilities and to bring all persons to the same level of mediocrity.[30]

The sickness he saw in Western culture led Nietzsche to welcome the death of God. The demise of a transcendent grounding for morality opened the way for the "transvaluation of values," the development of an authentic "will to power." The ideal of this new order is the Superhuman *(Übermensch)*.

While proclaiming this vision of the human potential, Nietzsche avoids lapsing into modern utopianism. He does not anticipate a golden age ready to burst upon the shores of Western society. It is not his intent to inspire his readers with new possibilities but simply to bring to light the illusions of the Enlightenment preachers of his day. Consequently, he speaks of the Superhuman only rarely, and he provides only a sketchy outline of the figure. In fact, his description of the Superhuman may be more an expression of disgust with human beings as they are than an expression of hope for what they might become. Nietzsche even muses that "the last man" will not be the Superhuman but a feeble bourgeois so thoroughly content with life that he says, "We have invented happiness."[31]

Despite his pessimism, Nietzsche does pour some content into the concept of the Superhuman. For one thing, in connection with his doctrine of "the eternal return," Nietzsche differentiates the Superhuman from his nineteenth-century contemporaries on the point of love of one's fate.

The concept of "eternal return" is central to the work that Nietzsche considered to be his most important, *Thus Spoke Zarathustra*.[32] In essence, it is Nietzsche's expression of his belief that whatever has happened will happen an infinite number of times. He appears to have formulated this doctrine in reaction to the nineteenth-century bourgeois myth of progress and the Christian conception of redemption.[33] Christian eschatology affirms that the apparently meaningless events of life gain their meaning in eternity. Nietzsche's doctrine

> This life as you live and have lived it, you will have to live once more and also innumerable times more; and there will be nothing new in it, but every pain and every joy and every thought and sigh and everything unutterably small or great in you life will have to return to you, all in the same succession and sequence.
>
> Nietzsche, *The Gay Science*, trans. Walter Kaufmann (New York: Random House, 1974), §341, p. 273.

of the eternal return asserts to the contrary that no event ever gains meaning; it simply happens again and again.

Nietzsche knows that his contemporaries, infected as they are with the slave morality, will find this thought horrifying. But he asserts that the Superhuman will consider it good news. Having lived life in every detail, Nietzsche's hero gladly wills to live it again.

The Rejection of the Enlightenment Philosopher. Like the Greeks before them, the philosophers of the Enlightenment tradition considered their task to be connected with the discovery and elucidation of absolute or ultimate truth. They sought to deduce the basic categories necessary for interpreting the nature of things. Consequently, Enlightenment philosophers emphasized the role of reason. By means of rational reflection, they hoped to provide the foundation for the enterprise of gaining conceptual knowledge about reality.

Nietzsche rejects this task. He denies what other philosophers held as axiomatic. We do not possess a faculty of reason that can know and explicate ultimate truth apart from life, he insists. But instead of bemoaning this loss of reason, knowledge, and an objective world, he calls for an active, aesthetic nihilism. He calls us to become the artists of our own existence, inventing a world suited to our being.[34]

According to Nietzsche, the philosopher's task is not to deduce metaphysical truths but to act as "a physician of culture." The philosopher is to be a free spirit who transforms our attitude to life. Denouncing the thinness and poverty of the ideas that dominate and shape contemporary Western society, the Nietzschean philosopher should foster the development of a more vigorous culture.[35]

Nietzsche clearly saw himself as the one who would create new values out of the ashes of bourgeois Christian civilization. But how could he accomplish this task? He constructs a proposal on the basis of two aspects of his understanding of how culture operates.

The first aspect focuses on the role of myth in cultural life. The rationalist method of the Enlightenment philosophers sought to undermine myth. Their program was to free society from bondage to irrational beliefs and superstitions that had no foundation in rational reflection. Nietzsche, in contrast, seeks to reintroduce the concept of myth. He maintains that myth is not only unavoidable but in fact essential to the health of human culture. In their wholesale efforts to destroy myth, says Nietzsche, modern philosophers robbed Western culture of an ordering myth and thereby inadvertently fostered an unwholesome nihilism.

In response, Nietzsche offered a myth he believed could save society from the nihilism that had cast its shadow over Western culture — the doctrine of the eternal return. He nowhere provides clear indication as to what "eternal return" actually means, why he considers himself justified in valuing the doctrine so highly, or how the idea embodies the social dimension inherent in a myth.[36] Nevertheless, he contends that

---

Without myth every culture loses the healthy natural power of its creativity: only a horizon defined by myths completes and unifies a whole cultural movement. Myth alone saves all the powers of the imagination and of the Apollonian dream from their aimless wanderings. The images of the myth have to be the unnoticed omnipresent demonic guardians, under whose care the young soul grows to maturity and whose signs help the man to interpret his life and struggles. Even the state knows no more powerful unwritten laws than the mythical foundation that guarantees its connection with religion and its growth from mythical notions.

Friedrich Nietzsche, *The Birth of Tragedy and the Case of Wagner,*
trans. Walter Kaufmann (New York: Vintage Books, 1967),
§23, p. 135.

---

this doctrine has the power to impart what had been lost in Western culture[37] — namely, a meaning or a pattern to human life.

The myth of the eternal return brings us to the second aspect out of which Nietzsche's program for Western culture emerges: his understanding of the nature and role of language.

On occasion, Nietzsche appears simply to conclude that although human language is a less than perfectly transparent medium for thought, it would nonetheless offer us a means to get the truth if we could somehow compensate for the distortions it introduces. But more generally he seems to be saying not that language distorts reality but that it *is* reality. By constructing an independent world, language creates "truth" through its metaphors and anthropomorphisms.[38]

Nietzsche views "truth" as a function of the internal workings of language itself. He contends that our beliefs are congruent with the language we employ because our language is simply a system of interpretation.[39] He also suggests that the objective "correctness" of the interpretation is less important than the "beautiful possibilities" it offers.[40] In championing this view, Nietzsche stands as a precursor to the postmodern deconstructionists. Following his lead, they concluded that there is no such thing as a *thing*. Every thing is simply a mask for some other thing — and every "other thing" turns out to be a mask as well.[41]

Nietzsche's assertion that language speaks its own truth is foundational to his proposal of a new myth for Western culture. We are introduced to his strategy for proposing the new myth in *Thus Spoke Zarathustra:* he presents himself as a "remystifier."[42] As Nietzsche tells the story, Zarathustra announces a world defined by the death of God. The teacher does not argue for his picture of the world; he merely seeks to work out the implications of his vision and then demands that we accept it. Those who acknowledge Zarathustra's vision enter into his realm of discourse. To those who cannot acknowledge his vision the teacher has nothing else to say.

Zarathustra is the model for the Nietzschean philosopher. Crucial to the inauguration of the new culture of the Superhuman is a new language (understood as a comprehensive system of interpretation). This new language embodies the myth of the Superhuman and the eternal return together with the values it teaches. At the same time, the language excludes all opposing systems.

The difference between the new and the old is not a matter of one being "correct" and the other "incorrect." Consequently, Nietzsche does not presume to facilitate the transition to the new by means of rational argumentation. The new reality is inaugurated through an interpretive "will to power." The cultural physician arbitrarily announces the new language, and, by virtue of its very existence, the new system of interpretation will bring into being the new reality that corresponds to it.[43]

In short, the philosopher of the Superhuman calls us to accept his language, his myth of the eternal return. He recognizes that it is merely a free-floating aesthetic universe, but he holds out the hope that once we come to live within it, we just might be transformed into his ideal.[44]

The Problem of Hermeneutics

Building from, but going beyond the work of the post-Kantian philosophers, Nietzsche sounded an alarm: modernity was poised for a catastrophic collapse. Together with his idealist colleagues, Nietzsche raised the issues that marked the beginning of the demise of the transcendental self so carefully constructed by the giants of modern philosophy, Descartes and Kant. But the role of the German idealists was largely preparatory. They left to others the task of focusing the issues that would eventually undermine modernism and prepare the way for the postmodern era.

Nietzsche brought Western philosophy face to face with the knotty issue of the nature of interpretation. He articulated the question and left other thinkers to seek the answers. One path they took in their search was to explore the domain of hermeneutics, understood as the theory of the interpretation of written texts.

The Genesis of Modern Hermeneutics:
Friedrich Schleiermacher

The modern discussion of hermeneutics predates Nietzsche by half a century. It was inaugurated not by a philosopher but by a theologian, the "father of modern theology," Friedrich Schleiermacher (1768-1834).[45]

Schleiermacher's quest began with his discovery that biblical texts are not systematic theological treatises. Instead, they are the products of creative minds responding to particular circumstances. On this basis, the nineteenth-century theologian argues that in order to understand a text, an interpreter must set it in context within the life of the author, must get behind the printed words to the mind that wrote them.

To this end, Schleiermacher differentiated between two aspects of interpretation, grammatical and psychological. The grammatical understanding looks for meaning in the words and phrases of the work itself. The psychological understanding seeks to go behind the words to the mind of the author which the written text expresses.[46]

Schleiermacher's method embodies a philosophical analysis of the conditions that make understanding possible.[47] Its underlying assumption is that in order to understand a work, we have to reconstruct it by retracing the process by which it came to be. It also assumes that the original creative process arose primarily from the author's personal outlook and life within the context of a larger social environment.

Ultimately, Schleiermacher's optimism concerning the interpreter's ability to re-create the mind of the author shows the influence of Romanticism. He works from the assumption that both author and interpreter are manifestations of universal life. There has to be some connection of this sort for the interpreter to complete the hermeneutical task, for in the end interpreters must not only gain an understanding of the world of the author but must in a sense transform themselves into the author.[48]

Historicism and Hermeneutics: Wilhelm Dilthey

Schleiermacher laid the foundation for the hermeneutical discussion of the past two centuries. But the transitional point in the discussion came with another German thinker, a contemporary of Nietzsche, Wilhelm Dilthey (1833-1911). Dilthey embedded the hermeneutical task within the horizon of history. But in accomplishing this goal, he took a step toward dismantling the transcendental self of the German idealists, for he also embedded the human person in a historical context.

Foundational to Dilthey's entire program is his turn to experience.

Kant's theory of the active mind declares that the knowing self constructs the world of objects it perceives by means of certain transcendental principles (e.g., space and time). These are a priori principles: they originate in the mind or understanding itself.

Dilthey denies that the structures of thought are a priori. They do not belong inherently to the mind, he says; they arise out of and derive their meaning from *experience*. Consequently, Dilthey has no place for a "timeless world" of meanings, essences, or rational principles. Nor does he subscribe to notions of a metaphysical subject or a transcendental self. Dilthey views the human person as a mind-body unity living in interaction with the physical and social environment. He maintains that all experience and hence all thought arise out of this interaction.[49] Thought is governed at every point by the ever-shifting confrontations of the living self and the surrounding world.[50]

Dilthey does not totally dismantle the Cartesian-Kantian self, however. Rather, he links the self to the construction of historically and socially conditioned "worldviews."

According to Dilthey, we are heirs to an accumulation of human wisdom expressed in social custom and tradition. This growing body of experience assists us in ordering the flux of our experience by helping us construct a coherent metaphysical system — a worldview *(Weltanschauung)*. This worldview includes our knowledge and beliefs about the world, our value judgments, the meaning we find in the world, and the ends, ideals, and principles of conduct that guide our living in our world.[51]

Implicit in each worldview is the claim that it is "true." However, no single *Weltanschauung* has yet commanded universal adherence. In fact, humans adhere to worldviews that are not merely different but irreconcilable. Dilthey argues that the variegated nature of life itself lies at the foundation of the multitude of worldviews. We must recognize that our experiences of the world are finite, he says, and avoid claiming complete and exclusive truth for any worldview we construct. Only then will we able to enlarge our own vision by understanding other worldviews and thereby begin to approach the full and balanced view of things that Dilthey holds out as a worthy goal.[52]

In a similar manner, Dilthey argues, philosophers must avoid the temptation to believe that there is one universally valid system of metaphysics.[53] He claims that the purpose of enterprises such as religion, art, and philosophy is not to discover some objective world order but to give expression to the various ways in which human minds endeavor to unify their experience of the world.[54]

More important for Dilthey than judging the truth claims of competing worldviews is observing the changes that they undergo in history. Such observations lead him to make a crucial differentiation between the natural sciences and the sciences of the human spirit. The natural sciences focus on classifying phenomena and understanding general laws, he declares; the social sciences do not. Human life does not come to us as data to be catalogued but as life already lived — lived through interpretations and meaning. We can understand human behavior only because we are able to view it "from the inside" and thereby recognize the meaning in what people say and do. Scientists "impose" categories or meanings on natural phenomena, but philosophers merely "read" the meanings already evident in words, acts, and gestures as well as in human social institutions, which represent vast complexes of interpretations.

Dilthey points out that the meaning associated with human activity is always embedded in a historical context. For this reason, he is often hailed as the primary figure in a movement called "historicism." He argues that we can never escape from our own historical circumstances. Not even philosophers can claim to view history from a transcendental standpoint outside history. Their understanding is necessarily limited by their own "horizon," says Dilthey, by the historical context in which they stand. They inevitably interpret the past through the concepts and concerns of the present.[55]

Dilthey's historicism leads him to the study of hermeneutics, to what he calls "the systematic interpretation of human experience." The goal of this enterprise is to understand the social and cultural meaning systems that underlie those past expressions of human experience that remain available for study in the present. He contends that the most readily available and the hence most important of these expressions are writings, and so he contends that the focus of hermeneutics is language.[56]

But the task of understanding texts is complicated at its inception by what Dilthey calls the "hermeneutical circle." Foundational to the problem is the common realization that complex wholes and their parts are always inseparably intertwined. We can comprehend a whole only by appeal to its parts, but the parts acquire their meaning only within the whole. Or, to put it another way, we can understand a complex system only if we first understand the particular expressions that manifest it, but we can understand any particular manifestation only if we already understand the system as a whole.[57]

The connection between words and a sentence provides an illuminating example. We can understand the imperative "Hand me my club" only as we grasp the meaning of the individual words. But we cannot select the appropriate meaning of "club" or realize that "hand" is a verb, not a noun, when we realize what the entire sentence means.[58]

According to Dilthey, the problem associated with this part-whole relationship pervades all aspects of the human world and is especially acute in the area of historical studies. We can understand the thinking of individuals only by comprehending the cultural environment in which they lived, but our comprehension of the culture of a given historical era requires an understanding of the thinking of individuals who lived at that time.[59]

The hermeneutical circle undercuts all hopes of finding a transcendent starting point or a self-evident, self-contained certainty on which we can construct an edifice of unconditioned knowledge. Dilthey himself admits that the circle is theoretically irresolvable. Nevertheless,

---

Here we encounter the general difficulty of all interpretation. The whole of a work must be understood from individual words and their combination but full understanding of an individual part presupposes understanding of the whole. This circle is repeated in the relation of an individual work to the mentality and development of its author, and it recurs again in the relation of such an individual work to its literary genre. . . . Theoretically we are here at the limits of all interpretation; it can only fulfil its task to a degree; so all understanding always remains relative and can never be completed.

Wilhelm Dilthey, "The Development of Hermeneutics," in
Dilthey: Selected Writings, ed. H. P. Rickman
(Cambridge: Cambridge University Press, 1976), p. 259.

---

he suggests that certain methods of exposition can solve the problem in practice. Specifically, we can approach an understanding of complex situations through an inductive, to-and-fro movement, reaching provisional conclusions and progressively refining and revising them. From the parts we obtain a preliminary sense of the whole. We then use this sense to determine more precisely the significance of the parts. With a better idea of the significance of the parts, we test and correct our idea of the whole, and so on.

The inductive exegetical process has its limitations, however. Dilthey argues that it can bring to light the structure immanent in the particular data we are studying, rendering them a coherent whole.[60] But it will only bring us *close* to the truth. We should not imagine that the process is a means to discovering a universal law. And what is true of the hermeneutical circle in general applies to the sciences of the human spirit in particular. Although he holds out the hope of our being able to see beyond our own horizons, Dilthey offers no guarantee that our inductive study of history will lead us to any necessary and universal meaning that ties all humankind together.

Schleiermacher maintained that the purpose of biblical interpretation is to capture the spirit of the author. Dilthey extended Schleiermacher's concern for hermeneutics to encompass all texts and, indeed, all human activities. He believed that every human enterprise has a meaning that an interpreter can illumine. In the twentieth century, such thinkers as Martin Heidegger and Hans-Georg Gadamer pursued these ideas.

The Hermeneutic of Difference: Martin Heidegger

Perhaps no twentieth-century philosopher has been more widely discussed and more variously understood than Martin Heidegger (1884-1976). His interpreters customarily divide his literary activities into two segments. They contrast the earlier, more existentialist Heidegger with the later, more poetic Heidegger.

For most of the century his greatest importance lay in his acknowledged status as the "father of German existentialism" (a designation that he himself eschewed).[61] His writings have been cited even by such

Christian thinkers as Rudolf Bultmann and John Macquarrie as providing the philosophical foundation for existentialist theology. In this connection, Heidegger has been acclaimed for his penetrating insight into the existential implications of the fact that human beings are conscious of their own impending death.[62]

The advent of postmodernism has shifted the focus away from the existential concerns of the early Heidegger to the literary concerns of the later Heidegger. Postmoderns read him as one of the first thinkers who tried "to take Nietzsche seriously as a thinker."[63] But in what sense was he a harbinger of the postmodern spirit?

Heidegger was born in 1889. He attended the university in Freiburg, Germany. After teaching for eight years at his alma mater, he became professor of philosophy at Marburg (1923), only to return to Freiburg in 1929 as successor to the well-known philosopher Edmund Husserl. After the fall of the Third Reich in 1945, Heidegger was dismissed from his post because of alleged Nazi sympathies during the war. At this point, he retired in seclusion near Freiburg.

Early in his career, Heidegger declared that the fundamental question of metaphysics is the question of Being: "Why is there anything at all rather than nothing?"[64] This question led him to a radical critique of the reigning philosophy of his day.

Heidegger claims that the Western philosophical tradition is based on an erroneous quest. From the ancient Greeks to his own day, he declares, philosophers sought definitive judgments about things-in-being (or things "out there"). By analyzing the opposites of Being (e.g., becoming and appearance), they tried to discover essential categories, hoping to transcend these opposites and arrive at Being.

In so doing, however, they failed to see that their main focus should have been on "being there," on being-in-the-world. Heidegger sought to discover Being or reality (what he later called "a new ground of meaning")[65] by beginning with authentic human existence.

This project introduces us to the cornerstone of his early work, the concept of *Dasein* ("being-in," or literally, "being there"). Although *Dasein* is a difficult, nearly indefinable concept,[66] Heidegger seems to link it closely with human existence. *Dasein* is that reality which is concerned with the nature of its own being. *Dasein* wonders, What am I? How did I come to be? and What does my existence mean? *Dasein* is always raising these questions; no final answers ever emerge. According to Heidegger, we have to "work out" rather than simply "find out" who (or what) we are. And we do this through living in the world.

Rather than a static "thing," therefore, *Dasein* is an activity — our working out of living in the world. In Heidegger's language, *Dasein* is fundamentally "being-in," or "being-in-the-world."[67]

In promoting the concept of *Dasein* as "being-in" Heidegger offers a bold rejection of the Cartesian-Kantian concept of the self, the knowing subject that encounters the world as as object. Descartes — and the entire Enlightenment tradition following him — begins with the discovery of the thinking subject: "I think, therefore I am." Heidegger, in contrast, declares that the starting point for philosophy is not a self-aware thinking being but simply a "being there."

Replacing the thinking self confronting its object with "being-in" opens the way for a more holistic understanding of reality. It provides a way to avoid the subject-object dualism and the two-part experience of "self" and "world" in favor of a unitary phenomenon, the "being-present-at-hand-together" of subject and object.[68] This vision of being-in the world as a seamless whole enables Heidegger to wage a relentless attack on the dualism that he says has beset philosophy (and literary theory) since Descartes.[69] His goal is to dislodge such traditional dichotomies as mind and body, self and world, subject and object, self and other.[70] In particular, he wants to dispose of the notion of the subject as an independent substance existing above time and human society or inhabiting some eternal, transcendent realm detached from life.[71]

Heidegger's insistence on our embeddedness in the world leads to what has become perhaps the most important aspect of his thought for the postmodern philosophers who claim his legacy: he provides a challenging critique of the Western philosophical understanding of "presence."

Heidegger claims that philosophers since Plato have confused Being with "presence." In keeping with the Western philosophical tradition, we view existence from the perspective of a single temporal mode, "the present." We declare that things exist in that they present themselves to us in the here-and-now.[72] Heidegger objects to the focus on the present on the grounds that it reinforces the fatal Cartesian dichotomy

between subject and object. It maintains the distinction between ourselves as conscious, thinking selves and the physical world, which we
see as the object of our knowing.

Heidegger calls us to understand Being in connection with all three
dimensions of temporality — past, present, and future. Doing so will
allow us to discover that Being includes absence as well as presence, he
says. An existing thing is not merely what presents itself to us in the
present; it is also what is not now present to us, because it is either past
or future.

Confronting Heidegger's thesis, postmodern philosophers pose a
crucial question: What connects the presence and absence involved in
Being?[73] What lies between any pair of apparent opposites, whether
presence and absence, identity and difference, or being and nonbeing?
Jacques Derrida grapples with this question and Heidegger's discussion
of "difference" in formulating his concept of *differance*.[74] But postmodern thinkers have on the whole been less interested in Heidegger's
views on philosophical issues of this sort than they have been in the
questions of the nature of "truth" and language that he explores in his
later writings.

Heidegger is critical of the transformation of truth into the certainty of representational thinking that he says is characteristic of the
Western tradition.[75] That is, he rejects the common assumption that
truth consists in a correspondence between our statements and a fully
formed reality that exists outside of us. He contends that the demand
for certainty connected with this correspondence theory leads us in the
wrong direction. Truth is not absolute and autonomous, he argues; it
is relational.[76] The dominant view is inadmissible simply because the
concept of an external world is itself nonsensical. We have only the
world of experience in which we are embedded as participants. Consequently, we can speak about truth only insofar as we are "in" it, not
searching for it outside of experience.

Truth is not a reward in a quest for the certainty of propositions,
says Heidegger. Truth has to do with "revelation," with the "disclosure"
of Being. To gain this truth, he argues, requires an "openness to the
mystery" that occurs only as we move away from our modern fixation
with calculative thinking and engage in "meditative thinking."[77] He
contends that our vaunted conceptual categories are insufficient to help

Art then is the becoming and happening of truth. Does truth, then, arise out of nothing? It does indeed if by nothing is meant the mere not of that which is, and if we here think of that which is as an object present in the ordinary way, and thereafter comes to light and is challenged by the existence of the work as only presumptively a true being.

Martin Heidegger, *Poetry, Language, Thought*, trans. Albert Hofstadter (New York: Harper & Row, 1971), p. 71.

us come to grips with the truth of Being; we need a new, more rigorous type of thinking that is neither merely theoretical nor practical but that precedes such distinctions.[78]

But what kind of thinking does the presence of Being shine through? Here Heidegger returns to the aestheticism pioneered by Nietzsche. He looks beyond conceptual discourse to artistic expression. He asserts that art is not merely a vehicle for the *revelation* of truth (and hence of Being) but that it can in fact become the means for the *creation* of truth.[79] In fact, Heidegger suggests that a work of art creates its own world.[80]

Heidegger does not consign ultimate world-creating power solely to the realm of art, however. Like Nietzsche before him, he attributes this power more broadly to language, and especially to poetry as the quintessential linguistic expression.[81]

Language takes precedence over art because it is more closely connected with thought. In fact, according to Heidegger, language and thought are nearly reciprocal in that the experience of language is thought's experience of itself.[82] Like Nietzsche, Heidegger believes that through its connection with thought, language plays a crucial role in bringing the human world into existence.[83]

Yet, at this point Heidegger seems to step farther than even Nietzsche dared to tread. He asserts that we do not so much create language as move within it.[84] Our "being-in" language allows us to discover that language (which for Heidegger *is* reality or Being) gives itself to us. As we enter into this kind of genuine experience with language, Heidegger believes, we will be transformed.[85]

107

In the naming, the things named are called into their thinging. Thinging, they unfold world, in which things abide and so are abiding ones.

Martin Heidegger, *Poetry, Language, Thought*, pp. 199-200.

Enlightenment philosophy begins with the assumption that the experience of meaning centers on the object known. Meaning occurs as the subject encounters an object and comes to know it. Nietzsche elevated the knower, who as an artist creates a personal world through language. Heidegger cuts language free from the artist. In so doing, however, he leaves us with what some critics call "a view from nowhere," a mystical encounter that is neither objective nor subjective.[86]

Despite making this seemingly radical move beyond modernism, in a sense Heidegger remains indebted to the Enlightenment project. He has turned his back on the notion of the self attaining in any way to some transcendent essence. Indeed, he rejects the notion that there is any such essence lying beyond life in the world. Nevertheless, Heidegger retains the post-Enlightenment, Romantic ideal of the subject discovering itself. His philosophy of the self's quest for self-discovery remains a nostalgic, world-weary, last-ditch defense of the concept of the self as a unified totality.[87]

Heidegger's postmodern heirs borrowed the mystical, antimetaphysical strand of this thought to eliminate the final remnant of nineteenth-century utopianism from the estate he bequeathed to them.

The Rebirth of Hermeneutics: Hans-Georg Gadamer

In 1960, Hans-Georg Gadamer published his *magnum opus, Wahrheit und Methode,* in which he revives the use of the term *hermeneutics,* which Schleiermacher had pioneered.[88] His interest lies not in the area of the specific task of biblical exegesis, however; rather, following Dilthey, Gadamer is interested in hermeneutics as a philosophical issue. Specifically, pulling into view all human experience of the world, he raises anew Kant's question of how understanding is possible.[89]

The purpose of my investigation is not to offer a general theory of interpretation and a differential account of its methods . . . but to discover what is common to all modes of understanding and to show that understanding is never subjective behaviour toward a given "object," but toward its effective history — the history of its influ- ence; in other words, understanding belongs to the being of that which is understood.

> Hans-Georg Gadamer, *Truth and Method*, trans. and ed. Garrett Barden and John Cumming (New York: Crossroad, 1984), p. xix.

In a manner reminiscent of Nietzsche and Heidegger, Gadamer turns to the experience of art for a means of critiquing the modernist centering of hermeneutics on rationality. Through a work of art, he argues, we experience truth that we cannot attain in any other way. The experience of art challenges the scientific consciousness to acknowledge its own limits. From this starting point — the justification of the truth of art — Gadamer attempts to develop a new understanding of knowl- edge and truth. He insists that this understanding must correspond to the whole of our experience of coming to know the world.[90] In pursuing this goal, he seeks to steer a course between two "heresies" — objectiv- ism and relativism.

Gadamer begins with the assumption that the old objectivist posi- tion is no longer viable, that there is no single, timeless truth existing "out there" independent of particular perspectives or methods, waiting to be discovered by means of scientific procedures and personal em- pathy. Contrary to Schleiermacher's belief, says Gadamer, the interpreter cannot come to grasp the mind and intention of the author.[91] Nor can the researcher recover the past "as it actually was."[92] Gadamer faults Dilthey for extending the objectivist principle to history in its entirety and erroneously concluding that the interpreter can discover the mean- ing of history as a whole.[93]

He also rejects the solution proposed by the German idealists. These nineteenth-century thinkers looked to the subject (the self) as the ground for meaning in the world, but, says Gadamer, they failed to see the obvious corollary: the world itself might have different meanings rather than a single "true" meaning.

While eschewing objectivism, Gadamer does not want to embrace the relativism of perspectivist thinkers such as Nietzsche.[94] He charges that they erroneously assert that there can be no such thing as "the truth." He rejects their assertion that one can speak only about perspectives or about a variety of incommensurable truths that change through history and from culture to culture.

To accomplish the seemingly impossible feat of treading a path between these two alternatives, Gadamer draws on Heidegger's concept of "being-in-the-world."[95] He credits Heidegger for pointing out that human existence is thoroughly "in the world" or historical. Because we stand within the world, we can never escape our historical context. But because we stand in different places in the world, we naturally develop different perspectives on the world and different interpretations of the world. In this light, Gadamer follows Heidegger in arguing that history is not an external object from which we stand detached but is rather an ongoing process that embraces us.[96]

But Gadamer denies that this necessarily leads to relativism. Lying behind the Babel of competing interpretations is a shared reality — a world, a tradition, a language. Because of this common dimension, we can anticipate experiencing a "fusion of horizons."[97] This occurs, says Gadamer, through a kind of conversation in which we compare and contrast our various interpretations. The conversation creates a common language and fosters a "communion" in which we no longer remain what we were.[98]

Gadamer's idea of a "fusion of horizons" offers him a point of departure for interpreting literary texts. Meaning is not merely a matter of what the author intended, lying in the text, waiting to be unlocked by means of scientific and empathetic interpretation. Rather, meaning emerges as the text and the interpreter engage in a dialogue, in a "hermeneutical conversation."[99] The goal of this dialogue is an intersection of the horizon of the author and the horizon of the interpreter.

Because meaning emerges within a conversation, the goal of hermeneutics is not to discover the "one meaning" of the text. The meaning of the text is not that strictly circumscribed: the limits of a text's meaning are not confined to just the author's intent or the reader's understanding.[100] In fact, we can never claim that any one interpretation is correct

110

"in itself."[101] Nonetheless, each text can lead to many instances in which an interpreter experiences a fusion of horizons.

Gadamer is not merely presenting a new theory of literature here. His assertions have far-reaching implications for the issue of the meaning of reality as a whole. Like Nietzsche and Heidegger, he appeals to artistic experience in order to understand the connection between language and the world, he concludes that our relationship to the world is fundamentally linguistic, and he affirms that meaning emerges from the artistic or linguistic enterprise.

By implication, then, Gadamer's position (like Nietzsche's and Heidegger's) undermines the Enlightenment epistemological program. Meaning does not inhere in our world, waiting to emerge as the Cartesian "knowing self" unlocks it. The knower does not discover a "preexisting" meaning "out there"; rather, meaning emerges as the interpreter

---

We can now see that it was this speculative movement at which we were aiming. . . . The being of the work of art was not a being-in-itself which was different from its reproduction or the contingency of its appearance. Only by a secondary thematicisation of the two things is it possible to make this kind of 'aesthetic distinction.' Similarly, that which offers itself for our historical study from tradition or as tradition, the significance of an event or the meaning of a text, is not a fixed object that exists in itself, whose nature we have simply to establish. The historical consciousness, in fact, also involved mediation between past and present. By seeing that language was the universal domain of this mediation, we were able to extend our enquiry from its starting-points, the critiques of aesthetic and historical consciousness and the hermeneutical approach that would replace them, to universal dimensions. For man's relation to the world is absolutely and fundamentally linguistic in nature, and hence intelligible.

Hans-Georg Gadamer, *Truth and Method*, trans. and ed. Garrett Barden and John Cumming (New York: Crossroad, 1984), pp. 432-33.

---

engages in a dialogue with the "text" of the world, and the ongoing hermeneutical conversation gives rise to many experiences of the fusion of horizons between the interpreter and the world.

But Gadamer provides an even broader foundation for the dismissal of the Cartesian self and of the rationality of the modern mind. In a manner that prefigures the postmodern philosophers, he asserts that our conversation with a text is less an event in which we take the initiative than a game in which we participate.[102] In fact, as he describes it, we do not even take the initiative of getting into the game; rather, it is the game itself that plays, drawing us as players into itself. In a similar manner, we do not engage in the language game: the play of language addresses us. And when we come to understand a text, what is meaningful in it "charms" us (as beauty charms us), even before we are in a position to test the claim to meaning that the text is making.[103]

The Problem of Language

Friedrich Nietzsche lobbed the first shell in the bombardment that eventually brought down modernity. The structure of Enlightenment philosophy was not able to withstand the new sorts of questions that he introduced. Among these, the linguistic questions — especially those focusing on matters of interpretation — proved to be the most decisive.

In the wake of Nietzsche's attack on modernity, some of his heirs struggled with the nature of hermeneutics. Others took up another equally troubling problem. They found what they believed to be a far-reaching challenge concerning the nature of language itself in Nietzsche's work. The responded to this challenge with a proposition that marked a radical change from nineteenth-century thinking on this issue: they asserted that language is socially structured. In making this assertion, they reconstructed the very nature of language.

Language as Game: Ludwig Wittgenstein

The reconstruction of the nature of language that occurred during the first half of the twentieth century was a result of the efforts of several thinkers working nearly simultaneously. One important player in this development was the Austrian philosopher Ludwig Wittgenstein (1889-1951).

Wittgenstein's first major treatise was the *Tractatus Logico-Philosophicus* (1921). The book's focus on elementary facts and its assertion that the purpose of language is to state facts made it greatly influential in the rise of what has been called "logical positivism." But its importance for postmodern thought lies elsewhere. Wittgenstein declares that language "pictures" the world.[104] In making his case for this view, he links thought, language, and knowledge.

Overall, the *Tractatus* is a model of logic and systematic order. Yet Wittgenstein ends the work on a surprisingly mystical note. Certain matters defy words, he notes, and "what we cannot speak about we must pass over in silence."[105] Some interpreters see in this statement the whole purpose of the book. They contend that Wittgenstein wants the reader to realize that rational thought should be transcended.[106]

What Wittgenstein only hints at in the *Tractatus* becomes more evident in two of his later writings, the so-called *Blue and Brown Books* and the *Philosophical Investigations*. These volumes reflect the changes that Wittgenstein's thought had undergone during and after the 1930s. Perhaps the most radical development was his refutation of the assertion he had made in the *Tractatus* that language has a single purpose. In the later works he argues that we use language not only to state facts but to offer prayer, to make requests, to convey ceremonial greetings, and so on.

This change in view led Wittgenstein to formulate his well-known concept of "language games." Essentially, he asserts that each use of language occurs within a separate and apparently self-contained system complete with its own rules. In this sense, says Wittgenstein, our use of language is similar to playing a game. We require an awareness of the operative rules and significance of the terms within the context of the purpose for which we are using language. Each use of language constitutes a separate "language game," and the various games may have little to do with one another.[107]

To adopt the concept of "language game" is to take an important step toward rejecting the idea of objective reality. In his later works, Wittgenstein explicitly abandons the concept of truth as correspondence with reality or a picturing of reality, characterizing it instead as an internal function of language. No proposition can be limited to a single meaning, he says, because its meaning is necessarily dependent on its context, the "language game" in which it appears. Thus, any sentence has as many meanings as the contexts in which it is used. Taken to its logical conclusion, this position implies that we can never claim to be stating the final truth or truth in any ultimate sense; at most, we can produce utterances that are true within the context in which they are spoken.[108]

Wittgenstein's metaphor carries an additional, far-reaching implication. The characterization of language as a "game" implies a subtle attack on the notion that language can have any sort of "private" meaning. It presumes that language is not a private phenomenon, arising when an individual mind grasps a truth or fact about the world and then expresses it, but rather that language is a social phenomenon, acquiring its meaning in social interaction. This observation lies at the foundation of the postmodern understanding of language.

Language as Social Convention: Ferdinand de Saussure

Wittgenstein introduced the phrase "language game" into popular parlance, but that in itself did not put in place the foundation for an entirely new understanding of language. That task was completed by a Swiss linguist who predated Wittgenstein by a generation, Ferdinand de Saussure (1857-1913).

Saussure never put his viewpoint into print. Notes taken by students provided outlines for the posthumous recreation of his lectures in Geneva. This re-creation, published in 1916 under the title *Course in General Linguistics,* is the single most influential source of the linguistic theory we have come know as "structuralism."[109]

Saussure's importance stems from his successful attack on the nineteenth-century's reigning "historical" understanding of linguistics. This older view approached the study of language by focusing on actual linguistic behavior (human speech, what Saussure calls *parole*). It traced the development of words and expressions over the course of time, inquiring into the influences of geography, migration, population shifts, and other external features that affect human linguistic behavior.[110]

Rather than focusing on the historical development of individual linguistic expressions, Saussure calls for an antihistorical approach that views language as a complete and internally coherent system (a *langue*). He thus proposes a "structuralist" theory of language to replace the "historicist" approach of his predecessors.

Saussure suggests that language is like a work of music. To understand a symphony, for example, we must focus on the whole work rather than on individual performances (which, among other things, might include mistakes on the part of individual musicians).[111] Similarly, to understand language, we must conceive of it "synchronically," as a network of interrelated sounds and meanings, rather than atomistically, as a category of individual linguistic expressions. Saussure thus calls into question the whole Enlightenment approach to the study of language, which dealt with the subject in bits and pieces and "from the outside" (i.e., in the mode of a detached scientist). He insists on treating language as a freestanding whole — hence the designation of his approach as "*structural* linguistics."[112]

This understanding of linguistic method provides the foundation for the radical conclusion that Saussure bequeathed to postmodern thought. His predecessors viewed language as a natural phenomenon that develops according to fixed and discoverable laws. They maintained that the structure of our sentences reflects the logic of our thought processes. For example, the logical categories of "substance" and "quality" give rise to the grammatical categories of "noun" and "adjective." Or, turning it around, we might say that our words serve as labels for independently identifiable things and hence that language is a nomenclature.[113] Saussure proposes to the contrary that language is a social phenomenon.[114]

Saussure's view constitutes a significant break not only from nineteenth-century linguistic theory but also from Enlightenment epistemology. For if language is in fact a social phenomenon, as Saussure claims, then each linguistic system, each system of linguistic signs, is determined by nothing else than social convention. As Saussure puts it, language is autonomous: the structure of language is not a reflection of the structure of thought or the representation of independently given "facts" but is entirely internal to the language itself.[115]

Furthermore, if language is a social phenomenon, then linguistic signs are arbitrary. We can offer no logical reasons to explain why words (or linguistic expressions) mean what they do. The most we can say is that this is how the language functions. In contemporary jargon, the bond between the "signifier" (the linguistic expression) and the "signified" (what the expression connotes) is arbitrary; the signifier has no natural connection with the signified.[116] We can define signifiers (or "signs") only in terms of their relationships within the system of language — and these relationships are culturally determined.[117]

In the end, the synchronic study of language is essentially the study of social facts. The linguist observes the linguistic conventions and relations operative at a given time that endow the signs of the system with the values they have.[118] In keeping with this understanding, Saussure calls for a new science — "semiology" — to explore the nature of signs.

If words stood for pre-existing concepts, they would all have exact equivalents in meaning from one language to the next; but this is not true. . . . Instead of pre-existing ideas . . . we find . . . *values* emanating from the system. When they are said to correspond to concepts, it is understood that the concepts are purely differential and defined not by their positive content but negatively by their relations with other terms of the system. Their most precise characteristic is in being what the others are not. . . . Everything that has been said up to this point boils down to this: in language there are only differences. Even more important: a difference generally implies positive terms between which the difference is set up; but in language there are only differences *without positive terms*. Whether we take the signified or the signifiers, language has neither ideas nor sounds that existed before the linguistic system, but only conceptual and phonic differences that have issued from the system.

Ferdinand de Saussure, *Course in General Linguistics*, ed. Charles Bally, Albert Sechehaye, and Albert Riedlinger, trans. Wade Baskin (New York: Philosophical Library, 1959), pp. 116, 117, 120.

Saussure's focus on relations has another important result: it elevates the category of "difference." He maintains that it is impossible to formulate absolute definitions of individual words. Hence, in his search for meaning he turns to the domain of the relationships among terms. Specifically, he contends that language is essentially a *system of relations* and that words take on meaning only in the context of these relations. In essence, he says, a linguistic system is merely a series of differences of sound combined with a series of differences of ideas.[119]

The Dissolved Self: Structuralism

Saussure's understanding of language as a socially based system provided the foundation for an entirely new way of viewing not only language but the human phenomenon in general. This view has come to be known as structuralism.[120] At the heart of structuralism is the assertion that an objective, universal cultural system "structures" our mental processes and that this structure is evident in both human language and social institutions.[121] Because of its far reaching implications, structuralism has proved appealing not only to linguists but also to specialists in a variety of fields.

Many early followers of Saussure developed a "Platonized" structuralism. They worked from the assumption that all cultures reflect a common, largely invariant structure of relations.[122] They focused their study on basic elements of human activity — actions and words — in an attempt to discover the structures that bring all such activity into ordered relations.[123]

Some structuralists believe that this structure is reflected in a universal grammar common to all languages. Tzvetan Todorov, for example, claims that a universal grammar is the source of all universals — that, in effect, it defines humankind. This grammar is universal not only because it informs all the systems of signification in the universe, argues Todorov, but because it coincides with the structure of the universe itself.[124]

Later structuralists, especially those in the field of literary criticism, have focused more on the significance of Saussure's insights for the interpretation of texts. Literary structuralists draw from Saussure's concept of *langue* to elevate the concept of the "cultural frame" for the meaning of a literary work.[125] They speak of each particular style of expression and each type of analysis as a different, self-sufficient *langue.* Hence, they cast interpreters and literary critics in the role of "translators" who express in one of the "languages" of their own day the formal system that the author of the work developed under the social conditions of another time.

These literary critics use the categories and methods of linguistics to uncover the structures that produce the meaning of specific works. They focus on the relations between texts and particular linguistic, psychoanalytic, metaphysical, logical, sociological, or rhetorical structures and processes. They view the discovery of such meaning-mediating structures as more important than any purported "true" meaning or "correct" implication of the work itself. They are far less interested in the intent of the author than in the language and structure of the work.[126]

Perhaps the most important implications of structuralism for postmodern thought have been worked out in the context of literary criticism. In this arena, structuralism has overturned modern understandings of the meaning of texts and indeed of the knowing self.

The subversion of modernity begins when the author of the text disappears behind the structures of language. Structuralists build from the assumption that there is no single genius behind a work. They insist that the modern idea of the creative self is a construct, a product of cultural systems over which the individual person has no control. In addition to dissolving the author into the social context, structuralists

---

Text means *Tissue:* but whereas hitherto we have always taken this tissue as a product, a ready-made veil, behind which lies, more or less hidden, meaning (truth), we are now emphasizing, in the tissue, the generative idea that the text is made, is worked out in a perpetual interweaving.

Roland Barthes, *The Pleasure of the Text,* trans. Richard Miller
(New York: Hill & Wang, 1975), p. 64

---

tend to undermine the traditional view of a text as "having" a meaning. The text is not a "given" that the interpreter approaches with the goal of uncovering the meaning already present within it, they say; rather, it is a kind of formless material on which structured modes of reading impose a shape.[127]

The destruction of the Enlightenment "self" is evident in the writing of one of the most influential structuralists of the twentieth century, the anthropologist Claude Lévi-Strauss (b. 1908).[128] He works out as much as anyone the structuralist shift in emphasis from the human conscious self to universal structures.

Underlying Lévi-Strauss's work is the assumption that each human being is completely embedded in a cultural and conceptual context. On this basis he contends that in order to discover what is truly important about humans, we have to explore not human consciousness as such but rather human cultural expressions.

In pursuit of this goal, Lévi-Strauss combines the insights of structuralist linguistics with the tools of the anthropologist in an attempt to bring to light the basic similarities that unite the seemingly different myths, rituals, and religious customs of human societies. His ultimate goal is to uncover the universal social structure that he believes all societies reproduce in a partial and incomplete manner. He maintains that this social structure, in turn, reflects the structures of the human brain.

In Lévi-Strauss's analysis, the individual fades into the social structure in which all humans participate. He categorically rejects the assertion that the Cartesian dictum — or indeed the Cartesian self — is the proper starting point for understanding the human phenomenon. But it is not just the idea of the self that he rejects: he also rejects subjectivity. He views human beings as primarily social creatures, the products of genetics, language, and culture-bound education. He maintains that the

---

I believe the ultimate goal of the human sciences to be not to constitute, but to dissolve man.

Claude Lévi-Strauss, *The Savage Mind*
(Chicago: University of Chicago Press, 1966), p. 247.

---

human sciences should not be directed toward making the human person an object of knowledge but should rather be directed toward making the self disappear under structural analysis.

The dissolution of the self evident in the work of Lévi-Strauss and other structuralists is the logical result of the outworking of Saussure's linguistics. Saussure argued that human language is not a developing historical phenomenon but a self-contained system of relations and that the meaning of any unit of language is the product of "difference." Only a small step moves structuralists from this linguistic assertion to a corresponding anthropological assertion — namely, that, like the unit of language, the human person (of whose mind language is the highest expression) is essentially a structure of intersecting relations.[129] Like a linguistic expression, the self finds identity only through its place in the larger system.

The advent of structuralism signals the destruction of the Enlightenment self. Nevertheless, the ascendancy of the structuralist approach does not in itself signal a complete shift from modernity to postmodernity. Despite the radical implications of their position, structuralists retain a remnant of the Enlightenment project.

Structuralists remain committed to the task of interpreting texts — whether the literary text or the "text" of the world. They do not step beyond their predecessors by denying the presence of any meaning in the text. Instead, they offer an innovative method of exploring a certain type of meaning. Borrowing from Saussure, structuralists seek to discover the relations within a linguistic system that can account for the form and meaning of literary works.

No longer a coherent *cognito,* man now inhabits the interstices, "the vacant interstellar spaces," not as an object, still less as a subject; rather, man is the *structure,* the generality of relationships among those words and ideas that we call the humanistic, as opposed to the pure, or natural, sciences.

Edward Said, *Beginnings: Intention and Method*
(New York: Basic Books, 1975), p. 286.

An equally telling vestige of the Enlightenment project lies in the structuralist epistemology. Structuralists remain convinced that some type of systematic knowledge is possible. Lévi-Strauss offers an illuminating example with his references to a universal social structure. At the very least, his work emerges from a conviction that knowledge about human nature as such is possible. Ultimately, his quest for such knowledge motivates Lévi-Strauss's interest in discovering universal structures.

The presence of these remnants of the Enlightenment make postmodern thinkers uneasy with the structuralist agenda. This discomfort has driven some of them beyond structuralism into "post-structuralism."

Some thinkers have been called post-structuralists because they have rejected the structuralist literary agenda after pointing out the ways in which the structuralist project is subverted by the workings of the texts themselves. More importantly, however, post-structuralists are characterized by their affirmation of postmodern assumptions in general. For one thing, they reject the pretense to knowledge that keeps their structuralist colleagues tied to the Enlightenment project. Post structuralist thinkers claim to know only one thing: the impossibility of knowing.[130]

Postmodern thinkers have taken a step beyond the developments in hermeneutics and linguistics that we have surveyed. Michel Foucault, for example, has pursued to its ultimate, radical conclusion the "language game" that leads to the dissolution of the self. His aim is to exorcise entirely the ghost of the Enlightenment ideal — the disinterested observer — from the structuralist scholar. Foucault demands that scholars leave behind all pretense of neutrality and accept the fact that it is their task to bring to light the authorless, subjectless, anonymous system of thought present within the language of an epoch. This is the way in which the postmodern critic seeks to gain freedom from the faith of rationality.[131]

CHAPTER 6

The Philosophers
of Postmodernism

On June 25, 1984, "the single most famous intellectual in the world" died.[1] In a sense, Michel Foucault's death at the age of fifty-seven marked the coming of age of postmodernism. Suddenly the collage of juxtaposed "limit experiences" that had characterized the life of this architect of postmodernism had added one additional feature. Now the montage included the gruesome face of a person cut down in the prime of life and at the peak of his influence by the scourge of the early postmodern era — AIDS.

At the heart of postmodern philosophy is a sustained attack on the premises and presuppositions of modernism. Postmoderns reject as pretentious the modern focus on the self. They scoff at the modern confidence in human knowledge. And they decry the duplicity inherent in the modern assumption that all people everywhere are ultimately as we are.[2]

Many voices have joined the postmodern chorus. But of these, three loom as both central and paradigmatic — Michel Foucault, Jacques Derrida, and Richard Rorty. They constitute a trio of postmodern prophets who sometimes sing in unison but more often produce the kind of discordant music that we would expect in the postmodern era.[3]

Rather than offering a thoroughly modern, objective account of the writing of these three philosophers, I want to try to view them through postmodern lenses. In the pages that follow, we will look for those particular strands of thought within the whole of their work that provide a philosophical foundation for the superstructure of postmodernism.

Knowledge as Power: Michel Foucault

Michel Foucault (1926-1984) epitomizes the postmodern scholar. At the time of his death, social critics and scholars were grappling with the questions he raised about the limits of knowledge and its connection to power. They were debating his attack on the foundations of morality. And they were taking seriously his radical reformulation of the task of historical inquiry as well as his new understanding of the nature of personal identity.[4]

Foucault is often classified as a cultural historian, but he preferred the designation "archaeologist of knowledge." Near the end of his life he referred to himself as a philosopher. But above all, Foucault is the quintessential Nietzschean. He has been called "Nietzsche's truest twentieth century successor"[5] and the "greatest of Nietzsche's modern disciples."[6] In many ways his entire life was a Nietzschean quest.[7]

Nietzsche's Truest Disciple

At his birth on October 15, 1926, Michel Foucault was christened "Paul Michel." He later dropped the "Paul" because he did not want to have the same name as the father whom he hated as an adolescent.[8] His father, like both his grandfathers, was a surgeon, as well as a professor of anatomy at the medical school in Poitiers, France. Although his parents were only nominally religious, their second child and firstborn son served as an acolyte and choirboy in the local Roman Catholic church. And when the Second World War cast its shadow over the local public school, Foucault's mother turned to the Catholic system for the completion of Michel's secondary education. He came away from his three-year experience in the Catholic school with a hatred for religion and monks.[9]

Michel's passion for history and literature led him to break with the family's professional association with medicine and turn instead to the study of philosophy in preparation for the entrance examinations for the Ecole Normale Supérieure (ENS). This quest led him to Paris in 1945. There he encountered the writings of the thinkers who would be most influential in the development of his thought — Hegel, Marx, Nietzsche, and Freud.

Foucault's subsequent educational track included the Sorbonne, where he gained his Licence de Philosophie in 1948 and his Licence de Psychologie in 1950. Finally in 1952 he was awarded the Diplôme de Psycho-Pathologie from the Université de Paris.

After serving as lecturer at the ENS (1951-55), Foucault left France for five years. During this self-imposed exile, he lived in Sweden, Poland, and Germany before returning in 1960 to serve as the director of the Institut de Philosophie at the Faculte des Lettres in Clermont-Ferrand. At this stage in his career, his political involvement was at least as significant as his academic prowess. Foucault was a budding young cultural attaché with connections to certain diplomats in the new government of Charles de Gaulle.

By the mid-1960s Foucault had gained a reputation as one of the younger lights of structuralism and as a new star in the French intellectual world. But when leftist student revolt shook the foundations of Gaullism in May 1968, he aligned himself with a radical Maoist cohort. Following a sojourn in Tunisia from 1966 to 1968, Foucault returned to Paris in 1969 to launch what would be a successful campaign for a chair at the Collège de France. From this position at the pinnacle of the French academic system, he not only engaged in writing but was involved in political activities and travel — to Iran, Poland, and the United States, especially California.

In California Foucault gave free reign to his homosexual impulses. In the spring of 1975 he plunged passionately into San Francisco's gay community, attracted especially by the consensual sado-masochistic eroticism that flourished in a number of bathhouses in the Bay City at that time.[10] Always eager to "transform the texture of his own daily life,"[11] Foucault now searched for the "complete total pleasure," the "limit experience" that he associated with death.[12] Through these California limit experiences, he sought to confirm dramatically his thesis that the body (like the soul) was in some sense socially constructed, so that at least in principle it was open to being changed.[13]

In fall 1983 Foucault made what would be his final trip to San Francisco. Apparently he was now preoccupied by AIDS and by his own possible death from the deadly disease.[14] Beyond madness, drugs, sexuality, and AIDS itself, death would be the ultimate "limit experience," which near the end of his life Foucault briefly defined as a form of being "that can and must be thought," a form of being "historically constituted" through "games of truth."[15]

Back in Paris, Foucault collapsed in his apartment on June 2, 1984. He had widely been assumed to be on the road to recovery, so his death on June 25 came as a shock. The hospital in which he died was a former mental institution that had formed the basis for one of his early books, *Madness and Civilization* (1961).

During his final hospitalization, Foucault was visited repeatedly by his lover, the author Herve Guibert. Guibert kept a diary of their conversations and later used them as the foundation for his novel *To the Friend Who Did Not Save My Life* (1990) and the short story "The Secrets of a Man." James Miller, Foucault's biographer, speculates that the philosopher knew what he was doing when he confided on his deathbed in a novelist and writer: in this act, the man who had devoted his life to undermining the idea of the individual subject was conceding his own inability to escape from his sense of duty to tell the truth about who he was and what he had become.[16]

The *bios philosophicos* is the animality of being human, renewed as a challenge, practiced as an exercise — and thrown in the face of others as a scandal.

Michel Foucault, in a lecture given at the College de France, 14 March 1984, as quoted by James Miller in *The Passion of Michel Foucault* (New York: Simon & Schuster, 1993), p. 363.

The Rejection of the Enlightenment

Through the way he lived and the way he wrote, Foucault launched a thoroughgoing rejection of the modern worldview. He was an untiring critic of the Enlightenment and the modern outlook it fostered.

The Rejection of the Self. As we have seen, the modern worldview is rooted in the concept of the self, the autonomous knowing subject who views the world as an object accessible to human knowledge. The modern thinker assumes that the perceptions of the inquiring self provide accurate representations of an external world and hence a valid basis for knowledge of that world. Foucault's critique of modernism begins with a rejection of this Cartesian-Kantian starting point.[17]

Rather than following the Enlightenment, Foucault draws on Nietzsche's emphasis on the richness and variety of reality. Reason and rational discourse are problematic, he argues, because they require that we squeeze the variety of reality into the artificial homogeneity that accommodates our concepts. In this way, rational discourse elevates sameness and universals at the expense of difference or "otherness."

Foucault seeks to expose this tendency by reversing it. Following Nietzsche, he gives preference to the specific and special, elevating them above the general and universal.[18] His writings advance otherness rather than sameness. His strategy in this enterprise is to deny the supposed universality and timelessness of categories by bringing them back into the historical flux.[19]

Of the universals that reason claims to know, none is more crucial in the modern era than what we call "human nature." In his analysis of this concept, Foucault avoids such abstract questions as "What is human nature?" and "Does human nature exist?" Instead he asks, "How has the concept of human nature functioned in our society?" Framing the question in this manner opens the way for his program of undermining the Enlightenment self.

Central to Foucault's attack on the self and the modern understanding of subjectivity is the focus on the social aspect of discourse that he inherited from the structuralists. Following their lead, he asserts that our subjective experience is socially and historically constituted by factors that we unconsciously internalize.[20] In fact, even our work is essentially social. For example, he contends that individuals practice medicine or write history not because they have gifts for the task but simply because they are able to follow the rules of the respective professions, which they take for granted. Foucault undertakes to bring to light the ways in which the rules that govern such rules have come to enforce what and how people think, live, and speak.[21]

A concern for the structures of language is especially evident in Foucault's writings in the 1960s.[22] Nevertheless, he was no mere structuralist.[23] Despite their innovations, structuralists preserve the modern assumption that some structure lies beneath the human phenomenon. Foucault insists that there are no such firm foundations. There is no original or transcendental "signified" to which all "signifiers" can ultimately refer.[24] There is no human nature that is displayed in the social structures that we study in the human sciences.

All of this is to say that Foucault moves us beyond structuralism to "post-structuralism." He moves us over the boundary between modernism from postmodernism (although he himself does not use the term).[25] Postmoderns like Foucault no longer engage in a quest for an independent self, a given reality governed by lawlike regularities. They tend to be engaged in something more like interpreting texts. And in this endeavor, they assume not that every text has a single unifying structure but, to the contrary, that texts are almost infinitely complex. In short, the postmodern paradigm, as exemplified by Foucault, celebrates *complexity*.[26]

The Rejection of Anthropology. Central to Foucault's rejection of the self is his attack on anthropology. In this connection he engages in lengthy studies of the various human sciences. Yet, he views himself not as a practitioner but as an analyst of the human sciences. His concern is to determine how they arise, the concepts around which they are formed, how they are used, and the effect they have had in Western culture.[27]

Central to Foucault's attack on anthropology is his claim that "humanity" (or "man," to use the older nomenclature) is a relatively recent phenomenon. Our present focus on the human person as an object of knowledge is the result of a historical shift that began in the seventeenth century. To understand this, he proposes a differentiation between "language" and "discourse." "Language" recognizes itself *as* the world; "discourse," in contrast, sees itself as *representing* the world. The sole function of discourse is to be a transparent representation of things and ideas standing outside it.

According to Foucault, "language" disappeared and "discourse" emerged in the early 1600s. But then, in the late 1700s, "language" reappeared, triggering the "dissolution" of humanity.[28]

The phrase, "the dissolution of humanity," refers to the disappearance of discourse about the human self, the loss of humanity as an object of our knowledge. Foucault calls the pursuit of the human self "anthropology" or "continuous history." Practitioners of continuous history seek to disclose the truth of the present by uncovering its origins in the past. Foundational to their work is the concept of historical continuity and the assumption that history is the unfolding of the essential attributes of humanity. Humanity can become the object of history precisely to the extent that humankind is history's subject.

One thing in any case is certain: man is neither the oldest nor the most constant problem that has been posed for human knowledge. Taking a relatively short chronological sample within a restricted geographical area — European culture since the sixteenth century — one can be certain that man is a recent invention within it. . . . In fact, among all the mutations that have affected the knowledge of things and their order . . . only one, that which began a century and a half ago and is now perhaps drawing to a close, has made it possible for the figure of man to appear. And that appearance was not the liberation of an old anxiety, the transition into luminous consciousness of an age-old concern. . . . It was the effect of a change in the fundamental arrangements of knowledge. As the archaeology of our thought easily shows, man is an invention of recent date. And one perhaps nearing its end.

If those arrangements were to disappear as they appeared . . . then one can certainly wager that man would be erased, like a face drawn in sand at the edge of the sea.

Michel Foucault, *The Order of Things: An Archaeology of the Human Sciences* (New York: Random House–Pantheon, 1970), pp. 386-87.

129

Foucault contends that "anthropology" has determined the path of philosophical thought since the time of Kant but that this focus is now disintegrating before our eyes.[29] Anthropology has been dethroned as the reigning science in contemporary Western society. Humanity is no longer the central concern of human knowledge. Foucault claims that we are now realizing that "humanity" is nothing more than a fiction composed by the modern human sciences. He argues that the credibility of this "illusion" has been destroyed by the contemporary interest in linguistics and by a growing skepticism that history can in fact provide us with the basis for a universal understanding of the human person. The self is no longer viewed as the ultimate source and ground for language; to the contrary, we are now coming to see that the self is constituted in and through language.

The foundation for Foucault's movement "beyond" the naive metaphysical certitudes of earlier thought lies in Nietzsche and Saussure. Saussure's contribution was a theory of language that leaves no room for the individual subject as the origin or locus of meaning. Nietzsche's contribution was a critique of all philosophies that identify truth with the quest for a distinctive human self-knowledge.[30] To use Foucault's metaphorical language, Nietzsche rediscovered the fact that the death of God and the promise of the Superhuman signify the imminence of the death of humanity. As a result, we can no longer think except in the void left by the disappearance of the human self.

Although he surveys a variety of human sciences, Foucault demonstrates a special interest in the discipline that he locates at the center of anthropology: *history*, the study of the unfolding of the self through time. As in his treatment of the other dimensions of anthropology, he does not approach history as a practitioner. Unlike modern historians, his goal is not to follow thinkers such as Hegel and engage in a search for a general theory of history. On the contrary, he views such a general theory as part of the current problem. He maintains that history — understood as the disinterested quest for knowledge of the past — is a Western myth that we need to lay to rest.

Foucault finds the discipline of history suspect at its very core. To present a continuous story, historians have dissolved the discontinuity and uniqueness of singular events and cloaked their work in the language of universals. They have violated the essence of their own reality

> To all those who still wish to think about man, about his reign or his liberation, to all those who still ask themselves questions about what man is in his essence, to all those who wish to take him as their starting-point in their attempts to reach the truth . . . to all these warped and twisted forms of reflection we can answer only with a philosophical laugh — which means, to a certain extent, a silent one.
>
> Michel Foucault, *The Order of Things*, pp. 342-43.

by intentionally seeking to erase any elements in their work that might reveal their dependence on their own particular time and place, their own personal preferences and prejudices.[31]

Knowledge as Power

The student uprising of 1968 produced a turning point in Foucault's thinking. It seemed to lead him to an appreciation for both the limits of insurrection and the extent to which the laws of discourse regulate human life.[32] From that point on, his central preoccupation — power — assumed center stage.[33]

According to Foucault, Western society has for three centuries made a number of fundamental errors. He argues that scholars have erroneously believed (1) that an objective body of knowledge exists and is waiting to be discovered, (2) that they actually possess such knowledge and that it is neutral or value-free, and (3) that the pursuit of knowledge benefits all humankind rather than just a specific class.[34]

Foucault rejects these Enlightenment assumptions. He denies the modern ideal of the disinterested knower. He denies that we can ever stand beyond history and human society, that there is any vantage point that offers certain and universal knowledge.[35] And hence, he denies the older understanding of truth as theoretical and objective, the belief that truth is a claim to knowledge that can be validated by procedures devised by the appropriate scholarly community.

131

But Foucault takes this rejection of the Enlightenment a step further. Because knowledge is embedded in the world, he says, it is involved in the power struggles and clashes that constitute our world. Hence, we cannot appeal to "objective knowledge" or "truth" as the way to stand above the fray.[36] On the contrary, knowledge is the product of what Foucault (echoing Nietzsche's will to power) calls a "will to knowledge" that arbitrarily establishes its own "truth." In this manner, he gives the word *discourse* a more precise definition, rooting it in relations of power — and particularly those forms of power embodied in specialized and institutionalized languages.[37]

Knowledge is inescapably linked to power because of its connection to "discourse." That is, knowledge is related to what Foucault calls a "discursive formation." Practices and institutions produce those claims to knowledge that the system of power finds useful. Discourse brings objects into being by identifying, specifying, and defining them. As an example, Foucault cites psychiatry, which declares that schizophrenics exist and then views them as the objects of therapy.[38]

Power produces knowledge. . . . Power and knowledge directly imply one another. . . . There is no power relation without the correlative constitution of a field of knowledge, nor any knowledge that does not presuppose and constitute at the same time power relations. These "power-knowledge relations" are to be analyzed . . . not on the basis of a subject of knowledge who is or is not free in relation to the power system, but, on the contrary, the subject who knows, the objects to be known and the modalities of knowledge must be regarded as so many effects of these fundamental implications of power-knowledge and their historical transformations. In short, it is not the activity of the subject of knowledge that produces a corpus of knowledge, useful or resistant to power, but power-knowledge, the processes and struggles that traverse it and of which it is made up, that determines the forms and possible domains of knowledge.

Michel Foucault, *Discipline and Punish: The Birth of the Prison,* trans. Alan Sheridan (New York: Vintage Books, 1977), pp. 27-28.

Foucault concludes from all this that "truth" is a fabrication or fiction, "a system of ordered procedures for the production, regulation, distribution, circulation and operation of statements." He further contends that this system of truth stands in a reciprocal relationship with systems of power that produce and sustain it.[39] Truth is just the product of the practices that make it possible.[40] The power of knowledge reveals itself in a discourse through which it arbitrarily, and for its own purposes, engages in the invention of "truth."[41] In this fashion, says Foucault, knowledge produces our reality.[42]

Obviously, Foucault's position undermines any conception of objective science. In fact, he characterizes "science" as an "ideology" and asserts that as such it is irremediably caught up within relations of power.

Like all forms of human discourse, says Foucault, history can make no claims to being value-free or neutral. He denies that the desire to know the past is driven by a disinterested quest for knowledge and truth; he argues that it arises out of the desire to domesticate and control the past in order to validate present structures.[43] The historian's seemingly neutral attempt to learn the truth about the past is merely a mask for the "will to knowledge."[44] This will to knowledge/power is evident in the way historical narratives invariably exclude certain objects while "privileging" (i.e., focusing on) others, says Foucault. It shows itself likewise in the tendency of historians to smooth out heterogeneous elements in order to secure the appearance of homogeneity in history and to advance the semblance of historical progress.

Foucault's connection between knowledge and power marks the postmodern end of the road that Francis Bacon charted at the beginning of the Enlightenment. According to Foucault, human knowledge does not merely allow us to exercise power over nature as Bacon had suggested; more significantly, knowledge is violence. The act of knowing, says Foucault, is always an act of violence.

On the basis of these considerations, Foucault collapses theory and practice into each other. He argues that theoretical activity must always have an entirely practical significance.[45] The purpose of theory is not to provide the foundation for action but to articulate strategies for such action. And Foucault considers the appropriate action of the scholar to be the perpetual critique of presently existing structures. Foundational

> Knowledge does not slowly detach itself from its empirical roots, the initial needs from which it arose, to become pure speculation subject only to the demands of reason. . . . Rather, it creates a progressive enslavement to its instinctive violence.
>
> Michel Foucault, "Nietzsche, Genealogy, History," in *Language, Counter-Memory, and Practice: Selected Essays and Interviews,* ed. Donald F. Bouchard, trans. Donald F. Bouchard and Sherry Simon (Ithaca, N.Y.: Cornell University Press, 1977), p. 163.

to this critique is his understanding of history as the means to propagate useful myths — myths that will "disorder" order and turn the present into a "past."[46]

To engage in the task of undermining presently existing structures, Foucault calls for an "effective history," in which historians acknowledge that their "histories" are conditioned by their own perspective.[47] Foucault's own writings serve this goal. In them he seeks to show how the form of historical narrative itself serves the interests of power and domination. He turns the vocabulary of history against those who had once used it for their own purposes.[48] And he brings into view the aspects of history that historians overlook in an attempt to bring "the Other" to speak across the barrier established by the "regime of reason."

It is evident in Foucault's writings that he views the world as discourse. And if that is in fact the nature of things, then the reigning order in the world is appropriately subject to discursive attack in the form of systematic suspicion of any order whatsoever.[49]

Genealogy

In his attack on "order," Foucault unleashes a powerful weapon that he draws from Nietzsche — genealogy.[50] His goal is to find a new discourse that enables one to take a stand outside of and against the "hegemonic" truth claims of reason. His method involves tracing the "genealogy" of a body of knowledge — that is, observing how the concepts of a disci-

134

> Let us give the term *genealogy* to the union of erudite knowledge and local memories which allows us to establish a historical knowledge of struggles and to make use of this knowledge tactically today. . . . What it really does is to entertain the claims to attention of local, discontinuous, disqualified, illegitimate knowledges against the claims of a unitary body of theory which would filter, hierarchize and order them in the name of some true knowledge and some arbitrary idea of what constitutes a science and its objects.
>
> Michel Foucault, "Two Lectures," in *Power/Knowledge: Selected Interviews and Other Writings. 1972-1977*, trans. Colin Gordon, Leo Marshall, John Mepham, and Kate Soper (New York: Pantheon Books, 1980), p. 83.

pline or human science came to be constructed. The idea is that, working in this manner, we can get a better understanding of how the present has come to be what it is. But genealogy also works to disrupt and disorient the present.

The principal targets of Foucault's genealogies are the grand unifying theories of society, history, and politics that regulate life in modern Western society.[51] The goal of modern thinkers has been to devise an overarching description of human history under the theme of the progress or emancipation of humankind — precisely the kind of "global systematic theory" or reductionistic "true discourse" that Foucault rejects.[52] He charges that such theories ultimately function as "regimes of truth" that only seek to legitimize present social structures and thereby mask the will to power that is operative through them.[53] And because modern scholarship assumes that knowledge is neutral, he says, the proponents of "true discourse" remain blind to the will to power that pervades their own scholarly endeavors. In this manner, modern scholarship actually masks the truth rather than reveals it.[54]

The task of Foucault's genealogists, then, is not to produce yet more "truths" but rather to unmask all forms of "true discourse" by determining the conditions that allow it to exist and by bringing to light its political effects.[55]

135

As we noted earlier, Foucault asserts that anthropology (or continuous history) has been the prevailing "true discourse" in Western society since the eighteenth century. He maintains that the historian's commitment to historical continuity both uses the past to sanctify the present and privileges the present as the vantage point from which we can definitively know the past.

Foucault's goal is to dismantle systematically the devices that historians traditionally use to construct a comprehensive view of history.[56] His project involves replacing the unifying concepts of human-centered history (e.g., tradition, influence, development, evolution, source, and origin) with their opposites (discontinuity, rupture, threshold, limit, and transformation).[57] He thus rejects the traditional historian's focus on continuity and focuses instead on the *dis*continuity between the present and the past, in order to undermine the legitimization of the present order that the traditional historian provides.

Foucault wants to establish the point that the present is not the inevitable outworking of the past, that it is not simply the latest stage in the ongoing story of progress and emancipation. Genealogy is the tool he uses to make this point. According to Foucault, the practice of genealogy informs us that history is not controlled by destiny or some regulative mechanism but is the product of haphazard conflicts.[58] History, in short, has no meaning.[59] And to undermine the presumption of meaning within history, the genealogist must dispense with humanity as the assumed subject of history.[60]

Foucault's genealogy, therefore, is not a theory of history in the traditional sense. In fact, we might call it an "anti-theory." The genealogist offers a method for analyzing established theories in terms of their effects. Foucault's genealogies describe how some of our ways of thinking dominate us "by the production of truth."[61] They do not so much explain reality as criticize all attempts to grasp reality within a reductionistic unifying theory.

According to Foucault, traditional "continuist" histories tend to legitimate rather than criticize present structures and to obscure conflicts and struggles in the past. Genealogies seek to reverse this tendency as well. Foucault's studies point to paths in history that were not taken, to unactualized possibilities, and to events that do not fit within the traditional historian's narrative of progress. It is his intent in focusing on such things to ignite a guerrilla war, an "insurrection of subjugated knowledges" against the established order.[62]

Foucault's attack on the existing order is not motivated by a desire to replace it with some other specific order. He is not looking to install any specific subjugated knowledge in the position of dominance. Unlike Marx and his followers, Foucault has no interest in pursuing an Enlightenment utopia, and he offers no vision of a better society. Rather, he engages in a never-ending crusade on behalf of subjugated knowledge in general.[63] He challenges order itself. His target is not merely some existing social system but the very notion of order itself. He believes that thought, interpretation, discourse, and language pose as great a threat of enslavement as any social system.[64]

In the end, argues Foucault, thought becomes discourse, and discourse makes and unmakes our world.[65] No natural order lies behind what we invent through our use of language. In making this assertion, Foucault reveals himself to be the quintessential postmodern. Central to postmodernism is the attempt to unmask the falsehood — the false claim to being "natural" or ontologically valid — that underlies every "given" order.

History as Fiction

Foucault's works fall into two categories: works of history and methodological treatises designed to make possible the writing of historical works.[66] But his histories are not simply about the past. His project is to describe the mechanisms of order and exclusion that have operated within Western society since the late 1700s. His prime concern is to represent (and hence to legitimate) neither the past nor the present but rather to mount an attack against the existing "order of things."[67] To this end, Foucault envisages a Nietzschean genealogy of discourses that study the shifting configurations of knowledge and power. In contrast to the works of modern historians, these genealogies would not focus on individual authors of the past. Foucault denies the idea of single authorship as a modern fiction; he insists that all works are ultimately socially produced.

Foucault acknowledges that his histories are likewise fictions but

The author does not precede the works, he is a certain functional principle by which, in our culture, one limits, excludes, and chooses; in short, by which one impedes the free circulation, the free manipulation, the free composition, decomposition, and recomposition of fiction. . . . One can say that the author is an ideological product, since we represent him as the opposite of his historically real function. . . . The author is therefore the ideological figure by which one marks the manner in which we fear the proliferation of meaning.

Michel Foucault, "What Is an Author?" in *Textual Strategies: Perspectives in Post-Structuralist Criticism*, ed. Josue V. Harari (Ithaca, N.Y.: Cornell University Press, 1979), p. 159.

contends that they serve the important function of producing myth. Affirming that knowledge arises out of a specific perspective, Foucault does not seek to provide objective truth but rather to produce a particular impact on his readers. He sets forth what he calls "effective history," which introduces discontinuity into our frame of reference and deprives us of the reassuring stability of life.[68]

Foucault works from the premise that historical analyses should be a real part of a political struggle rather than merely attempts to relate the theoretical foundations of the struggles. To this end, he "fictions" the past in order to open our eyes to the reality of the present.[69] His works *read* like history — he even presents them as histories — but they are double-coded: he deliberately incorporates the fictional character of all historical interpretation into his work. This double-coding serves to give his writings their rhetorical power.

The Deconstruction of Logocentrism: Jacques Derrida

If Foucault is the most flamboyant philosopher of postmodernism, Jacques Derrida is its most rigorous.[70] And if Foucault is Nietzsche's "truest" twentieth-century disciple, Derrida is his most significant postmodern reinterpreter.

Jacques Derrida was born in 1930 to Jewish parents in El Biar, Algiers. While working on his baccalaureate degree, he was drawn to the study of philosophy. He left his home and went to France to serve in the military. After completing his duties, he remained in the country to attend the Ecole Normale Supérieure (ENS). Like Foucault, he studied under Jean Hyppolite, the French translator of the works of the German phenomenologist Edmund Husserl (1859-1938). As his graduate work progressed, Derrida abandoned plans to write a thesis for the state doctorate. He was gaining an awareness of the problems created for philosophy vis-à-vis literature. He was coming to what seemed to him the inescapable conclusion that philosophy is a literary genre.

Derrida launched his career as an academic philosopher in 1955. He has held teaching posts at both the ENS and the Sorbonne. In 1972 he began to divide his time between teaching in Paris and lecturing in various American universities, including Johns Hopkins and Yale.

Derrida's writings are exceedingly difficult to interpret. At the foundation of much of what he does is his concern to call philosophy to task for its tendency to stand in judgment over other literary expressions while resisting the suggestion that it is itself a kind of writing. Derrida objects to the tendency of philosophers to claim to be objective observers with the prerogative to raise foundational questions about other disciplines, such as "What is literature?" or "What is poetry?"

To combat this tendency, Derrida seeks to throw philosophy off balance. He himself makes no claim to a vantage point outside or above other types of literary activities. Rather, by drawing other forms (such as poetry) into the domain of the philosopher, he indirectly and discreetly interrogates philosophy's attempt to divide one type of writing from another.[71] This strategy gives Derrida's writings an iconoclastic edge. They oscillate between a certain playfulness and a deliberate parody of accepted literary conventions.

Derrida uses several techniques to achieve his desired result. Many of his works consist of engagements with a series of writings by the great philosophers and other writers. His prose often juxtaposes one style or tone with another. Sometimes he juxtaposes two texts by running them together over the course of several pages split either vertically or horizontally. Other times he offers conversations including several voices or a main voice interrupted by interlocutors. Through it all,

The end of linear writing is indeed the end of the book, even if, even today, it is within the form of a book that new writings — literary or theoretical — allow themselves to be, for better or for worse, encased. It is less a question of confiding new writings to the envelope of a book than of finally reading what wrote itself between the lines in the volumes. That is why, beginning to write without line, one begins also to reread past writing according to a different organization of space. If today the problem of reading occupies the forefront of science, it is because of this suspense between two ages of writing. Because we are beginning to write, to write differently, we must reread differently.

Jacques Derrida, Of Grammatology,
trans. Gayatri Chakravorty Spivak (Baltimore:
The Johns Hopkins University Press, 1976), pp. 86-87.

Derrida emerges as a master of double-coding and the hidden meaning. He calls us to new ways of reading and writing.

The Nature of Language

Foucault attacks what he characterizes as the modern illusion of knowledge. In particular, he trains his sights on anthropology as the study of "humanity" and brings the weapon of genealogy to bear on its legitimization of the "order of things." He investigates scholarly fields of discourse in order to uncover the hidden connections between knowledge and power. The focus of Derrida's attack on the modern project, in contrast, is "logocentrism."

In a sense, Derrida begins where Kant leaves off. He raises the question "What foundation can we offer for our use of reason?"[72] But he questions the modern trust in reason chiefly by undertaking a ruthless exploration of the nature of language and its relation to the world. In this enterprise, Derrida offers a critique of the so-called "realist" understanding of language — the view that our statements are representations of the world as it actually is apart from human activity. Derrida denies that language has a fixed meaning connected to a fixed reality or that it unveils definitive truth. He wants to divest us of this modern concept and open us up to the "hermeneutical" possibilities of the written word, the possibilities that arise as we engage in an ongoing conversation with texts.[73]

Derrida sees a crucial roadblock to this sort of conversation in a mistaken understanding of literature that has characterized Western thought. To get at this problem, he points to a distinction between "speech" and "writing."[74] "Speech" entails the possibility of direct contact with truth; "writing" entails the realization that we have no such immediate connection.

These two dimensions of language are appropriate metaphors for the contrast Derrida seeks to illumine. By its very nature, speaking is more closely connected with its source than writing is. When we speak, what we say is broadcast immediately into the world and then quickly disappears. Speech, therefore, carries a sense of immediacy. When we write, however, our writing quickly becomes disengaged from us. It is no longer dependent on us for its existence. In fact, what we have written can remain long after we are gone. Because writing is not dependent on the presence of its origin,[75] it is removed from the immediacy that speech connotes.

Derrida criticizes Western philosophy for eschewing "writing" in the pursuit of "speech."[76] Modern thinkers assume that their literary efforts can bring to light an immediately present truth or meaning, he notes, but, ironically, philosophy takes the form of writing — the mode of language that indicates absence, not presence.

Derrida labels this tendency in Western philosophy "logocentrism." As the term indicates, "logocentrism" refers to the philosophical method that looks to the *logos*, the word, or language — especially written language — as the carrier of meaning.

Logocentrism is connected to what Derrida calls the "metaphysics of presence." Western philosophers assume that there is at the foundation of our language a "presence" of being or an essence that we can come to know.[77] And they are convinced that language (the system of linguistic "signs") is able to "signify" or represent this given reality in its essential nature. Consequently, they search for some ultimate "word," presence, essence, truth, or reality to serve as the foundation for our thought, language, and experience (the "transcendental signified").[78] They offer a variety of labels for this foundation (the "transcendental signifier") — God, the Idea, the World Spirit, the Self. Along these lines, some philosophers assert that we have access to the divine mind or to the infinite understanding that God possesses. Others assume the existence of an infinitely creative subjectivity or speak of the human self present to and fully known to itself.[79]

Imbued with the "myth of presence," says Derrida, the Western philosophical tradition makes claims it cannot possibly defend and exudes a confidence it cannot possibly sustain. This "onto-theological tradition" refuses to consider the possibility that there is in fact no such ultimate grounding for our systems of thought and language. But if such a transcendental signifier did exist, Derrida points out, it would have to lie beyond the linguistic system. It could not be tainted by the play of linguistic differences or in any way be entangled in the language it is supposed to anchor.[80]

Derrida is thus concerned with the question of meaning: How does language derive its meaning? And he is not happy with the modern answer. He charges that Western philosophers err in attempting to locate meaning in the ability of our thoughts and statements to represent an objective, given reality. He also criticizes them for viewing writing as a representation of speech.[81]

Difference and Differance

The initial object of Derrida's attack on logocentrism is the "phenomenalism" of Edmund Husserl.

Husserl renews the perennial modern attempt to provide an indisputable foundation for reason and language. Reminiscent of Descartes, he sets out to discover the primordial structures of thought and perception. He is convinced that this is facilitated by elevating knowledge that arises from authentic "self-presence" above knowledge based on memory, anticipation, or traces of an absent experience. This differentiation, in turn, requires a demarcation between the "now," where the subject is located, and the receding horizons of past and future.

Central to Husserl's project is a distinction between two modes of language — "expressive" and "indicative." Expressive signs indicate personal intention. Indicative signs signify but are not the carriers of animating intention (e.g., dark clouds may portend a storm but not someone's intention to rain on a planned parade). Husserl maintains that expressive signs (and not indicative signs) offer the key to understanding the meaning of language.[82] He argues that the study of language must focus on the self-reflective, solitary consciousness — the individual mental life — and not the realm of interpersonal discourse.

In challenging Husserl's "logic of presence" Derrida picks up on the concept of "difference" pioneered by Saussure and others.[83] But he adds an interesting twist. Under his artistic direction, "difference" becomes *"differance."*[84]

The French noun *differance* is Derrida's own coinage. Its etymological root lies in the verb *differer*, which means both "to differ" and "to defer." *Differance* sounds exactly like *difference*. But by appending the *ance*-ending, which in French produces verbal nouns, Derrida constructs a new form that means literally both "differing" and "deferring."

Differance embodies Derrida's rejection of Husserl's project. Derrida appeals to Saussure's observation that a linguistic signifier (e.g., a word) does not possess a fixed meaning within itself but derives its meaning from its relations within the language system.[85] Meaning is produced by the difference between signifiers in the language chain. But language is more than just a composite of independently meaningful units. The signs we use to express intention are caught up in a network of linguistic relations. This being the case, Derrida argues, it is clear that meaning does not lie buried within Husserl's isolated, self-reflective consciousness. Husserl's "presence" (or the meaning of the present) and the self are not autonomous givens: they are necessarily contextual, arising from their positive and negative relations to other elements.

But Derrida takes the matter a step farther. *Differance* entails not only "differing" but also "deferring."

Following Saussure's lead, Derrida differentiates between a phonic signifier (i.e., the word itself) and its corresponding mental signified (the concept, idea, perception, or emotion to which the word is connected).[86] Our use of phonic signifiers to express mental signifieds creates a crucial difference between language and the mental process to which we seek to give expression. The meanings of the words we use arise out of their relations within the immediate context in which they appear (their "textual location") and not necessarily out of any connection to mental signifieds.

Derrida concludes that in the end language is merely "self-referential." A sign, he argues, will always lead to another sign. Thus, a language is a chain of signifiers referring to other signifiers, in which each signifier in turn becomes what is signified by another signifier. And because the textual location in which a signifier is embedded constantly changes, its meaning can never be fully determined. Derrida thus holds that meaning is never static, never given once-for-all. Instead, meaning changes over time and with changing contexts. For this reason, we must continually "defer" or postpone our tendency to attribute meaning.[87]

Presumption of a similarity between meaning and consciousness is crucial to Derrida's view. He argues that both are dependent on language. There is no signified that exists apart from the signifier — no mental concept that exists apart from the word that we attach to that thought.[88] Because of this link between mental activity and language, *differance* — the interplay of passive differing and active deferring — provides a radical critique of the concept of the self as an entity existing apart from its context. In fact, the concept implies that there is no self standing beneath or preceding linguistic activity.

But how do we account for our experience of existing as a self in the "now"? Derrida suggests that the experience of a singular, objective "present" is an illusion. What we experience in the present is actually the result of a complex web of meanings that is constantly changing. Through language and concepts, we impose the sense of objective meaning on the flux of experience.

To see how this is so, let us suppose that I claim to see a mug on a desk in a room. Our tendency is to assume that this is an objective, given occurrence. Yet, there is no single correct statement that objectively describes the experience. On the contrary, I could offer many possible descriptions of it. And each description would actually alter and color the experience itself. Depending on the circumstances, I may anticipate enjoying a refreshing drink in my work area, see another example of my son's untidiness, or view the situation as an opportunity to hurl a missile at an attacker.[89]

Derrida's goal is to bring to light this dimension of language, especially written language. He wants to chasten the modern pretension to assign fixed meanings to the flux of experience.

The change from "difference" to *"differance"* has another function as well. The replacement of the *e* with an *a* is not readily noticeable in speaking. It is evident only when written. Derrida's use of *differance* thus contains an implicit criticism of the classical Western idea that writing is simply the representation of human speech, which is more foundational and immediate. In this playful manner, he seeks to subvert the classical theory of meaning, which moves from thought to speech to written language.[90]

An additional implication arises as well. Derrida's consistent use of *differance* reminds the reader that the term *difference* is absent from the text, even though its meaning is very much present there.[91] This phenomenon supports Derrida's thesis, drawn from Heidegger, that the meaning of writing arises from an interplay between presence and absence. Meaning occurs because of the presence of a "trace" of a now-absent reality or a trace of its former connections to other elements. Derrida's new style of writing seeks to expose this situation.

It is a question . . . of producing a new concept of writing. This concept can be called *gram* or *differance*. . . . Whether in the order of spoken or written discourse, no element can function as a sign without referring to another element which itself is not simply present. This interweaving results in each "element" — phoneme or grapheme — being constituted on the basis of the trace within it of the other elements of the chain or system. This interweaving, this textile, is the *text* produced only in the transformation of another text. Nothing, neither among the elements nor within the system, is anywhere ever simply present or absent. There are only, everywhere, differences and traces of traces. The gram, then, is the most general concept of semiology — which thus becomes grammatology.

Jacques Derrida, *Positions*, trans. Alan Bass (Chicago: University of Chicago Press, 1981), p. 26.

145

Derrida's attack on Husserl's concept of the "present" also dismantles the idea of a linear succession of "presents" (i.e., history). In this connection, it also undermines the notion of writing — or the "book" — as a deposit of lived experiences.[92] For Derrida, there is no "outside the text." All we have is the text itself, not some external meaning to which the text points.[93] The "book" is actually our "reading" of the text.

Postmoderns draw far-reaching implications from Derrida's conclusions. They find in his critique a refutation of the notion of singular meaning. A text consists of no more than the play of linguistic signifiers, they say; there is no place outside the discourse itself from which to establish metaphysical boundaries for the linguistic play.[94] But this means that the text is fluid. It has no fixed origin, identity, or end. Moreover, the process of interpreting the text can never reach a conclusion; each act of reading the text is a preface to the next.[95] We are left solely with the repetition of the act of interpretation — and interpretation becomes unqualified free play divested of ontological anchors.

The absence of a transcendental signified extends the domain and the play of significations infinitely.

Jacques Derrida, *Writing and Difference*, trans. Alan Bass (Chicago: University of Chicago Press, 1978), p. 280.[96]

Like Foucault's agenda, therefore, Derrida's program leads to questioning the order that dominated Western thought in the modern era. His appraisal of the situation, however, differs from that of his compatriot. Foucault asserts that the "order of things" is the product of selective readings of the past that "privilege" the powerful. Derrida contends that the problem lies deeper, that it arises from the unavoidable logocentric structure that makes possible the employment of reason. This being the case, he argues, we must question this order. But we can only do so from within the order itself. This is Derrida's goal. He calls for the strategic questioning of reason by reason, the relentless querying

The unsurpassable, unique, and imperial grandeur of the order of reason, that which makes it not just another actual order or structure (a determined historical structure, one structure among other possible ones), is that one cannot speak out against it except by being for it, that one can protest it only from within it. . . .

But if no one can escape this necessity, and if no one is therefore responsible for giving in to it, however little he may do so, this does not mean that all the ways of giving in to it are of equal pertinence. The quality and fecundity of a discourse are perhaps measured by the critical rigor with which this relation to the history of metaphysics and to inherited concepts is thought. Here it is a question both of a critical relation to the language of the social sciences and a critical responsibility of the discourse itself. It is a question of explicitly and systematically posing the problem of the status of a discourse which borrows from a heritage the resources necessary for the deconstruction of that heritage itself.

Jacques Derrida, *Writing and Difference*, trans. Alan Bass (Chicago: University of Chicago Press, 1978), pp. 36, 289.

of our Western metaphysical tradition *using the tools we inherit from the tradition.*

Deconstruction

In Foucault's attack on anthropology, his patron saint is Nietzsche, his weapon is genealogy, and his goal is to produce an "effective history" — new myths that can continuously overturn the present order. In Derrida's attack on language, his mentor is Heidegger — or, to be more precise, Nietzsche as read by Heidegger.[97]

But in contrast to his predecessors, Derrida is not a maker of new myths.[98] He does not attempt to construct something new on the foundation of the old. Rather, his goal is largely negative or destructive — namely, to disabuse the Western tradition of its logocentrism. Derrida wants to dismantle the modern ideal that views philosophy as pure, disinterested inquiry and to repudiate as well the common notion that there is some sort of straightforward correspondence between language and the external world. The weapon Derrida relies on to accomplish this goal is *deconstruction*.

Deconstruction is a difficult term to define. In fact, it defies definition, if for no other reason than that Derrida has shrewdly placed obstacles along the path. He begins by insisting that deconstruction is not a method, a technique, a style of literary critique, or even a procedure for textual interpretation.[99] He warns us not to replace the actual activity of deconstructive reading with a description or conceptualized understanding of that activity.[100]

Despite the difficulty of defining it, we can say something about deconstruction, however. At its heart, deconstruction concerns language. In a sense, it is all those things that Derrida said it is not. That is, deconstruction involves the use of certain philosophical or philological assumptions to launch an assault on logocentrism, understood as the assumption that something lies beyond our system of linguistic signs to which a written work can refer to substantiate its claim to be an authentic statement.[101]

Derrida's primary goal is to divest us of logocentrism by showing the impossibility of drawing a clear line between reality and our linguistic representations. His chief focus, of course, is written language — texts. He wants to wean us from too quickly assuming that we can discover the meaning inherent in a text, and he does this by demonstrating the difficulties of any theory that defines meaning in a univocal way, whether by appeal to what the author intends, what literary conventions determine, or even what a reader experiences.[102] After all our theorizing, there still remains "the free play of meaning," which is the result of what Derrida calls "the play of the world." The text always provides further connections, correlations, and contexts and hence always has the potential to yield further meanings.

The immediate target of deconstruction is philosophy. Derrida believes that the Western philosophical tradition is hopelessly logocentric or objectivistic. It is fixated on a search for an ultimate grounding for our language. But no written work is held static by a metaphysical anchor, says Derrida. Writing has no extralinguistic referent. Con-

Deconstruction cannot limit itself or proceed immediately to a neutralization: it must, by means of a double gesture, a double science, a double writing, practice an *overturning* of the classical opposition *and* a general *displacement* of the system. It is only on this condition that deconstruction will provide itself the means with which to *intervene* in the field of oppositions that it criticizes, which is also a field of nondiscursive forces. Each concept, moreover, belongs to a systematic chain, and itself constitutes a system of predicates. There is no metaphysical concept in and for itself. There is a work — metaphysical or not — on conceptual systems. Deconstruction does not consist in passing from one concept to another, but in overturning and displacing a conceptual order, as well as the nonconceptual order with which the conceptual order is articulated. For example, writing, as a classical concept, carries with it predicates which have been subordinated, excluded, or held in reserve by forces and according to necessities to be analyzed. It is these predicates (I have mentioned some) whose force of generality, generalization, and generativity find themselves liberated, grafted onto a "new" concept of writing which also corresponds to whatever always has *resisted* the former organization of forces, which always has constituted the *remainder* irreducible to the dominant force which organized the — to say it quickly — logocentric hierarchy. To leave to this new concept the old name of writing is to maintain the structure of the graft, the transition and indispensable adherence to an effective *intervention* in the constituted historic field. And it is also to give their chance and their force, their power of *communication*, to everything played out in the operations of deconstruction.

But what goes without saying will quickly have been understood . . . as a disseminating operation *separated* from presence (of Being) according to all its modifications, writing, if there is any, perhaps communicates, but does not exist, surely. Or barely, hereby, in the form of the most improbable signature.

Jacques Derrida, "Signature Event Context," in
Derrida, *Margins of Philosophy*, trans. Alan Bass
(Chicago: University of Chicago Press, 1982), pp. 329-30.

sequently, no attempt to construct such a referent can produce anything more than a fiction created out of words. According to Derrida, philosophy's "first principle" ought not to be an illusory unifying ground for all language but rather a system of symbols that is not propped up by anything outside language. Further, the purpose of philosophy ought not to be to defend or account for these systems but to deconstruct them.[103]

But the implications of deconstruction run deeper. Saussure asserts that linguistic meaning arises from structures of relations rather than from some ideal correspondence between sound and sense; Derrida insists that this insight is relevant to more than just written language. In all its forms, language is always a system of differential signs. That being the case, says Derrida, the classical definition of writing applies to every form of language and even to thinking itself.[104]

For this reason, Derrida asserts that we must abandon the logocentric quest for a meaning that exists outside and beyond the differential play of language (i.e., the quest for the "transcendental signified"). Deconstruction is a perpetual reminder that the origin of language lies with writing (the "sign of a sign") and not with some assumed immediate experience of the correspondence of thought with object. Not even thought can escape the endless supplementarity of the linguistic system.

In the wake of Derrida's work, avant-garde postmoderns conclude that we can no longer assume an ontological ground for certain knowledge. Derrida's attack on the "center," they declare, has forever shattered traditional appeals to the author's intention. In fact, it has undermined appeals to anything located beyond the text.

What should we do in this situation? Derrida's followers counsel us simply to learn to live with the anxiety that results from his deconstruction of logocentrism and the demise of the metaphysics of presence. We must abandon the older understanding of reading as an attempt to gain entrance into the text in order to understand its meaning and embrace instead the idea that reading is a violent act of mastery over the text.[105]

The Pragmatic Utopia: Richard Rorty

Saturday evening, March 19, 1994, a humanities professor from the University of Virginia was scheduled to deliver a public lecture on the campus of the University of British Columbia in Vancouver. This academic event evoked such interest that thirty minutes before its scheduled beginning, the lecture hall was filled to capacity. To accommodate the crowd, the University had to provide closed-circuit television feeds to two adjacent lecture halls. The lecturer, Richard Rorty, has emerged as one of the most popular academic philosophers in contemporary North America.

Rorty has never been reluctant to affix labels to his own view. At one time he aligned himself with postmodernism, referring to his position as "postmodernist bourgeois liberalism."[106] He has since concluded that the term *postmodern* is overused and that we ought not to "periodize" culture.[107] Yet one description Rorty has consistently welcomed is "pragmatism."

The New Pragmatism

If Foucault is Nietzsche's truest twentieth-century disciple, and Derrida's patron saint is Heidegger, then Richard Rorty is unabashedly the protégé of John Dewey.[108] So important is this connection that Rorty has been hailed as "the central figure behind the renewed interest in the American pragmatist tradition."[109]

If Foucault is difficult to understand and Derrida nearly impossible to comprehend, Rorty's clear prose is a breath of fresh air. But what else would we expect from an American philosopher who employs writing and philosophical argumentation as the means to convince the reader of the validity of a position he calls "pragmatism"?[110]

The Pragmatist Outlook. At the heart of the pragmatist tradition is a specific understanding of the nature of truth. At the heart of Rorty's pragmatism is the abandonment of a idea that has reigned in philosophy since the Enlightenment — namely, that the mind is the "mirror of nature."[111] We can gain a sense of the immense shift in thinking Rorty proposes by drawing on a series of comparisons that he sprinkles throughout his writings.

151

The pragmatist view of truth is nonrealist rather than realist. The realist works from the assumption that we have direct access to the world independent of language and that our language follows from our observations of this objective, given world. Thus, we say, "Snow is white," because in the real world snow is in fact white. *Truth,* in turn, is a metaphysical term that means "what accurately represents objective reality."

The nonrealist, in contrast, begins with the assumption that our access to the world is mediated by language. We say "Snow is white" simply because we have chosen our categories in this way. As a result, truth is not primarily a metaphysical concept but a matter of human convention.[112]

In addition to being nonrealists, pragmatists hold to a nonessentialist rather than essentialist understanding of truth. Essentialists believe that an object or thing has both "intrinsic" and "relational" properties. Intrinsic properties are the essential qualities that the thing has "in itself," and relational properties are qualities that it has merely in relation to other things, especially human desires and interests.

Nonessentialists focus on relational properties. We cannot speak of the essential nature of a thing in isolation, they argue, but only in relation with other things. Hence, for nonessentialists like Rorty, "objects" are what we find useful to speak about in order to cope with the stimulations that come our way.[113]

Rorty draws a connection between his own nonessentialism and that of the pioneers of the new linguistics, such as Saussure and Wittgenstein, as well as their heir Derrida.[114] He lauds the linguistic philosophers for rejecting the essentialist understanding in the field of language. They point out that the significance of a sentence derives from its place in a web of other sentences (as the significance of beliefs and desires derives from their place in webs of other beliefs and desires). They are thus asserting that both linguistic signs and thoughts are context sensitive. The signs and thoughts are not "things" with intrinsic properties but nodes on a web of relations.

Rorty's goal is to extend this assertion from linguistic signs to all objects in our discourse — to everything from quarks and tables to people and social institutions.[115] His version of pragmatism is simply nonessentialism applied to all the "objects" of philosophical theorizing — truth, knowledge, and morality as well as language.[116]

152

In addition, pragmatists propose a nonrepresentationalist, rather than a representationalist understanding of truth. Representationalists assign a certain objectivity not only to the world but also to human language. They assume that our discourse can represent the world as it actually is. Any proposition that correctly represents the "real" world is true. Such a statement "re-presents" — brings into the present of the thinker or speaker — what the assertion is correctly describing. And knowledge, in turn, is the compilation of correct propositions.

Nonrepresentationalists deny that language has the capability to represent the world in this manner. Representation cannot mean "re-presentation," they say, because language cannot bring what is absent into our presence. As nonrepresentationalists, pragmatists like Rorty do not view knowledge as a matter of "getting reality right." They seek instead to acquire habits of action for coping with reality.[117]

Because it is nonrealist, nonessentialist, and nonrepresentationalist, the pragmatist view of truth elevates coherence rather than correspondence. The modern epistemological project is grounded in the correspondence theory of truth. Rorty characterizes the goal of this theory as penetrating the veil of appearances in order to glimpse things as they are in themselves. Measured by the correspondence criterion, statements always have a clear truth value: they are either true or false. And we can discover the veracity of an assertion by checking whether or not it corresponds to the reality it purports to describe.

Following Dewey, Rorty refers to the correspondence theory as the "spectator theory of knowledge," and he dismisses it as simply unworkable. It assumes that we can attain a perspective outside the world — what Hilary Putnam calls a "God's-eye point of view" of things.[118]

Rorty credits Dewey for pointing us in a more helpful direction. In place of the assumption that beliefs represent reality, Dewey substitutes the idea that beliefs are tools for dealing with reality; they are maxims that dictate the behavior of the one that holds them.[119]

Following Dewey, Rorty seeks to distance us from the correspondence theory of truth. In its place he advocates a type of coherence theory, while eschewing the idea of proposing any specific theory of truth.[120] Borrowing from Wittgenstein, he declares that statements are "true" insofar as they cohere with the entire system of beliefs — the "vocabulary" — that we hold. The aim of inquiry, in turn, is to make our beliefs and desires coherent.[121]

More importantly, pragmatists understand truth as what works rather than what is theoretically correct. According to Rorty, pragmatism is the "vocabulary" of practice rather than of theory. It focuses on action rather than contemplation.[122] Pragmatists frame questions about what is "right" in terms of what is "useful."[123] They ask, "What difference will this belief make to our conduct?"[124] It is on these grounds that Rorty calls for an "edifying philosophy."[125]

In the philosophical venture, pragmatists are nominalists. They maintain that a word has no intrinsic meaning, that it is merely a convention, the regular use of a mark or noise. Language, in turn, is a tool — human beings using marks and noises to get what they want.[126]

Rorty's pragmatism has significant implications for the scientific enterprise. Citing Thomas Kuhn and John Dewey, he proposes that we give up the idea that the goal of science is to produce models that correspond perfectly with reality. Instead, we should understand that scientific discourse is merely one vocabulary among many. Our question ought to be, "Which vocabulary works better than the others for the purpose we have in view."[127]

This kind of pragmatism also motivates Rorty to chastise Heidegger and Derrida for seeking to escape from the "onto-theological tradition" of Western philosophy. In typical pragmatist fashion, he suggests that instead of discarding the tradition *in toto,* we should seek to discover which "bits" of the tradition might be useful for some current purpose.[128]

Postmodern Pragmatism. But Rorty is not merely repackaging the older pragmatism. He gives a distinctively postmodern twist to the tradition pioneered by Dewey and others.

In promoting the notion that our statements are true insofar as they cohere with our entire system of beliefs, he does not go so far as to champion the idea that we can attain a system of beliefs that is perfectly consistent internally. Just as we have no access to a perspective outside the world, so we have no access to a perspective of objective rationality or morality outside our own particular historically conditioned vocabulary from which we can judge that vocabulary.[129]

Like the heirs of the new linguistics, Rorty takes for granted "the

154

It is useless to ask whether one vocabulary rather than another is closer to reality. For different vocabularies serve different purposes, and there is no such thing as a purpose that is closer to reality than another purpose. . . . Nothing is conveyed by saying . . . that the vocabulary in which we predict the motion of a planet is more in touch with how things really are than the vocabulary in which we assign the planet an astrological influence. For to say that astrology is out of touch with reality cannot *explain* why astrology is useless; it merely restates that fact in misleading representationalist terms.

Richard Rorty, in his introduction to John P. Murphy's *Pragmatism: From Peirce to Davidson* (Boulder: Westview Press, 1990), p. 3.

relativity of thinghood to choice of description."[130] Properties do not inhere in isolated objects; rather, a thing's properties are dependent on the language we use to describe them. Rorty readily admits that, in the end, truth becomes in essence truth *for us*.[131]

Rorty's postmodern pragmatism finds no epistemological difference between truth about what ought to be and truth about what is. Nor will he admit any metaphysical difference between morality and science. He views ethics and physics as equally objective, and he refuses to accede to the modern tendency to elevate scientists as more objective, logical, methodological, or devoted to truth than anyone else. He finds only one reason to elevate science among the scholarly disciplines: scientific institutions are models to the rest of culture of tolerance (or "unforced agreement") and human solidarity.[132]

This leveling of the plain between the natural sciences and the human sciences gives a postmodern twist to Rorty's nominalism. With other representatives of this long tradition, he sees language as a tool that we use to satisfy a variety of wants: food, sex, an understanding of the origin of the universe, an enhanced sense of human solidarity, and perhaps even a personal identity attained by developing one's own private, autonomous philosophical language. Rorty acknowledges that a single vocabulary could serve several of our varied aims, but, in postmodern fashion, he questions the existence of "any great big meta-vocabulary" under which we could subsume all the various types of human discourse. He finds no reason to lump together in the category of language "all the various uses of all the various marks and noises which we use for all these various purposes."[133]

The Pragmatist's Self and the Human Community

In the context of his appraisal of science, Rorty introduces his understanding of the self and community. It is here that the postmodern sensitivities of his thought come into sharp focus.

First, Rorty joins the postmodern assault on the modern concept of the self. He rejects Descartes's view of the self as an autonomous thinking substance, characterizing it instead as a centerless and ever-changing web of beliefs and desires that produces action.[134]

Further, Rorty rejects the Kantian quest for the universal human self, which often takes the form of a search for a coherent image that will fit the entire species to which we belong. Instead, he encourages us to tailor a coherent personal identity for ourselves that can serve as the foundation for our own behavior.[135] This task is expedited, he says, if we view our lives as episodes within larger historical narratives.

Rorty's introduction of the concept of "narrative" in the context of our search for a personal sense of identity gives an indication of the extent to which he places the individual (as well as truth) squarely in a social context. Indeed, Rorty is adamant that the way we think and act is thoroughly embedded in our temporal and cultural context. Consequently, he proposes an "ethnocentric" view of the justification of truth claims.[136] He argues that one cannot go beyond one's own society's procedures of justification. Everything one can say about truth or rationality is embedded in the understanding and concepts unique to the society in which one lives.[137]

However, Rorty is less concerned about carving out a philosophical foundation for a social view of the self than he is about counteracting what he says is the unhelpful tendency of Western philosophy and culture to assume that the knowing self can occupy a position beyond the ebb and flow of our historical context. Western "Platonists" assert that reality is ultimately ahistorical and nonhuman in nature, he says.

They erroneously imagine that they can transcend the vocabulary and practices of their own time and discover a universal, timeless, necessary, ahistorical "truth." In seeking the answer to such questions as "Why believe what I take to be true?" and "Why do what I take to be right?" they find it necessary to appeal to absolutes beyond the ordinary, concrete reasons that lie in their historical and social context.[138]

Rorty cites a variety of methods that Western thinkers have proposed for reaching this realm of timeless truth. Christians propose that we seek to become attuned to the voice of God in the heart. Cartesians attempt to empty the mind of all doubtful propositions and discover what cannot be doubted. The followers of Kant look to the foundational structure of inquiry, language, or social life.

Rorty eschews all such attempts. He asserts that it is impossible to find a starting point for our discourse that lies beyond the contingency of our own temporal context. Specifically, he contends that it is impossible for us to rise above human communities.[139] That being the case, he cautions against any attempt to endow any interpretation with timeless, universal authority.[140]

But rather than bemoaning the loss of a transcendental vantage point, Rorty welcomes the new situation. It is beneficial, he says, because it builds our sense of community. As we acknowledge the contingency of starting points, we realize that our inheritance from and our conver-

---

If we give up this hope [to become a properly programmed machine], we shall lose what Nietzsche called "metaphysical comfort," but we may gain a renewed sense of community. Our identification with our community — our society, our political tradition, our intellectual heritage — is heightened when we see this community as *ours* rather than *nature's, shaped* rather than *found,* one among many which men have made. In the end, the pragmatists tell us, what matters is our loyalty to other human beings clinging together against the dark, not our hope of getting things right.

Richard Rorty, "Pragmatism," in *The Consequences of Pragmatism*
(Minneapolis: University of Minnesota Press, 1982), p. 166.

157

sation with our fellow human beings is our only source of guidance.[141] He contends that an awareness of this fact can help us to move from confrontation to conversation in our ongoing inquiries.[142]

Lying behind Rorty's denial of any objective starting point for knowledge and truth is a far-reaching rejection of the quest for a theory of knowledge (i.e., epistemology). At least since the Enlightenment, philosophy has been motivated by the belief that despite the apparent differences and conflicting opinions of individual human beings, we are nonetheless united by an underlying common rationality. Driven by this belief, philosophers have sought to outline a fixed neutral framework for judging human discourse, a theory of knowledge that brings to light the hidden rationality we all share.

Rorty, however, is an antifoundationalist. He denies that the philosopher can set forth "first principles" or canons of rationality that provide the foundation for our discovery of truth and certain knowledge. We cannot derive a foundation for human discourse by appeal to the nature of the objects of our inquiry, the mind, or the rules of language, he says. The scholarly enterprise is no longer ruled by purportedly objective extracultural constraints. We simply cannot bring human discourse under a set of rules of rationality: there is no set of transcendent rules that will help us determine how to resolve conflicting assertions.[143]

We should not seek an objective, external foundation for the human inquiry into truth, says Rorty; we need only conform ourselves to the constraints that arise through our conversations with our fellow inquirers.[144] The only valid guidelines we will ever be able to find are those of the community in which we participate. The only foundation we will ever be able to assemble is the give-and-take of the conversation among competing interpretations. The proper goal of philosophy is not to uncover objective truth but to maintain the discussion among these differing interpretations.[145]

As an antifoundationalist, Rorty calls for a move from epistemology to hermeneutics.[146] In issuing the call to abandon the quest for a universal theory of knowledge in favor of engaging in an ongoing conversation, Rorty proves himself heir to a trajectory that begins with Schleiermacher and Dilthey, runs through Heidegger and Gadamer, and leads to Foucault and Derrida. Rorty completes the postmodern turn from knowledge to interpretation. In the midst of the discordant noise of competing interpretations, he insists that the philosopher no longer can play the role of neutral arbiter. The postmodern philosopher can only "decry the notion of having a view while avoiding having a view about having views."[147]

The New Utopianism

Foucault's attack on "the order of things" inaugurates a never-ending state of siege on behalf of "subjugated knowledge." Derrida's assault on the bastions of logocentrism leaves us in the position of being able to do little more than cope with the anxiety produced by living in a centerless world. In contrast to the seemingly bleak implications of the others, Rorty's pragmatism appears refreshingly hopeful. Unlike the anti-utopia of Derrida and the negative utopia of Foucault, Rorty leads his followers into a new postmodern utopianism.

Rorty's utopianism is evident in his adamant rejection of the relativism that his critics often attribute to him. He categorically denies that trading foundationalism for an understanding that embeds "truth" within community leads to a self-refuting relativism. His thesis is that we have no choice but to begin within the social networks in which we find ourselves and the communities with which we presently identify. But he repudiates the suggestion that this makes every community as good as every other one. In fact, he argues that if we assume this kind of relativism, we are implicitly adopting the very stance he cautions us to avoid: we are presuming to stand above history and claim a God's-eye view of the world. Only God could conclude that all communities are equally good.[148]

Although Rorty's utopianism is evident in his denial of relativism, its basis lies elsewhere. Rorty is a utopian philosopher because he believes that inquiry leads to a positive goal and that this goal can be achieved even in a postmodern era. He defines this goal as "the attainment of an appropriate mixture of unforced agreement with tolerant disagreement."

Rorty advocates the kind of thoroughgoing cultural pluralism that is in keeping with the spirit of tolerance that has made constitutional

159

democracies possible. He affirms that such cultural pluralism will be possible only to the extent that public institutions remain neutral on the central questions about the goal or purpose of human existence.[149] True to his ethnocentric view of truth, however, Rorty looks to the social community to determine through trial and error what counts as an "appropriate mixture" of agreement and disagreement within the context of this pluralism.[150]

Rorty is confident that the pragmatists' enterprise can rid our society of the bugaboos that now beset it. By following the pragmatic agenda, he says, we could divest ourselves not only of the correspondence model of truth but also of the subject-object model of inquiry and the "child-parent" model of moral obligation.[151]

Like a true utopian, Rorty sees signs that the pragmatist's paradise is already dawning. He welcomes the work of the European postmoderns, including Derrida's assault on essentialism and logocentrism. Rorty sees pragmatism and Continental philosophy as engaging in a common task — namely, the debunking of the reigning conception of philosophy. They agree that philosophy is not endowed with the ability to decide issues of ultimate significance for human life, that the philosopher is no "super-scientist."[152]

Rorty maintains that the contemporary attack on the modern view is simply the latest stage in a gradual and continuous development in our understanding of our relation to the rest of the universe, a trajectory that led from the worship of gods to the worship of sages to the worship of empirical scientific inquirers. But he hopes this trajectory will lead one step farther: he hopes that we will be able to divest ourselves of the worship of anything.[153]

His commitment to this goal lies behind his critique of the attempt by the natural scientist to step into the cultural role vacated by the philosopher. In the pragmatist's ideal society, the role of super-scientist must remain forever unfilled.[154]

Rorty is not concerned that we will have to sacrifice anything valuable in order to attain the pragmatist utopia. He sees only benefits in the full flowering of cultural pluralism. After the "high altars" are gone, he suggests, the wholesome aspects of culture will multiply — galleries, book displays, movies, concerts, museums. We will be leaving behind nothing more than a privileged central discipline or practice.[155]

CHAPTER 7

The Gospel and
the Postmodern Context

Evangelicalism shares close ties with modernity. A child of the Reformation, pietism, and revivalism, the evangelical movement was born in the early modern period. And North American evangelicalism reached maturity in the mid-twentieth century — at the height of the modern era.

As modern thinkers, evangelicals have always used the tools of modernity, such as the scientific method, the empirical approach to reality, and commonsense realism.[1] But the these tools became especially important in the twentieth century, as evangelical intellectuals attempted to understand and articulate the gospel with eyes turned toward the challenge posed by the worldview of late modernity — secularism.

Twentieth-century evangelicals have devoted much energy to the task of demonstrating the credibility of the Christian faith to a culture that glorifies reason and deifies science. Evangelical presentations of the gospel have often been accompanied by a rational apologetic that appeals to proofs for the existence of God, the trustworthiness of the Bible, and the historicity of Jesus' resurrection. Evangelical systematic theologies have generally focused on the propositional content of the faith, seeking to provide a logical presentation of Christian doctrine.

In short, modern evangelicals have done well in developing a vision of the Christian faith for the old *Star Trek* society.

But we are now moving into a new context. The Western world — from pop culture to academia — is jettisoning the Enlightenment principles that formed the foundation for modernity. We are entering a postmodern era.

The postmodern ethos is especially influential within the emerging generation — among younger adults who take for granted the information age, endless channels of cable programming, and MTV. This generation has been nurtured in a context shaped less by commitment to the Enlightenment project embodied in *Star Trek* than by the postmodern vision represented in *Star Trek: The Next Generation* and its successors. In this new context, Foucault's suspicion of every "present order," Derrida's questioning of reason by reason, and Rorty's thoroughgoing pragmatism are common parlance, even for those who have never heard the names of these philosophical gurus of postmodern culture.

The shift from the familiar territory of modernity to the uncharted terrain of postmodernity has grave implications for those who seek to live as Christ's disciples in the new context. We must think through the ramifications of the phenomenal changes occurring in Western society for our understanding of the Christian faith and our presentation of the gospel to the next generation.

How then should we respond to the intellectual ethos of the emerging postmodern world? With a view toward facilitating reflection on this question, I want to conclude my survey of postmodernism by offering a preliminary assessment of the postmodern phenomenon.[2]

The Postmodern Critique of Modernism

As I have noted repeatedly in these pages, the quest to jettison the Enlightenment project of modernity is foundational to postmodernism. Whatever it may eventually become, postmodernism has begun as a rejection of the modern mind-set launched under the conditions of modernity. In keeping with this largely negative orientation, this rejection of the immediate past, postmodern intellectuals have generally not sought to provide any constructive new proposals. Their goal has primarily been to set forth a stinging critique of the Enlightenment project on the basis of its own underlying principles.

How should we appraise this critique?

Standing Our Ground: *Rejecting the Rejection of the Metanarrative*

Christians confronted for the first time with the ideas of such thinkers as Foucault, Derrida, and Rorty may well be inclined to recoil in horror, fearing that the postmodern rejection of the Enlightenment project goes too far.

Concerning one important aspect of the postmodern agenda, such fears are well founded. Postmodernism has tossed aside objective truth, at least as it has classically been understood. Foucault, Derrida, and Rorty stand against what has for centuries been the reigning epistemological principle — the correspondence theory of truth (the belief that truth consists of the correspondence of propositions with the world "out there"). This rejection of the correspondence theory not only leads to a skepticism that undercuts the concept of objective truth in general; it also undermines Christian claims that our doctrinal formulations state objective truth.

But the clash of postmodernism with Christian sympathies runs at a deeper level than the debate over which epistemological theory we should follow. More radical than the rejection of the correspondence theory of truth is the postmodern despair concerning the quest to discover all-encompassing truth. In fact, the postmodern ethos arises from the assumption that there is no unified whole that we can call "reality." Postmodern thinkers have given up the search for universal, ultimate truth because they are convinced that there is nothing more to find than a host of conflicting interpretations or an infinity of linguistically created worlds.

The abandonment of the belief in universal truth entails the loss of any final criterion by which to evaluate the various interpretations of reality that compete in the contemporary intellectual realm. In this situation, all human interpretations — including the Christian world-

163

view — are equally valid because all are equally invalid. (In fact, as adjectives objectively describing interpretations, *valid* and *invalid* become meaningless terms.) At best, say the postmoderns, we can judge these interpretations only on the basis of pragmatic standards, on the basis of "what works."

Postmodern skepticism, therefore, leaves us in a world characterized by a never-ending struggle among competing interpretations. It puts us in a situation reminiscent of Hobbes's war of all against all.

Our commitment to the God revealed in Christ compels us to stand squarely against at least one aspect or outworking of the radical skepticism of postmodernism: the loss of a "center."

As Christians, we can go only so far with Derrida, for example, in his unrelenting attack on the "metaphysics of presence" and "logocentricism." In contrast to postmodern thought, we believe that there is a unifying center to reality. More specifically, we acknowledge that this center has appeared in Jesus of Nazareth, who is the eternal Word present among us.

To put this in another way, we might say that because of our faith in Christ, we cannot totally affirm the central tenet of postmodernism as defined by Lyotard — the rejection of the metanarrative. We may welcome Lyotard's conclusion when applied to the chief concern of his analysis — namely, the scientific enterprise. Indeed, we can live quite well without such myths as the progress of knowledge. But we cannot accede to the extension of Lyotard's thesis to reality as a whole.

Our world is more than a collection of incompatible and competing local narratives. Contrary to the implications of Lyotard's thesis, we firmly believe that the local narratives of the many human communities do fit together into a single grand narrative, the story of humankind. There *is* a single metanarrative encompassing all peoples and all times.

As Christians, we claim to know what that grand narrative is. It is the story of God's action in history for the salvation of fallen humankind and the completion of God's intentions for creation. We boldly proclaim that the focus of this metanarrative is the story of Jesus of Nazareth, who, we testify, is the incarnate Son, the second Person of the triune God.

Postmodern thinkers rightly alert us to the naïveté of the Enlightenment attempt to discover universal truth by appeal to reason alone. Ultimately the metanarrative we proclaim lies beyond the pale of reason either to discover or to evaluate. Therefore, we agree that in this world we will witness the struggle among conflicting narratives and interpretations of reality. But we add that although all interpretations are in some sense invalid, they cannot all be *equally* invalid. We believe that conflicting interpretations can be evaluated according to a criterion that in some sense transcends them all. Because we believe that "the Word became flesh" in Jesus Christ, we are convinced that this criterion is the story of God's action in Jesus of Nazareth.

In short, we simply cannot allow Christianity to be relegated to the status of one more faith among others. The gospel is inherently an expansive missionary message. We believe not only that the biblical narrative makes sense for *us* but is also good news for *all*. It provides the fulfillment of the longings and aspirations of all peoples. It embodies *the* truth — the truth of and for all humankind.

Common Ground: The Rejection of the Enlightenment Epistemology

As Christians we must stand against the postmodern rejection of the metanarrative. We simply do not share the despair over the loss of universality that leads to the radical skepticism of the emerging era. At the same time, we dare not allow our resounding "No!" to postmodernism at this central point to blind us to the validity of its critique of modernity. On the contrary, closer inspection of the phenomenon should convince us that we are in fundamental agreement with the postmodern rejection of the modern mind and its underlying Enlightenment epistemology.[3]

As we noted earlier, modernity is built on the assumption that knowledge is certain, objective, and good. Postmodernism rejects this supposition. Unfortunately, evangelicals have often uncritically accepted the modern view of knowledge despite the fact that at certain points the postmodern critique is more in keeping with Christian theological understandings.

The Certainty of Knowledge. Postmodernism questions the Enlightenment assumption that knowledge is certain and that the criterion for certainty rests with our human rational capabilities.

165

In a similar manner, the Christian faith entails a denial that the rational, scientific method is the sole measure of truth. We affirm that certain aspects of truth lie beyond reason and cannot be fathomed by reason. As Blaise Pascal put it, "The heart has its reasons which reason cannot know."

In addition, Christians take a cautious, even distrustful stance toward human reason. We know that because of the fall of humankind, sin can blind the human mind. And we realize that following the intellect can sometimes lead us away from God and truth.

The Objectivity of Knowledge. Similarly, we ought to commend the postmodern questioning of the Enlightenment assumption that knowledge is objective and hence dispassionate.

As we have seen, modern epistemology was built on the model of the Cartesian self encountering the Newtonian universe as an external object. But in contrast to the modern ideal of the dispassionate observer, we affirm the postmodern discovery that no observer can stand outside the historical process. Nor can we gain universal, culturally neutral knowledge as unconditioned specialists. On the contrary, we are participants in our historical and cultural context, and all our intellectual endeavors are unavoidably conditioned by that participation.

Postmodern epistemologists are actually echoing Augustine when they assert that our personal convictions and commitments not only color our search for knowledge but also facilitate the process of understanding.

The Goodness of Knowledge. Finally, we can affirm the postmodern rejection of the Enlightenment assumption that knowledge is inherently good.

Events of the twentieth century bear poignant witness that, despite its benefits, the knowledge explosion is not going to produce a utopia. Technological advances bring not only the possibility of good but also the possibility of evil. An obvious example is the splitting of the atom. This discovery opened the door to a nuclear Armageddon and a whole new type of nondisposable waste. We can only wonder what dire results may flow from investigations into the human genetic structure.

The Christian understanding of the human situation provides its own foundation for a rejection of the Enlightenment assumption of the inherent goodness of knowledge. We believe that the human problem is a matter not merely of ignorance but also of a misdirected will. We believe that the myth of knowledge dispelling ignorance and thereby bringing in the golden age is based on a dangerous half-truth. We must not only be saved from our ignorance but also undergo a renewal and redirection of our will.

Contours of a Postmodern Gospel

Part of the Christian calling is to appraise any new ethos that shapes the culture in which God calls believers to live as his people. One goal of this task is to equip the church to articulate and embody the gospel in the context of that culture. Today we are challenged to live out our Christian commitment in the midst of a culture and to proclaim the gospel to a generation that is increasingly postmodern in its thinking.

This mandate demands that we explore the contours of the gospel in a postmodern context. What biblical emphases concerning God's saving work resonate with the longings and concerns of the emerging generation? And how can we express the gospel in the categories of the new social context?

The postmodern situation requires that we embody the gospel in a manner that is *post-individualistic, post-rationalistic, post-dualistic,* and *post-noeticentric.*

A Post-Individualistic Gospel

First, a postmodern articulation of the Christian gospel will be post-individualistic.

One of the hallmarks of modernity is the elevation of the individual. The modern world is an individualistic world, a realm of the autonomous human person endowed with inherent rights.

This modern focus corresponds with certain central dimensions of scriptural teaching. Consequently, we dare not entirely lose the emphasis on the importance of the individual human person indicative of modernity. Indeed, we must always keep in view the biblical themes of God's concern for each person, the responsibility of every human

167

before God, and the individual orientation that lies within the salvation message.

In addition, twentieth-century examples of totalitarianism are stark reminders that we must continually stand against the tyranny of the collective in all its various forms.

But while maintaining an individual focus in our presentations of the gospel, we must shake ourselves loose from the radical individualism that has come to characterize the modern mind-set. We must affirm with postmodern thinkers that knowledge — including knowledge of God — is not merely objective, not simply discovered by the neutral knowing self.

Here we can learn from contemporary communitarian scholars who have joined the postmodern assault on the modern epistemological fortress. They reject the modern paradigm with its focus on the self-reflective, self-determining, autonomous subject who stands outside any tradition or community. In its place the new communitarians offer a constructive alternative: the individual-within-community.

Communitarians point out the unavoidable role of the community or social network in the life of the human person. For example, they affirm that the community is essential in the process of knowing. Individuals come to knowledge only by way of a cognitive framework mediated by the community in which they participate. Similarly, the community of participation is crucial to identity formation. A sense of personal identity develops through the telling of a personal narrative, which is always embedded in the story of the communities in which we participate.[4] The community mediates to its members a transcendent story that includes traditions of virtue, common good, and ultimate meaning.[5]

We must take seriously the discoveries of contemporary communitarians.[6] They are echoing the great biblical theme that the goal of God's program is the establishment of community in the highest sense.

In the postmodern world, we can no longer follow the lead of modernity and position the individual at center stage. Instead, we must remind ourselves that our faith is highly social. The fact that God is the social Trinity — Father, Son, and Spirit — gives us some indication that the divine purpose for creation is directed toward the individual-in-relationship. Our gospel must address the human person within the context of the communities in which people are embedded.

With its focus on community, the postmodern world encourages us to recognize the importance of the community of faith in our evangelistic efforts. Members of the next generation are often unimpressed by our verbal presentations of the gospel. What they want to see is a people who live out the gospel in wholesome, authentic, and healing relationships. Focusing on the example of Jesus and the apostles, a Christian gospel for the postmodern age will invite others to become participants in the community of those whose highest loyalty is to the God revealed in Christ. Participants in the inviting community will seek to draw others to Christ by embodying that gospel in the fellowship they share.

A Post-Rationalistic Gospel

In addition to being post-individualistic, a postmodern articulation of the Christian gospel will be post-rationalistic.

A second hallmark of modernity is its elevation of reason. The focus on logical argumentation and the scientific method has freed us from a host of superstitions that plagued premodern peoples. This focus has also provided us with the tools to construct the modern society, which offers so many benefits to its citizens.

Despite the challenges to faith that troubled Christians in the age of reason, Christianity was able to find a home in the modern world. Modern evangelicals contributed to this process. They painstakingly demonstrated that the Christian faith is not necessarily unreasonable. In response to modern skeptics, they boldly claimed that no one need commit intellectual suicide to be a Christian.

A postmodern embodiment of the gospel ought not to become anti-intellectual and wholly abandon the gains of the Enlightenment. Yet the postmodern critique of modernity stands as a needed reminder that our humanity does not consist solely in our cognitive dimension. We are intellectual beings, but we amount to more than just Aristotle's "rational animal." And we must acknowledge that intellectual reflection and the scientific enterprise alone cannot put us in touch with every dimension of reality or lead us to discover every aspect of God's truth.

169

This means that we cannot simply collapse truth into the categories of rational certainty that typify modernity. Rather, in understanding and articulating the Christian faith, we must make room for the concept of "mystery" — not as an irrational complement to the rational but as a reminder that the fundamental reality of God transcends human rationality. While remaining reasonable, therefore, the appeal of our gospel must not be limited to the intellectual aspect of the human person. It must encompass other dimensions of our being as well.

Central to our task in thinking through the faith in a postmodern context is an obligation to rethink the function of assertions of truth or propositions. We must continue to acknowledge the fundamental importance of rational discourse, but our understanding of the faith must not remain fixated on the propositionalist approach that views Christian truth as nothing more than correct doctrine or doctrinal truth.

We can gain assistance in this task from postmodern social theorists. These thinkers are attempting to replace the individualistic foundational rationalism of modern Western thinking with an understanding of knowledge and belief that views them as socially and linguistically constituted.[7] Along the way they are offering helpful insights into the role of propositions in our lives.

No experience occurs in a vacuum; no transformation comes to us apart from an interpretation facilitated by the concepts — the "web of belief" — we bring to it. To the contrary, experience and interpretive concepts are reciprocally related. Our concepts facilitate our understanding of the experiences we have in life, and our experience shapes the interpretive concepts we employ to speak about our lives.

At the heart of being a Christian is a personal encounter with God in Christ that shapes and molds us. On the basis of this encounter, we seek to bring into an understandable whole the diverse strands of our personal lives by appeal to certain categories. Prominent among these are "sin" and "grace," "alienation" and "reconciliation," "helplessness" and "divine power," "having been lost" but "now being saved." It is in this context of making sense out of life by means of recounting the story of a transformative religious experience that doctrinal propositions find their importance. Thus the encounter with God in Christ is both facilitated by and expressed in categories that are propositional in nature. The categories that form the cradle for this experience in turn constitute the grid through which the believer comes to view all of life.

Propositions can thus be said to have a second-order importance. They both serve the conversion experience and arise out of our new status as believers. Consequently, our goal in proclaiming the gospel should not merely be to bring others to affirm a list of correct propositions. Rather, we should employ theological propositions such as "sin" and "grace" in order that others might encounter God in Christ and then join us on the grand journey of understanding the meaning of that encounter for all of life.

A postmodern articulation of the gospel is post-rationalistic. It no longer focuses on propositions as the central content of Christian faith. Instead, it takes seriously a dynamic understanding of the role of the intellectual dimension of human experience and our attempts to make sense of life.

A Post-Dualistic Gospel

Third, a postmodern articulation of the gospel will also be post-dualistic. It must draw courage from the postmodern critique of modern dualism to develop a biblical holism.

The Enlightenment project was built on the division of reality into "mind" and "matter." This fundamental dualism affected the Enlightenment view of the human person as "soul" (thinking substance) and "body" (physical substance).

We cannot deny that this dualism has long been influential in Christian thinking. Christians who are imbued with the Enlightenment outlook often articulate a dualistic gospel. Their primary if not sole concern is that of saving "souls." They may entertain a secondary concern for "bodies," but they are convinced that the physical dimension of the human person has no eternal importance.

If we would minister in the postmodern context, however, we must realize that the next generation is increasingly interested in the human person as a unified whole. The gospel we proclaim must speak to human beings in their entirety. This does not mean merely placing more emphasis on emotion or the affective aspects of life alongside the rational.

171

Rather, it involves integrating the emotional-affective, as well as the bodily-sensual, with the intellectual-rational within the one human person. In other words, to borrow from *Star Trek: The Next Generation,* we must be willing to acknowledge the interdependency of the Counselor Troi alongside the Spock (or Data) in each of us.

But postmodern Christian holism must go beyond reuniting the soul and body torn asunder in the Enlightenment. As we noted earlier, our gospel must also put the human person back into the social and environmental context that forms and nourishes us. We must not dwell merely on the individual in isolation but also on the person-in-relationships.

Our anthropology must take seriously the biblical truth that our identity includes being in relationship to nature, being in relationship with others, being in relationship with God, and, as a consequence, being in true relationship with ourselves. All these emphases are evident in the ministry of our Lord, who spoke about and ministered to people as whole persons and as persons-in-relationship.

A Post-Noeticentric Gospel

Finally, a postmodern articulation of the gospel will be post-noeticentric. That is to say, our gospel must affirm that the goal of our existence encompasses more than just the accumulation of knowledge. We must declare that the purpose of correct doctrine is to serve the attainment of *wisdom.*

The Enlightenment gave humankind a great legacy through its elevation of knowledge. It focused human efforts on the quest for knowledge, which came to be viewed as inherently good.

Indeed, knowledge is *a* good. And as Christian heirs of the Enlightenment, we ought to center our intellectual efforts on the discovery of knowledge about God in its various forms. We can also affirm that right thinking is an important goal in the process of sanctification, for we are convinced that right beliefs and correct doctrines are vital to Christian living.

However, we must not restrict our goal to the amassing of a wealth of knowledge for its own sake. Nor should we be under any illusion that the possession of knowledge — even biblical knowledge or correct doctrine — is inherently good. Paul adamantly rejected such beliefs among the Corinthians (1 Cor. 8:1). Knowledge is good only when it facilitates a good result — specifically, when it fosters wisdom (or spirituality) in the knower.

A post-noeticentric Christian gospel emphasizes the relevance of faith for every dimension of life. It refuses to allow commitment to Christ to remain merely an intellectual endeavor, a matter solely of assent to orthodox propositions. Commitment to Christ must also take its lodging in the heart. In fact, the postmodern world provides the occasion for us to reappropriate the older pietist belief that a right head has no value apart from a right heart. The Christian gospel is concerned not only with the reformulation of our intellectual commitments but also with the transformation of our character and the renewal of our entire lives as believers.

To this end, a post-noeticentric gospel fosters a proper ordering of activism and quietism. No longer can we follow the modern outlook, which looks to overt activity, conduct, or specific decisions as the sole measure of spirituality. In the end, this emphasis leads only to spiritual aridity and burnout. The postmodern ethos correctly understands that activism must arise from inner resources. The postmodern gospel will remind us that we will be able to sustain right action only when it flows from the resources of the Holy Spirit, who continually renews our inner person.

This focus returns us to the ancillary role of knowledge. Beliefs are important because they shape conduct. Our fundamental belief structure is reflected in our actions. As Christians, then, we should be concerned to gain knowledge and to hold to correct doctrine *in order* that we might attain wisdom for living so that we might please God with our lives.

In the opinion of many, our society is in the throes of a monumental transition, the movement from modernity to postmodernity. For better or worse, the emerging generation — those who belong to the world of *Star Trek: The Next Generation* and its successors — is imbued with many aspects of the postmodern mind. Our task is not to defend modernism, to turn the intellectual tide back to the Enlightenment. Rather, we are called to understand the new intellectual climate, to view it through Christian eyes.

This project involves using the tools of our faith to assess the strengths and weaknesses of the postmodern ethos. And postmodernism comes up short at many points. Therefore, we dare not simply "move with the times" and embrace uncritically the latest intellectual trend. At the same time, critical engagement with postmodernism cannot end with a simplistic rejection of the entire ethos. Our critical reflections must lead us to determine the contours of the gospel that will speak to the hearts of postmodern people. We must engage postmodernism in order to discern how best to articulate the Christian faith to the next generation.

The gospel of Jesus Christ has gone forth in every era with power to convert human hearts. Today that gospel is the answer to the longings of the postmodern generation. Our task as Christ's disciples is to embody and articulate the never-changing good news of available salvation in a manner that the emerging generation can understand. Only then can we become the vehicles of the Holy Spirit in bringing them to experience the same life-changing encounter with the triune God from whom our entire lives derive their meaning.

Notes

Notes to Chapter 1

1. See, e.g., Diogenes Allen, *Christian Belief in a Postmodern World: The Full Wealth of Conviction* (Louisville: Westminster/John Knox Press, 1989), p. 2.

2. Some thinkers have boldly sought to describe the new postmodern mood, but their portraits tend to reflect their own sympathies. E.g., Sallie McFague includes among the postmodern assumptions "a greater appreciation for nature, a recognition of the importance of language to human existence, a chastened admiration for technology, an acceptance of the challenge that other religions present to the Judeo-Christian tradition, an apocalyptic sensibility, a sense of the displacement of the white, Western male and the rise of those dispossessed due to gender, race, or class, perhaps most significantly, a growing awareness of the radical interdependence of life at all levels and in every imaginable way" (*Metaphorical Theology* [Philadelphia: Fortress Press, 1982], pp. x-xi).

3. For a discussion of the early uses of the term, see Margaret Rose, "Defining the Post-Modern," in *The Post-Modern Reader,* ed. Charles Jencks (New York: St. Martin's Press, 1992), pp. 119-36.

4. Craig Van Gelder, "Postmodernism as an Emerging Worldview," *Calvin Theological Journal* 26 (1991): 412.

5. For a short discussion of the Enlightenment period and its impact on Christian theology, see Stanley J. Grenz and Roger E. Olson, *Twentieth-Century Theology: God and the World in a Transitional Age* (Downers Grove, Ill.: InterVarsity Press, 1992).

6. Van Gelder, "Postmodernism as an Emerging Worldview," p. 413.

7. On the modernist presumption of the objectivity of knowledge, see James M. Kee, "'Postmodern' Thinking and the Status of the Religions," *Religion and Literature* 22 (Summer-Autumn 1990): 49.

8. Richard Luecke, "The Oral, the Local and the Timely," *Christian Century,* 3 October 1990, p. 875.

9. Klaus Hedwig, "The Philosophical Presuppositions of Postmodernity," *Communio* 17 (Summer 1990): 168.

10. Merold Westphal, "The Ostrich and the Boogeyman: Placing Postmodernism," *Christian Scholar's Review* 20 (December 1990): 115.

11. Ted Peters, "Toward Postmodern Theology," *Dialog* 24 (Summer 1985): 221.

12. At first the Enlightenment project appeared to be a friend of religion, offering to place belief on the surer footing of human reason. Later thinkers, however, no longer accepted the understanding of God and the world that had been salvaged earlier. Their new skepticism led to the atheistic-materialistic worldview of late modernity. Specifically, the ideas of Descartes and Newton undergirded a body/soul dichotomy and posited an absolute gulf between the human soul and the rest of creation. Late moderns found it difficult to conceive of God's action in this dualistic world. Difficulty in understanding how soul and body could interact led to the characterization of the mind as an *epiphenomenon*, a by-product of the brain, and then the elimination of concept of the human soul on the grounds that it was an unsubstantiated "ghost in the machine." See David Ray Griffin, *God and Religion in the Postmodern World: Essays in Postmodern Theology* (Albany: State University of New York Press, 1989), pp. 21-23, 54-56.

13. "Structuralism," in *Dictionary of Philosophy and Religion,* ed. W. L. Reese (Atlantic Highlands, N.J.: Humanities Press, 1980), p. 553.

14. This proposal is often credited to Hans-Georg Gadamer. See, e.g., *Truth and Method* (New York: Crossroad, 1984), p. 261.

15. Derrida, *Of Grammatology,* trans. Gayatri Chakravorty Spivak (Baltimore: The Johns Hopkins University Press, 1976), p. 50.

16. Foucault, "Truth and Power," in *Power/Knowledge: Selected Interviews and Other Writings, 1972-1977,* ed. Colin Gordon (New York: Pantheon Books, 1980), p. 133.

17. Rorty, *Philosophy and the Mirror of Nature* (Princeton: University of Princeton Press, 1979), p. 393.

18. Women are not stereotyped into affective roles, however; the ship's chief medical officer is a woman.

19. Marsden, "Evangelicals, History, and Modernity," in *Evangelicalism and Modern America,* ed. George M. Marsden (Grand Rapids: William B. Eerdmans, 1984), p. 98.

Notes to Chapter 2

1. Steven Connor, *Postmodernist Culture* (Oxford: Basil Blackwell, 1989), p. 69.

2. Jencks, *The Language of Post-Modern Architecture,* 4th ed. (London: Academy Editions, 1984), p. 9. See also Jencks, "The Post-Modern Agenda," in *The Postmodern Reader,* ed. Charles Jencks (New York: St. Martin's Press, 1992), p. 24.

3. Jencks, "The Post-Modern Agenda," p. 11.

4. For a helpful discussion of the origins of the term, see Margaret Rose, "Defining the Post-Modern," in *The Post-Modern Reader,* pp. 119-36.

5. Already in the 1930s it served as the designation for certain developments in the arts. Craig Van Gelder, "Postmodernism as an Emerging Worldview," *Calvin Theological Journal* 26 (November 1991): 412.

6. Jencks, *What Is Post-Modernism?* 3d ed. (New York: St. Martin's Press, 1989), p. 8.

7. Steven Connor, *Postmodernist Culture* (Oxford: Basil Blackwell, 1989), p. 65.

8. For a discussion of Toynbee's use of the term and its meaning, see Rose, "Defining the Post-Modern," pp. 122-24. See also Margaret A. Rose, *The Post-Modern and the Post-Industrial: A Critical Analysis* (Cambridge: Cambridge University Press, 1991), pp. 9-11.

9. Thomas J. J. Altizer and William Hamilton, *Radical Theology and the Death of God* (Indianapolis: Bobbs-Merrill, 1961). For a short discussion of this movement, see Stanley J. Grenz and Roger E. Olson, *Twentieth-Century Theology: God and the World in a Transitional Age* (Downers Grove, Ill.: InterVarsity Press, 1993), pp. 156-61.

10. Fiedler, "The New Mutants," in *The Collected Essays of Leslie Fiedler*, vol. 2 (New York: Stein & Day, 1971), pp. 382, 389.

11. Connor, *Postmodern Culture*, p. 204.

12. Hassan, "The Question of Postmodernism," in *Romanticism, Modernism, Postmodernism*, ed. Harry R. Garvin (Toronto: Bucknell University Press, 1980), pp. 117-26.

13. Connor, *Postmodernist Culture*, p. 6.

14. Gary John Percesepe, "The Unbearable Lightness of Being Postmodern," *Christian Scholar's Review* 20 (December 1990): 18.

15. See, e.g., Paolo Portoghesi, "What Is the Postmodern?" in *The Post-Modern Reader*, p. 211.

16. Jencks, *What Is Postmodernism?* p. 44.

17. Jencks, *What Is Postmodernism?* p. 11.

18. Benjamin Barber, "Jihad vs. McWorld," *Atlantic Monthly*, March 1992, p. 53.

19. For a discussion of major works that herald the advent of a postindustrial age, see Rose, *The Post-Modern and the Post-Industrial*, pp. 21-39.

20. Foucault, *The Order of Things: An Archaeology of the Human Sciences* (New York: Pantheon Books, 1970), p. xviii.

21. For a detailed study, see Steven Connor, *Postmodernist Culture* (London: Basil Blackwell, 1989).

22. Fredric Jameson, "Postmodernism and Consumer Society," in *The Anti-Aesthetic: Essays on Postmodern Culture*, ed. Hal Foster (Port Townsend, Wash.: Bay Press, 1983), pp. 114, 115-16, 125.

23. For examples, see Jameson, "Postmodernism and Consumer Culture," pp. 116-17.

24. Wright, "Organic Architecture" (excerpt, 1910), in *Programmes and Manifestoes on Twentieth-Century Architecture*, ed. Ulrich Conrads, trans. Michael Bullock (London: Lund Humphries, 1970), p. 25.

25. Jencks, "The Post-Modern Agenda," p. 24.

26. Heinrich Klotz, "Postmodern Architecture," in *The Post-Modern Reader*, pp. 241-42.

27. Paolo Portoghesi, *After Modern Architecture*, trans. Meg Shore (New York: Rizzoli: 1982), p. 3.

28. Robert Venturi, *Learning from Las Vegas* (Cambridge: M.I.T. Press, 1977), pp. 135-36.

29. Greenberg is often credited with having provided modernist art with its most influential form of legitimation. See Connor, *Postmodernist Culture*, p. 81.

30. See Clement Greenberg, "Modernist Painting," in *Postmodern Perspectives: Issues in Contemporary Art,* ed. Howard Risatti (Englewood Cliffs, N.J.: Prentice-Hall, 1990), pp. 12-19. See also Greenberg, "Towards a Newer Laocoon," in *Pollock and After: The Critical Debate,* ed. Francis Frascina (London: Harper & Row, 1985), pp. 41-42.

31. David Harvey, "The Condition of Postmodernity," in *The Post-Modern Reader,* p. 308. Gregory L. Ulmer refers to Derrida as the Aristotle of montage in "The Objects of Post-Criticism," in *The Anti-Aesthetic,* p. 87.

32. Douglas Crimp, "On the Museum's Ruins," in *The Anti-Aesthetic,* p. 53.

33. For a discussion of Levine's intent, see Douglas Crimp, "The Photographic Activity of Postmodernism," *October* 15 (Winter 1980): 91-100.

34. Michel Benamou, "Presence as Play," in *Performance in Postmodern Culture,* ed. Michel Benamou and Charles Caramello (Milwaukee: Center for Twentieth Century Studies, 1977), p. 3.

35. See, e.g., Steven Connor, *Postmodernist Culture* (London: Basil Blackwell, 1989), p. 134.

36. Connor, *Postmodernist Culture,* p. 135.

37. Walter Truett Anderson, *Reality Isn't What It Used to Be: Theatrical Politics, Ready-to-Wear Religion, Global Myths, Primitive Chic, and Other Wonders of the Postmodern World* (San Francisco: Harper & Row, 1990), p. 49.

38. E.g., Antonin Artaud; see his essay "The Theatre of Cruelty: Second Manifesto," in *The Theatre and Its Double,* trans. Victor Corti (London: Calder & Boyers, 1970), pp. 81-87.

39. Patrice Pavis, "The Classical Heritage of Modern Drama: The Case of Postmodern Theatre," trans. Loren Kruger, *Modern Drama* 29 (1986): 16.

40. Bernard Dort, "The Liberated Performance," trans. Barbara Kerslake, *Modern Drama* 25 (1982): 62.

41. Henry Sayre, "The Object of Performance: Aesthetics in the Seventies," *Georgia Review* 37 (1983): 174.

42. For a discussion of fiction by an early postmodern literary thinker, see Ihab Hassan, *The Dismemberment of Orpheus: Towards a Postmodern Literature* (New York: Oxford University Press, 1971).

43. John Barth, "The Literature of Replenishment, Postmodernist Fiction," *Atlantic Monthly,* January 1980, pp. 65-71; Umberto Eco, "Postmodernism, Irony, the Enjoyable," in *Postscript to "The Name of the Rose"* (New York: Harcourt Brace Jovanovich, 1984), pp. 65-72.

44. Connor, *Postmodernist Culture,* p. 118.

45. William V. Spanos, "Heidegger, Kierkegaard and the Hermeneutic Circle: Towards a Postmodern Theory of Interpretation as Discourse," in *Martin Heidegger and the Question of Literature: Toward a Postmodern Literary Hermeneutics,* ed. William V. Spanos (Bloomington, Ind.: Indiana University Press, 1979), p. 135.

46. Edith Wyschogrod refers to such techniques using the term *differentiality.* See *Saints and Postmodernism: Revisioning Moral Philosophy* (Chicago: University of Chicago Press, 1990), p. xvi.

47. Anderson, *Reality Isn't What It Used to Be*, pp. 101-2.

48. Brian McHale, *Postmodernist Fiction* (New York: Methuen, 1987), pp. 59-60.

49. Andreas Huyssen, "Mapping the Postmodern," in *The Post-Modern Reader*, p. 66. See also Jameson, "Postmodernism and Consumer Society," p. 112.

50. Jim Collins, "Post-Modernism as Culmination: The Aesthetic Politics of De-centred Culture," in *The Post-Modern Reader*, p. 105.

51. See Walter Benjamin, "The Work of Art in the Age of Mechanical Reproduction," in *Illuminations*, trans. Harry Zohn (London: Fontana, 1970), pp. 219-54.

52. For a discussion of *Blue Velvet* as a postmodern film, see Norman K. Denzin, "*Blue Velvet*: Postmodern Contradictions," in *The Post-Modern Reader*, pp. 225-33.

53. Arthur Kroker and David Cook, *The Postmodern Scene: Excremental Culture and Hyper-Aesthetics* (New York: St. Martin's Press, 1986), p. 268.

54. For a discussion of this situation, see Neil Postman, *Amusing Ourselves to Death: Public Discourse in the Age of Show Business* (New York: Viking Press, 1985); and *Technolopoly: The Surrender of Culture to Technology* (New York: Vintage Books, 1993), pp. 73-82.

55. Jameson, "Post-Modernism and Consumer Society," pp. 111-25.

56. Lawrence Grossberg, "The In-Difference of Television," *Screen* 28 (1987): 28-45

57. Jean Baudrillard, "The Ecstasy of Communication," in *The Anti-Aesthetic*, pp. 126-34.

58. Connor, *Postmodernist Culture*, p. 186.

59. Connor, *Postmodernist Culture*, p. 151.

60. Connor, *Postmodernist Culture*, p. 191.

Notes to Chapter 3

1. Lyotard makes no pretense of having coined the term *postmodern*. In fact, he cites earlier uses of the term by such individuals as Alain Touraine, Daniel Bell, and Ihab Hassan (*The Postmodern Condition: A Report on Knowledge*, trans. Geoff Bennington and Brian Massumi [Minneapolis: University of Minnesota Press, 1984], p. 85n.1).

2. As Susan Rubin Suleiman puts it, "Most notably, it articulated the links between French poststructuralist philosophy and postmodern cultural practices ('culture' being understood to include science and everyday life as well as the arts), so that the latter could be seen — at least in the ideal sketched by Lyotard — as an instantiation of the former" ("Feminism and Postmodernism: A Question of Politics," in *The Post-Modern Reader*, ed. Charles Jencks [New York: St. Martin's Press, 1992], p. 318).

3. See Hilary Lawson's introduction to "Stories about Truth," in *Dismantling Truth: Reality in the Post-Modern World*, ed. Hilary Lawson and Lisa Appignanesi (New York: St. Martin's Press, 1989), p. 4.

4. Walter Truett Anderson, *Reality Isn't What It Used to Be: Theatrical Politics, Ready-to-Wear Religion, Global Myths, Primitive Chic, and Other Wonders of the Post-modern World* (San Francisco: Harper & Row, 1990), pp. x-xi, 8.

5. For a concise critique of realism, see Hugh Tomlinson, "After Truth: Post-Modernism and the Rhetoric of Science," in *Dismantling Truth,* pp. 46-48.

6. We will discuss Wittgenstein at greater length in Chap. 5. This brief introduction is based on Lyotard's description (*The Postmodern Condition,* p. 10).

7. "The collapse of belief we have been witnessing throughout the twentieth century comes with globalism," says Anderson. "The postmodern condition is not an artistic movement or a cultural fad or an intellectual theory — although it produces all of those and is in some ways defined by them. It is what inevitably happens as people everywhere begin to see that there are many beliefs, many kinds of belief, many ways of believing. Postmodernism *is* globalism; it is the half-discovered shape of the one unity that transcends all our differences" (*Reality Isn't What It Used to Be,* p. 231).

8. Anderson, *Reality Isn't What It Used to Be,* p. 255.

9. Thomas S. Kuhn, *The Structure of Scientific Revolutions,* 2d ed. (Chicago: University of Chicago Press, 1970), p. 206.

10. Hilary Lawson explains: "Through language, theory, and text, we close the openness that is the world. The closures we make provide our world. . . . We do not have different accounts of the same 'thing,' but different closures and different things" (*Reflexivity: The Post-Modern Predicament* [London: Hutchinson, 1985], pp. 128-29).

11. Hilary Putnam, *Reason, Truth and History* (Cambridge: Cambridge University Press, 1981), p. 74.

12. See Robert P. Scharlemann's introduction to *Theology at the End of the Century: A Dialogue on the Postmodern,* ed. Robert P. Scharlemann (Charlottesville: University Press of Virginia, 1990), p. 6.

13. Anderson offers a typical postmodern conclusion: "Lacking absolutes, we will have to encounter one another as people with different information, different stories, different visions — and trust the outcome" (*Reality Isn't What It Used to Be,* p. 183).

14. Tomlinson, "After Truth," p. 55.

15. Charlene Spretnak, *States of Grace: The Recovery of Meaning in the Postmodern Age* (San Francisco: HarperCollins, 1991), p. 4.

16. Greg Ulmer, *Applied Grammatology: Post(e)-Pedagogy from Jacques Derrida to Joseph Beuys* (Baltimore: The Johns Hopkins University Press, 1985).

17. Frederick Ferré speaks of the "religious world model," which he defines as "any image suggesting how *all things fundamentally should be thought* which also *expresses or evokes profound value responses*" (*Hellfire and Lightning Rods: Liberating Science, Technology, and Religion* [Maryknoll, N.Y.: Orbis Books, 1993], p. 75).

18. See, e.g., R. M. MacIver, *The Web of Government* (New York: Macmillan, 1947), p. 4.

19. See, e.g., Lyotard, *The Postmodern Condition,* p. 27.

20. Lyotard, *The Postmodern Condition,* p. 37.

21. Anderson somewhat erroneously contends that six stories are vying for loyalty in the postmodern world:

(1) the Western myth of progress . . . ; (2) the Marxist story of revolution and international socialism; (3) the Christian fundamentalist story about a return to a society governed on the basis of Christian values and biblical belief; (4) the Islamic fundamentalist story about a return to a society governed on the basis

of Islamic values and koranic belief; (5) the Green story about rejecting the myth of progress and governing societies according to ecological values; and (6) the "new paradigm" story about a sudden leap forward to a new way of being and a new way of understanding the world. (*Reality Isn't What It Used to Be*, pp. 243-44)

22. Lyotard, *Postmodern Condition*, p. 82.

23. Anderson, *Reality Isn't What It Used to Be*, p. 108.

24. Lyotard, *The Postmodern Condition*, p. 29.

25. Lyotard, *The Postmodern Condition*, pp. 31-36.

26. Lyotard, *The Postmodern Condition*, p. 37.

27. Lyotard, *The Postmodern Condition*, pp. 39-41.

28. Lyotard, *The Postmodern Condition*, p. 46.

29. Lyotard, *The Postmodern Condition*, p. 51.

30. Lyotard, *The Postmodern Condition*, p. 81.

31. Lyotard, *The Postmodern Condition*, p. xxv.

32. Lyotard, *The Postmodern Condition*, p. xxv.

33. Charles Jencks, "The Post Modern Agenda," in *The Postmodern Reader*, ed. Charles Jencks (New York: St. Martin's Press, 1992), p. 11.

34. See, e.g., Nancey R. Pearcey and Charles B. Thaxton, *The Soul of Science: A Christian Map to the Scientific Landscape* (Wheaton, Ill.: Crossway Books, n.d.), pp. 192-93.

35. David Bohm, "Postmodern Science and a Postmodern World," in *The Reenchantment of Science: Postmodern Proposals*, ed. David Ray Griffin (Albany, N.Y.: State University of New York Press, 1988), pp. 60-62.

36. For a recounting of the development of quantum physics, see Robert Matthews, *Unravelling the Mind of God* (London: Virgin Books, 1992), pp. 119-52.

37. See, e.g., James B. Miller, "The Emerging Postmodern World," in *Postmodern Theology: Christian Faith in a Pluralist World* (San Francisco: Harper & Row, 1989), p. 9.

38. Matthews, *Unraveling the Mind of God*, pp. 158-59.

39. Matthews, *Unravelling the Mind of God*, p. 193.

40. Miller, "The Emerging Postmodern World," pp. 9-10.

41. A perplexing illustration of this is the famous Paradox of Schrodinger's Cat, on which see Matthews, *Unravelling the Mind of God*, pp. 148-49.

42. Miller, "The Emerging Postmodern World," p. 10.

43. Miller, "The Emerging Postmodern World," p. 10.

44. See Matthews, *Unravelling the Mind of God*, pp. 144-46.

45. Tito Arecchi, "Chaos and Complexity," in *The Post-Modern Reader*, p. 351.

46. Miller, "The Emerging Postmodern World," p. 9.

47. See, e.g., Miller, "The Emerging Postmodern World," p. 11.

48. For a succinct summary of Kuhn's view from a postmodern perspective, see Anderson, *Reality Isn't What It Used to Be*, pp. 72-73. Among the earlier critics of the traditional modern view was Karl Popper, who pointed out that science is not simply a rational enterprise but ultimately depends upon the exercise of the creative human imagination, which often works in a nonlogical manner. See Miller, "The Emerging Postmodern World," pp. 11-12.

49. Kuhn, *The Structure of Scientific Revolutions*, p. 175.

50. Kuhn, *The Structure of Scientific Revolutions*, p. 126.

51. See H. M. Collins, "The Meaning of Experiment: Replication and Reasonableness," in *Dismantling Truth*, p. 88.

52. Anderson, *Reality Isn't What It Used to Be*, p. 77.

53. Robert N. Bellah, "Christian Faithfulness in a Pluralist World," in *Postmodern Theology*, p. 76.

54. Kuhn, *The Structure of Scientific Revolutions*, p. 110.

55. Kuhn, *The Structure of Scientific Revolutions*, p. 126.

Notes to Chapter 4

1. For this reason, Stuart Hampshire claims that Bacon "was rather the last philosopher of the Renaissance than the first philosopher of the seventeenth century" (*The Age of Reason: Seventeenth Century Philosophers* [New York: New American Library of World Literature, 1956], p. 17; see also pp. 19-20).

2. W. L. Reese, *Dictionary of Philosophy and Religion* (Atlantic Highlands, N.J.: Humanities Press, 1983), p. 48.

3. Nicholas Wolterstorff, *Reason within the Bounds of Religion*, 2d ed. (Grand Rapids: William B. Eerdmans, 1984), pp. 123-24.

4. Wolterstorff, *Reason within the Bounds of Religion*, pp. 124-25.

5. See, e.g., Hampshire, *The Age of Reason*, p. 11.

6. William C. Placher, *A History of Christian Theology* (Philadelphia: Westminster Press, 1983), pp. 237-38.

7. Carl L. Becker, *The Heavenly City of the Eighteenth-Century Philosophers* (New Haven: Yale University Press, 1932), p. 7.

8. The roots of this change lay likewise in the Renaissance. Giorgio de Santillana points to Erasmus as the one who transformed the meaning of rationalism from the medieval to the modern. See *The Age of Adventure* (New York: New American Library of World Literature, 1956), p. 27.

9. De Santillana, *The Age of Adventure*, p. 46.

10. Among those who have voiced this opinion is Laurence J. Lafleur, the translator of Descartes's *"Discourse on Method" and "Meditations"* (Indianapolis: Bobbs-Merrill, 1960), pp. vii, xvii. See also Hampshire, *The Age of Reason*, p. 12.

11. Hampshire, *The Age of Reason*, p. 17.

12. Robert C. Solomon, *Continental Philosophy since 1750: The Rise and Fall of the Self* (Oxford: Oxford University Press, 1988), p. 5.

13. Solomon, *Continental Philosophy since 1750*, pp. 5-6.

14. For a succinct summary of the lasting importance of Descartes, see Lafleur's introduction to the *"Discourse on Method" and "Meditations,"* pp. viii-xiv.

15. Justo L. Gonzales, *A History of Christian Thought*, vol. 3 (Nashville: Abingdon Press, 1975), p. 297.

16. Hampshire, *The Age of Reason*, pp. 12-13; and Isaiah Berlin, *The Age of Enlightenment* (New York: Mentor Books, 1956), pp. 16-17.

17. In his helpful study of theological history, Paul Tillich characterizes the Enlightenment mind-set using the first four of these principles. See *A History of Christian Thought* (New York: Simon & Schuster, 1968), pp. 320-41.

18. Becker, *The Heavenly City of the Eighteenth-Century Philosophers*, p. 65.

19. Becker, *The Heavenly City of the Eighteenth-Century Philosophers*, p. 118.

20. Isaiah Berlin, *The Age of Enlightenment* (New York: Mentor Books, 1956), p. 29.

21. E.g., in his essay *Christianity as Old as Creation*, Matthew Tindal (1655-1733) offers the representative argument that the Christian gospel means to show that a universal natural law lies at the basis of all religion.

22. E.g., John Toland (1670-1722), *Christianity Not Mysterious*.

23. Gonzales, *A History of Christian Thought*, 3:307. An early list of the principal beliefs of natural religion was offered by Lord Herbert of Cherbury in *De Religione Gentilium* (1663). For a delineation of these, see Arthur Cushman McGiffert, *Protestant Thought before Kant* (London: Duckworth, 1911), p. 212; and Placher, *A History of Christian Theology*, p. 242.

24. This view was articulated already in the seventeenth century by the Anglican archbishop John Tillotson but was further developed by Tindal. See McGiffert, *Protestant Thought before Kant*, pp. 195, 214.

25. E.g., Tindal, *Christianity as Old as the Creation*; and Thomas Chubb, *The True Gospel of Jesus Christ Asserted* (1738).

26. E.g., Anthony Collins, *A Discourse on the Grounds and Reasons of the Christian Religion* (1724)

27. E.g., the tracts of Thomas Woolston (1727) and especially David Hume's *Essay on Miracles* (1748).

28. Among those defending this position were John Tillotson, John Locke, and Samuel Clarke. See McGiffert, *Protestant Thought before Kant*, pp. 195-210.

29. David Hume was the exemplar of enlightened skepticism. For a discussion of this development, see McGiffert, *Protestant Thought before Kant*, pp. 230-51. Gotthold Lessing was a paradigmatic relativist. For a summary of his views, see Placher, *A History of Christian Theology*, pp. 249-50.

30. Hume presents these arguments in *Providence and a Future State* (1748), *Dialogues concerning Natural Religion* (1779), and *Natural History of Religion* (1757).

31. Hume agreed that such concepts were necessary for human knowing but declared that they were deduced from experience. Kant, in contrast, claimed that these concepts "sprang from the pure understanding" (*Prolegomena to Any Future Metaphysics*, trans. and ed. Paul Carus [Peru, Ill.: Open Court, 1967], p. 7).

32. Another well-known formulation of the categorical imperative emphasizes treating human beings as ends rather than means: "So act as to treat humanity, whether in thine own person or in that of any other, in every case as an end withal, never as means only" (Kant, *Fundamental Principles of the Metaphysic of Morals*, trans. Thomas K. Abbott [Indianapolis: Bobbs-Merrill, 1949], p. 46).

33. See Clement Greenberg, "Modernist Painting," in *Postmodern Perspectives: Issues in Contemporary Art*, ed. Howard Risatti (Englewood Cliffs, N.J.: Prentice Hall, 1990), pp. 12-13.

34. Solomon, *Continental Philosophy since 1750,* p. 40.
35. See Solomon, *Continental Philosophy Since 1750,* p. 6.
36. Solomon, *Continental Philosophy since 1750,* p. 7.
37. See Solomon, *Continental Philosophy since 1750,* p. 40.
38. Craig Van Gelder, "Postmodernism as an Emerging Worldview," *Calvin Theological Journal* 26 (1991): 413.

Notes to Chapter 5

1. Allan Megill, *Prophets of Extremity: Nietzsche, Heidegger, Foucault, Derrida* (Berkeley and Los Angeles: University of California Press, 1985), p. 2.
2. Even his critics have found lasting importance in Descartes's work. Above all, he reminds us that thought and consciousness are embedded in personal existence. Descartes leads us to speak not in the impersonal passive voice — "There is thought" — but rather in the first person: "I am a being who thinks." He focused thought and consciousness in the human person, not only making us conscious of localization but affirming that consciousness itself is localized. See, e.g., Emmaunel Levinas, *Existence and Existents,* trans. Alphonso Lingis (The Hague: Martinus Nijhoff, 1978), p. 68. See also Edith Wyschogrod, *Saints and Postmodernism: Revisioning Moral Philosophy* (Chicago: University of Chicago Press, 1990), p. 77.
3. Wyschogrod, *Saints and Postmodernism,* p. 76. For Descartes's response, see his "Objectives and Replies," in *The Philosophical Works of Descartes,* trans. Elizabeth R. Haldane and G. R. T. Ross (New York: Dover Publications, 1951) 2:201-2.
4. Wyschogrod, *Saints and Postmodernism,* p. 76.
5. Ryle, *The Concept of Mind* (New York: Barnes & Noble, 1949), pp. 11-24.
6. Heidegger, *Basic Problems of Phenomenology,* trans. Albert Hofstadter (Bloomington, Ind.: Indiana University Press, 1982), pp. 122-40.
7. See Fichte's preface to *Science of Knowledge,* ed. and trans. Peter Heath and John Lachs (New York: Appleton-Century-Crofts, 1970), p. viii.
8. For an interesting discussion of the "absolute self," see George H. Mead, *Movements of Thought in the Nineteenth Century,* ed. Merritt H. Moore (Chicago: University of Chicago Press, 1936), p. 101.
9. Robert C. Solomon, *Continental Philosophy since 1750: The Rise and Fall of the Self* (Oxford: Oxford University Press, 1988), p. 50.
10. For a discussion of the connection between Nietzsche and postmodern thinkers, see Megill, *Prophets of Extremity;* and Cornel West, "Nietzsche's Prefiguration of Postmodern American Philosophy," in *Why Nietzsche Now?* ed. Daniel T. O'Hara (Bloomington, Ind.: Indiana University Press, 1985), pp. 241-69.
11. See Geoffrey Clive's introduction to his edition of *The Philosophy of Nietzsche* (New York: Mentor Books, 1965), p. xi.
12. Nietzsche, "On Truth and Lie in an Extra-Moral Sense," in *The Portable Nietzsche,* ed. and trans. Walter Kaufmann (New York: Penguin Books, 1976), p. 46. See also Megill, *Prophets of Extremity,* p. 49.
13. Nietzsche, "On Truth and Falsity in an Extra-Moral Sense," in *"Early Greek*

Philosophy" and Other Essays, trans. M. A. Mügge, vol. 2 of *The Complete Works of Friedrich Nietzsche,* ed. Oscar Levy (New York: Russell & Russell, 1964), pp. 181-82.

14. Nietzsche, "On Truth and Lie in an Extra-Moral Sense," pp. 44-46.

15. For a discussion of this point, see Mead, *Movements of Thought in the Nineteenth Century,* pp. 123-26.

16. Nietzsche, *The Will to Power,* §853, trans. Walter Kaufmann and R. J. Hollingdale, ed. Walter Kaufmann (New York: Random House, 1967), pp. 451-52.

17. Nietzsche, *The Will to Power,* §15, pp. 14-15.

18. Megill, *Prophets of Extremity,* pp. 50, 59.

19. Nietzsche, *The Will to Power,* §493, p. 272.

20. Megill, *Prophets of Extremity,* p. 52.

21. Nietzsche, *The Will to Power,* §796, p. 419.

22. Megill, *Prophets of Extremity,* p. 33.

23. See Megill, *Prophets of Extremity,* pp. 58-59.

24. For a discussion of Nietzsche's understanding of the concept of "will to power," see Solomon, *Continental Philosophy since 1750,* p. 116.

25. Mark C. Taylor, *Deconstructing Theology* (New York: Crossroad, 1982), p. 90.

26. Nietzsche, *The Gay Science,* §301, trans. Walter Kaufmann (New York: Random House, 1974), pp. 241-42.

27. Nietzsche, *Beyond Good and Evil,* 1.13, trans. Helen Zimmern, in *The Philosophy of Nietzsche* (New York: Random House, 1937), p. 14.

28. W. L. Reese, *Dictionary of Philosophy and Religion* (Atlantic Highlands, N.J.: Humanities Press, 1980), pp. 391-92.

29. Nietzsche, "On Truth and Lie in an Extra-Moral Sense," p. 47.

30. Solomon, *Continental Philosophy since 1750,* p. 117.

31. Solomon, *Continental Philosophy since 1750,* pp. 124-25.

32. Megill, *Prophets of Extremity,* p. 61.

33. Megill, *Prophets of Extremity,* p. 84.

34. Megill, *Prophets of Extremity,* p. 34.

35. John Passmore, *A Hundred Years of Philosophy* (London: Gerald Duckworth, 1957), p. 99.

36. Megill, *Prophets of Extremity,* p. 83.

37. See Nietzsche, *The Will to Power,* §1, pp. 7-8.

38. Nietzsche, "On Truth and Falsity," p. 184.

39. Megill *Prophets of Extremity,* p. 95.

40. Nietzsche, *Beyond Good and Evil,* I.10, p. 9.

41. Megill suggests that this is Nietzsche's position as well (*Prophets of Extremity,* p. 85).

42. See Megill, *Prophets of Extremity,* p. 62.

43. Megill, *Philosophers of Extremity,* pp. 96-97.

44. See Megill, *Prophets of Extremity,* p. 99.

45. See F. D. E. Schleiermacher, *Hermeneutics: The Handwritten Manuscripts,* American Academy of Religion Texts and Translation Series, 1, ed. Heinz Kimmerle, trans. James Duke and Jack Forstman (Atlanta: Scholars Press, 1977).

46. German philosopher Wilhelm Dilthey characterizes Schleiermacher's distinc-

tion as follows: "Grammatical interpretation proceeds from link to link to the highest combinations in the whole of the work. The psychological interpretation starts with penetrating the inner creative process and proceeds to the outer and inner form of the work and from there to a further grasp of the unity of all his works in the mentality and development of their author" ("Development of Hermeneutics," in *Dilthey: Selected Writings*, ed. H. P. Rickman [Cambridge: Cambridge University Press, 1976], p. 259).

47. H. A. Hodges, *The Philosophy of Wilhelm Dilthey* (1952; reprint, Westport, Conn.: Greenwood Press, 1974), p. 13.

48. For this characterization of Schleiermacher's position, see Hans-Georg Gadamer, *Truth and Method*, trans. and ed. Garrett Barden and John Cumming (New York: Crossroad, 1984), pp. 166-67.

49. Hodges, *The Philosophy of Wilhelm Dilthey*, pp. xviii-xix.

50. Hodges, *The Philosophy of Dilthey*, p. 31.

51. Hodges, *The Philosophy of Dilthey*, pp. 85-86.

52. Hodges, *The Philosophy of Dilthey*, pp. 354-55.

53. Hodges, *The Philosophy of Dilthey*, p. 91.

54. Hodges, *The Philosophy of Dilthey*, pp. 93-94. Hodges is referring at this point to vol. 5 of Dilthey's *Gesammelte Schriften*, pp. 413-16.

55. Solomon, *Continental Philosophy since 1750*, p. 106.

56. "Re-creating and re-living what is alien and past . . . is dependent on permanently fixed expressions being available so that understanding can always return to them," writes Dilthey. "The methodical understanding of permanently fixed expressions we call *exegesis*. As the life of the mind only finds its complete, exhaustive and, therefore, objectively comprehensible expression in language, exegesis culminates in the interpretation of the written records of human existence. This method is the basis of philology. The science of this method is hermeneutics" ("Construction of the Historical World," in *Dilthey: Selected Writings*, p. 228).

57. Solomon, *Continental Philosophy since 1750*, pp. 106-7.

58. H. P. Rickman uses this example in his introduction to *Dilthey: Selected Writings*, pp. 10-11.

59. See Dilthey, "The Construction of the Historical World in the Human Studies," in *Dilthey: Select Writings*, p. 196.

60. Hodges, *Philosophy of Dilthey*, pp. 139-40. Hodges is referring at this point to vol. 7 of Dilthey's *Gesammelte Schriften*, pp. 220, 227.

61. Megill, *Prophets of Extremity*, pp. 150-51.

62. Heidegger speaks of authentic living as being "free for death": "Only Being-free *for* death, gives Dasein [existence, literally "being there"] its goal outright. . . . This is how we designate Dasein's primordial historizing, which lies in its authentic resoluteness and in which Dasein *hands* itself *down* to itself, free for death, in a possibility which it has inherited and yet has chosen." Being free for death occurs as we anticipate our death. In Heidegger's words, "If Dasein, by anticipation, lets death become powerful in itself, then, as free for death, Dasein understands itself in its own *superior power,* the power of its finite freedom, so that in this freedom, which 'is' only in its having chosen to make such a choice, it can take over the *powerlessness* of abandonment to its having done so, and can thus come to have a clear vision for the accidents of the Situation that

186

has been disclosed" (*Being and Time*, trans. John Macquarrie and Edward Robinson [New York: Harper & Row, 1962], pp. 435, 436).

63. Heidegger, "The Word of Nietzsche: 'God Is Dead,'" in *"The Question concerning Technology" and Other Essays*, trans. William Lovitt (New York: Harper & Row, 1977), pp. 54-55.

64. Heidegger, *An Introduction to Metaphysics*, trans. Ralph Manheim (New York: Doubleday-Anchor, 1961), p. 1.

65. For a discussion of this change, see John M. Anderson's introduction to Heidegger's *Discourse on Thinking*, trans. John M. Anderson and E. Hans Freund (New York: Harper & Row, 1966), pp. 19-21.

66. Concerning *Dasein*, Solomon declares, "It is an intentially vague, non-descriptive, almost vacuous designation, virtually a pointing gesture rather than a proper subject for a philosophy" (*Continental Philosophy since 1750*, p. 154).

67. Heidegger, *Being and Time*, p. 78.

68. Heidegger, *Being and Time*, p. 221.

69. Frank Lentricchia, *After the New Criticism* (Chicago: University of Chicago Press, 1980), p. 81.

70. Solomon, *Continental Philosophy since 1750*, p. 156.

71. Lentricchia, *After the New Criticism*, pp. 81, 85.

72. See, e.g., Heidegger, *Being and Time*, pp. 47, 101; and "Time and Being," in Heidegger, *On Time and Being*, trans. Joan Stambaugh (New York: Harper & Row, 1972), pp. 3, 12-15.

73. See, e.g., Mark C. Taylor, "The End(s) of Theology," in *Theology at the End of Modernity: Essays in Honor of Gordon D. Kaufman*, ed. Sheila Greeve Davancy (Philadelphia: Trinity Press International, 1991). Taylor is specifically engaging Heidegger's essay "The End of Philosophy and the Task of Thinking."

74. For Heidegger's discussion of "difference," see, e.g., his essay "Language," in *Poetry, Language, Thought*, trans. Albert Hofstadter (New York: Harper & Row, 1971), pp. 202-10.

75. Heidegger, "Metaphysics as History of Being," in *The End of Philosophy*, trans. Joan Stambaugh (New York: Harper & Row, 1973), pp. 19-26.

76. Heidegger criticizes the demand for certainty because it seeks a basis for truth "which no longer depends upon a relation to something else but rather is absolved from the very beginning from this relation, and rests within itself" ("Metaphysics as History of Being," p. 26).

77. Heidegger, "Memorial Address," in *Discourse on Thinking*, pp. 55, 46.

78. See Heidegger, "Letter on Humanism," in *Basic Writings*, ed. David Farrell Krell (New York: Harper & Row, 1976), pp. 235, 236.

79. See Megill, *Prophets of Extremity*, pp. 157-62.

80. "To be a work means to set up a world," says Heidegger (*Poetry, Language, Thought*, trans. Albert Hofstadter [New York: Harper & Row, 1971], p. 44).

81. Heidegger, *Poetry, Language, Thought*, pp. 73-74. On Heidegger's view of language in general, see Megill, *Prophets of Extremity*, pp. 162-70.

82. See Megill, *Prophets of Extremity*, p. 164.

83. "The word alone gives Being to the thing," says Heidegger ("The Essence of

Language," in *On the Way to Language,* trans. Peter D. Hertz [New York: Harper & Row, 1971], p. 62).

84. Heidegger, *What Is Called Thinking?* trans. Fred D. Wieck and J. Glenn Gray (New York: Harper & Row, 1968), p. 192.

85. Heidegger, "The Nature of Language," p. 57.

86. Solomon, *Continental Philosophy since 1750,* p. 167. Thomas Nagel provided the phrase in the title of his book *The View from Nowhere* (New York: Oxford University Press, 1986).

87. See Lentricchia, *Beyond the New Criticism,* pp. 99-100.

88. See Gadamer's foreword to the second edition of *Truth and Method,* p. xvi.

89. Gadamer, *Truth and Method,* p. xviii.

90. Gadamer, *Truth and Method,* pp. xi-xii.

91. Gadamer, *Truth and Method,* p. 168.

92. Megill, *Prophets of Extremity,* p. 22.

93. Gadamer, *Truth and Method,* p. xxiii.

94. See, e.g., Gadamer, *Truth and Method,* p. 308.

95. Gadamer, *Truth and Method,* pp. 227-34.

96. Lentricchia, *After the New Criticism,* p. 150. See Gadamer, *Truth and Method,* pp. 175, 245, 250, 258, 264-65.

97. See Gadamer, *Truth and Method,* pp. 273, 337, 340, 358.

98. Gadamer, *Truth and Method,* p. 341.

99. Gadamer, *Truth and Method,* p. 349.

100. Gadamer, *Truth and Method,* pp. 356-57.

101. Gadamer, *Truth and Method,* p. 358.

102. Lentricchia's critique of Gadamer suggests another connection to post-modernism as well:

> We can only be stunned by the implication of what he has uncritically to say about authority, the power of tradition, knowledge, our institutions, and our attitudes. . . . Just as soon as Gadamer begins to speak of a "nameless" traditional and institutional authority, it is clear that the terms "knowledge" and "intelligibility" are being used (perhaps unwittingly) in a Nietzschean sense, and that the primary issue by his own admission ("tradition has a justification that is outside the arguments of reason") is power. In other words, reason is arbitrary; reason is irrational. The question of the acquisition of power is indistinguishable from the question of the acquisition of knowledge and authority. Our willingness to assent to authority is no cool act of reason but a submission to the force that defines and appropriates tradition and knowledge and encloses our cognitive reason within their boundaries. (*After the New Criticism,* pp. 153-54)

103. Gadamer, *Truth and Method,* p. 446.

104. E.g., Ludwig Wittgenstein, *Tractatus Logico-Philosophicus,* 4.021, trans. D. F. Pears and B. F. McGuinness (London: Routledge & Kegan Paul, 1961), p. 39.

105. Wittgenstein, *Tractatus Logico-Philosophicus,* 7, p. 151.

106. Solomon, *Continental Philosophy since 1750,* p. 147.

107. See, e.g., the discussion beginning in Wittgenstein's *Philosophical Investigations* 1.65, trans. G. E. M. Anscombe (Oxford: Basil Blackwell, 1953), p. 32. See also Solomon, *Continental Philosophy since 1750*, p. 150.

108. See Hilary Lawson, "Stories about Stories," in *Dismantling Truth: Reality in the Post-Modern World*, ed. Hilary Lawson and Lisa Appignanesi (New York: St. Martin's Press, 1989), pp. xxiii-xxiv.

109. Lentricchia, *After the New Criticism*, p. 112.

110. See, e.g., the characterization of Emile Benveniste in *Problems in General Linguistics*, trans. Mary Elizabeth Meek (Coral Gables: University of Miami Press, 1971), p. 4.

111. Saussure, *Course in General Linguistics*, ed. Charles Bally, Albert Sechehaye, and Albert Riedlinger, trans. Wade Baskin (New York: Philosophical Library, 1959), p. 18.

112. See Benveniste, *Problems in General Linguistics*, pp. 5, 8. Actually, Saussure speaks of two branches of linguistics, with different subject matters. Synchronic linguistics studies *langue*, whereas diachronic linguistics is concerned with relations of succession between individual items: "*Synchronic linguistics* will be concerned with logical and psychological relations that bind together coexisting terms and form a system in the collective mind of speakers. *Diachronic linguistics*, on the contrary, will study relations that bind together successive terms not perceived by the collective mind but substituted for each other without forming a system" (*Course in General Linguistics*, p. 100). He contends that insofar as nineteenth-century linguists were concerned solely with historical questions, they were not concerned with language *(langue)* at all. See David Holdcroft, *Saussure: Signs, System, and Arbitrariness* (Cambridge: Cambridge University Press, 1991), p. 70.

113. Holdcroft, *Saussure*, p. 11.

114. Holdcroft, *Saussure*, pp. 7-8.

115. Holdcroft, *Saussure*, p. 10.

116. Saussure, *Course in General Linguistics*, pp. 67-69.

117. Holdcroft, *Saussure*, p. 2.

118. Holdcroft, *Saussure*, p. 135.

119. Sausure, *Course in General Linguistics*, p. 120.

120. Lentricchia, *After the New Criticism*, p. 115.

121. Charlene Spretnak, *States of Grace: The Recovery of Meaning in the Post-modern Age* (San Francisco: HarperCollins, 1991), p. 259.

122. Reese, *Dictionary of Philosophy and Religion*, p. 553.

123. See, e.g., Solomon, *Continental Philosophy since 1750*, p. 197.

124. Todorov, *Grammaire du Decameron* (The Hague: Mouton, 1969), p. 15. Lentricchia cites Todorov's assumption of a universal grammar as perhaps the most extreme expression of a "Platonized Saussure" (*After the New Criticism*, p. 116).

125. Lentricchia cites Jonathan Culler as an example of this sort of literary structuralist, arguing that Culler redefines Saussure "by making *langue* over into a system of reading which, within a given cultural frame, absolutely governs interpretation — just as the concept, within rationalist traditions, tyrannized the particular" (*After the New Criticism*, p. 116; Lentricchia is discussing Culler's book *Structuralist Poetics: Structuralism, Linguistics, and the Study of Literature* [Ithaca, N.Y.: Cornell University Press, 1975]).

126. Jonathan Culler, *On Deconstruction: Theory and Criticism after Structuralism* (Ithaca, N.Y.: Cornell University Press, 1982), pp. 21-22.

127. Lentricchia cites the dissolution of the author in the text and the transfer of the locus of meaning from the text to the process of reading as the two foundational motifs of structuralism (*After the New Criticism*, p. 108).

128. Lévi-Strauss is sometimes cited as the founder of structuralism. See, e.g., Reese, *Dictionary of Philosophy and Religion*, pp. 303, 553.

129. Taylor, *Deconstructing Theology*, p. 99.

130. Culler, *On Deconstruction*, p. 22.

131. Lawson, "Stories about Stories," p. xiii.

Notes to Chapter 6

1. James Miller, *The Passion of Michel Foucault* (New York: Simon & Schuster, 1993), p. 13.

2. Robert C. Solomon, *Continental Philosophy since 1750: The Rise and Fall of the Self* (Oxford: Oxford University Press, 1988), p. 196.

3. Foucault, Derrida, and Rorty are all complex thinkers, and each can be read in many different ways. In this chapter, we will be focusing on a single reading of each, looking at how they have served as heralds of postmodernism.

4. Miller, *The Passion of Michel Foucault*, p. 13.

5. Merold Westphal, *Suspicion and Faith: The Religious Uses of Modern Atheism* (Grand Rapids: William B. Eerdmans, 1993), p. 241.

6. Edward W. Said, "Michel Foucault, 1926-1984," in *After Foucault: Humanist Knowledge, Postmodern Challenges*, ed. Jonathan Arac (New Brunswick, N.J.: Rutgers University Press, 1988), p. 1.

7. For an intriguing account of this quest, see Miller, *The Passion of Michel Foucault*. See also Didier Eribon, *Michel Foucault*, trans. Betsy Wing (Cambridge: Harvard University Press, 1991).

8. Eribon, *Michel Foucault*, p. 5.

9. Eribon, *Michel Foucault*, p. 11.

10. Miller, *The Passion of Michel Foucault*, pp. 253, 27.

11. Miller, *The Passion of Michel Foucault*, p. 253.

12. Foucault, "The Minimalist Self," in *Politics, Philosophy, Culture: Interviews and Other Writings, 1977-1984*, ed. Lawrence D. Kritzman, trans. Alan Sheridan et al. (New York: Routledge, 1988), p. 12.

13. Miller, *The Passion of Michel Foucault*, p. 273.

14. Miller, *The Passion of Michel Foucault*, p. 29.

15. Foucault, *The Use of Pleasure*, vol. 2 of *The History of Sexuality*, trans. Robert Hurley (New York: Pantheon Books, 1985), pp. 6-7.

16. Miller, *The Passion of Michel Foucault*, p. 358.

17. In this context, we can view Foucault's *Archaeology of Knowledge* (trans. A. M. Sheridan Smith [London: Tavistock Press, 1972]) more as a parody of modern method than as a treatise on postmodern method as such. Foucault is attacking Cartesianism

in the sense of the whole subjectivist emphasis that he sees underlying modern science and technology. See Allan Mcgill, *Prophets of Extremity: Nietzsche, Heidegger, Foucault, Derrida* (Berkeley and Los Angeles: University of California Press, 1985), p. 228.

18. Said, "Michel Foucault, 1926-1984," pp. 5-7.

19. See Paul Rabinow's introduction to *The Foucault Reader*, ed. Paul Rabinow (New York: Pantheon Books, 1984), p. 4.

20. David Couzens Hoy, "Foucault: Modern or Postmodern?" in *After Foucault*, p. 27.

21. Said, "Michel Foucault, 1926-1984," p. 10.

22. Especially important are *The Order of Things: An Archeology of the Human Sciences* (New York: Random House–Pantheon, 1971) and *The Archaeology of Knowledge and the Discourse on Language* (1969), trans. A. M. Sheridan Smith (New York: Pantheon Books, 1972).

23. During his formative years, Foucault came under the influence of Claude Lévi-Strauss, Jacques Lacan, Roland Barthes, and Louis Althusser, and these associations may have led certain critics to label him as a structuralist. See, e.g., the placement of Foucault, s.v. "Structuralism," in William L. Reese's *Dictionary of Philosophy and Religion* (Atlantic Highlands, N.J.: Humanities Press, 1980), p. 553. Foucault himself vehemently objected to this characterization (see, e.g., *The Order of Things*, p. xiv). For a discussion of Foucault's connection with structuralism, see Megill, *Prophets of Extremity*, pp. 203-19.

24. Megill, *Prophets of Extremity*, p. 211.

25. For a discussion that reaches a similar conclusion, see David Couzens Hoy, "Foucault: Modern or Postmodern?" pp. 12-41.

26. Hoy, "Foucault: Modern or Postmodern?" p. 28.

27. See Rabinow's introduction to *The Foucault Reader*, p. 12.

28. Foucault, *The Order of Things*, pp. 81, 235-36, 303-4, 311, 385-86.

29. Foucault, *The Order of Things*, pp. 342-43.

30. Christopher Norris, *Derrida* (Cambridge: Harvard University Press, 1988), p. 218.

31. Foucault, "Nietzsche, Genealogy, History," in *Language, Counter-Memory, and Practice: Selected Essays and Interviews*, trans. Donald F. Bouchard and Sherry Simon (Ithaca, N.Y.: Cornell University Press, 1977), pp. 156-57.

32. See Said, "Michel Foucault, 1926-1984," p. 6.

33. Sheldon S. Wolin, "On the Theory and Practice of Power," in *After Foucault*, p. 181.

34. See Wolin, "On the Theory and Practice of Power," p. 186.

35. See Rabinow's introduction to *The Foucault Reader*, p. 4.

36. See Rabinow's introduction to *The Foucault Reader*, pp. 6-7.

37. See Foucault, *The Archaeology of Knowledge*; see also Foucault, "The Order of Discourse," in *Untying the Text: A Post-Structuralist Reader*, ed. Robert Young (London: Routledge & Kegan Paul, 1981), pp. 48-78.

38. Foucault, *The Archaeology of Knowledge*, 40-49.

39. Foucault, "Truth and Power," in *Power/Knowledge: Selected Interviews and Other Writings, 1972-1977*, trans. Colin Gordon, Leo Marshall, John Mepham, and Kate Soper (New York: Pantheon Books, 1980), p. 133.

40. See Wolin, "On the Theory and Practice of Power," pp. 191-92.

41. Megill, *Prophets of Extremity,* pp. 191-92.

42. Foucault, *Discipline and Punish: The Birth of the Prison,* trans. Alan Sheridan (New York: Pantheon Books, 1977), p. 194.

43. H. D. Harootunian, "Foucault, Genealogy, History: The Pursuit of Otherness," in *After Foucault,* p. 113.

44. Foucault, "Nietzsche, Genealogy, and History," p. 162.

45. Megill proposes this interesting interpretation in *Prophets of Extremity,* pp. 232-33.

46. Foucault, "Two Lectures," in *Power/Knowledge,* pp. 80-81.

47. Foucault, "Nietzsche, Genealogy, and History," p. 156.

48. Foucault, "Nietzsche, Genealogy, History," p. 154.

49. Megill, *Prophets of Extremity,* pp. 238-39.

50. Foucault, "Nietzsche, Genealogy, History," p. 152.

51. Jana Sawicki, "Feminism and the Power of Foucauldian Discourse," in *After Foucault,* p. 163.

52. Foucault, "Power and Strategies," in *Power/Knowledge,* p. 145.

53. Foucault, "Truth and Power," in *Power/Knowledge,* p. 131.

54. Foucault, *The Archaeology of Knowledge,* p. 219.

55. Isaac D. Balbus, "Discipling Women: Michel Foucault and the Power of Feminist Discourse," in *After Foucault,* p. 139.

56. Foucault, "Nietzsche, Genealogy, History," p. 153.

57. Douglas Crimp, "On the Museum's Ruins," in *The Anti-Aesthetic: Essays on Postmodern Culture,* ed. Hal Foster (Port Townsend, Wash.: Bay Press, 1983), p. 45.

58. Foucault, "Nietzsche, Genealogy, History," pp. 146, 154.

59. Charles C. Lemert and Garth Gillan, *Michel Foucault: Social Theory and Transgression* (New York: Columbia University Press, 1980), p. 91.

60. Foucault, "Truth and Power," in *Power/Knowledge,* p. 117.

61. Foucault, "Questions of Method: An Interview with Michel Foucault," in *After Philosophy: End of Transformation?* ed. Kenneth Baynes, James Bohman, and Thomas McCarthy (Cambridge: MIT Press, 1987), p. 108.

62. Foucault, "Two Lectures," in *Power/Knowledge,* p. 81.

63. See Foucault, "Two Lectures," p. 80.

64. Foucault declares that thought "cannot help but liberate and enslave" (*The Order of Things,* p. 328).

65. In one of his final studies, Foucault applies this idea to sexuality, arguing that discourse about sexuality produces sexuality. His goal in making this argument is to divorce sexuality from nature.

66. Megill, *Prophets of Extremity,* p. 192.

67. Megill, *Prophets of Extremity,* pp. 192-93.

68. Foucault, "Nietzsche, Genealogy, History," p. 154.

69. E.g., Foucault, "The History of Sexuality," in *Power/Knowledge,* p. 193.

70. There has been some debate over whether Derrida is in fact a postmodern philosopher. See, e.g., Megill, *Prophets of Extremity,* pp. 263, 337.

71. See Peggy Kamuf's remarks in *A Derrida Reader: Between the Blinds,* ed. Peggy Kamuf (New York: Columbia University Press, 1991), pp. 143-44.

72. Christopher Norris, *What's Wrong with Postmodernism: Critical Theory and the Ends of Philosophy* (Baltimore: The Johns Hopkins University Press, 1990), p. 197.

73. Megill, *Prophets of Extremity,* p. 271.

74. Some contend that he himself later "deconstructs" this distinction. See Megill, *Prophets of Extremity,* p. 286.

75. Derrida, *Of Grammatology,* trans. Gayatri Chakravorty Spivak (Baltimore: The Johns Hopkins University Press, 1976), p. 37.

76. Derrida, *Of Grammatology,* p. 35.

77. See Derrida, *Of Grammatology,* pp. 11-12. See also Spivak's preface to the volume, p. lxviii.

78. Derrida, *Of Grammatology,* p. 49.

79. Derrida, *Of Grammatology,* p. 73.

80. Terry Eagleton, *Literary Theory* (Minneapolis: University of Minnesota Press, 1983), p. 131.

81. Norris, *Derrida,* p. 121.

82. Norris, *What's Wrong with Postmodernism,* pp. 201-2.

83. Derrida, *Of Grammatology,* p. 52.

84. For an example of his description of the term *differance,* see his essay "Differance," in Derrida, *Margins of Philosophy,* trans. Alan Bass (Chicago: University of Chicago Press, 1982), pp. 1-27.

85. Saussure, *Course in General Linguistics,* trans. W. Baskin (New York: Philosophical Library, 1959), p. 120.

86. See, e.g., Derrida, *Of Grammatology,* p. 63. See also Charlene Spretnak, *States of Grace: The Recovery of Meaning in the Postmodern Age* (San Francisco: HarperCollins, 1991), p. 234.

87. Derrida, *Positions,* trans. Alan Bass (Chicago: University of Chicago Press, 1981), pp. 28-29.

88. Frank Lentricchia, *After the New Criticism* (Chicago: University of Chicago Press, 1980), p. 168.

89. For the basis of this example, see Hilary Lawson, "Stories about Stories," in *Dismantling Truth: Reality in the Post-Modern World,* ed. Hilary Lawson and Lisa Appignanesi (New York: St. Martin's Press, 1989), p. xxv.

90. Jonathan Culler, *On Deconstruction: Theory and Criticism after Structuralism* (Ithaca, N.Y.: Cornell University Press, 1982), p. 97.

91. See Spivak's preface to *Of Grammatology,* p. xliii.

92. Derrida, *Of Grammatology,* p. 86.

93. Derrida, *Of Grammatology,* p. 158.

94. Lentricchia, *After the New Criticism,* p. 160.

95. See Spivak's preface to *Of Grammatology,* p. xii.

96. Elsewhere Derrida writes, "The domain and the interplay of signification are extended *ad infinitum*" ("Structure, Sign, and Play in the Discourse of the Human Sciences," in *Structuralist Controversy: The Language of Criticism and the Sciences of Man,*

ed. Richard Macksey and Eugenio Donato [Baltimore: The Johns Hopkins University Press, 1972], p. 249). See also Derrida, *Of Grammatology*, p. 50.

97. For an example of Derrida's evaluation of Heidegger, see Derrida, *Of Spirit: Heidegger and the Question*, trans. Geoffrey Bennington and Rachel Bowlby (Chicago: University of Chicago Press, 1989). For an example of Derrida's use of Nietzsche, see his essay "The Ends of Man," in *Margins of Philosophy*, pp. 109-36. Concerning the point that Derrida is drawing on Nietzsche as read by Heidegger, see Spivak's preface to *Of Grammatology*, p. xxxiii.

98. See Megill, *Prophets of Extremity*, p. 333.

99. Derrida, "Letter to a Japanese Friend," *A Derrida Reader: Between the Blinds*, ed. Peggy Kamuf (New York: Columbia University Press, 1991), p. 273.

100. See Norris, *Derrida*, p. 20.

101. See Walter Truett Anderson, *Reality Isn't What It Used to Be: Theatrical Politics, Ready-to-Wear Religion, Global Myths, Primitive Chic, and Other Wonders of the Postmodern World* (San Francisco: Harper & Row, 1990), p. 90.

102. Culler, *On Deconstruction*, pp. 131-34.

103. Anderson, *Reality Isn't What It Used to Be*, p. 91; and Solomon, *Continental Philosophy since 1750*, p. 201.

104. Derrida, *Of Grammatology*, p. 50.

105. Lentricchia, *After the New Criticism*, p. 179.

106. Rorty chose this phrase as the title of one of his essays. In this essay, he refers to his mentor John Dewey as "a postmodernist before his time" ("Postmodernist Bourgeois Liberalism," in *Objectivity, Relativism, and Truth* [Cambridge: Cambridge University Press, 1991], p. 201).

107. Rorty, "Introduction: Pragmatism and Post-Nietzschean Philosophy," in *Essays on Heidegger and Others* (Cambridge: Cambridge University Press, 1991), p. 1.

108. Rorty repeatedly acknowledges his deep indebtedness to Dewey. See, e.g., Rorty, "Introduction: Antirepresentationalism, Ethnocentrism, and Liberalism," in *Objectivity, Relativism, and Truth*, pp. 16-17.

109. See Hilary Lawson's Introduction to "Stories about Truth," in *Dismantling Truth*, p. 4.

110. For Rorty's three-point summary of his brand of pragmatism, see "Pragmatism, Relativism, and Irrationalism," in *The Consequences of Pragmatism* (Minneapolis: University of Minnesota Press, 1982), pp. 160-66.

111. This is the central thesis of Rorty's major treatise, *Philosophy and the Mirror of Nature* (Princeton: Princeton University Press, 1979).

112. Rorty, *The Consequences of Pragmatism*, pp. xvi-xvii.

113. Rorty, "Inquiry as Recontextualization: An Anti-dualist Account of Interpretation," in *Objectivity, Relativism, and Truth*, pp. 106-7.

114. For a discussion of Rorty and Derrida, see Norris, *Derrida*, pp. 150-55; and Culler, *On Deconstruction*, p. 153.

115. Rorty, "De Man and the American Cultural Left," in *Essays on Heidegger and Others*, pp. 130-31.

116. Rorty, "Pragmatism, Relativism and Irrationalism," in *The Consequences of Pragmatism*, p. 162.

117. Rorty, "Introduction: Antirepresentationalism, Ethnocentrism, and Liberalism," p. 1.

118. Putnam, *Reason, Truth, and History* (Cambridge: Cambridge University Press, 1981), pp. 49-50.

119. See Rorty's introduction to John P. Murphy's *Pragmatism: From Peirce to Davidson* (Boulder: Westview Press, 1990), p. 2.

120. Rorty, "Solidarity or Objectivity," in *Objectivity, Relativism, and Truth*, p. 24.

121. Rorty, "Inquiry as Recontextualization," p. 106.

122. Rorty, "Pragmatism, Relativism and Irrationalism," p. 162.

123. Rorty, "Introduction: Pragmatism and Post-Nietzschean Philosophy," in *Essays on Heidegger and Others*, pp. 4-5.

124. See Rorty's introduction to *Essays on Heidegger and Others*, p. 2.

125. Rorty, *Philosophy and the Mirror of Nature*, p. 373.

126. Rorty, "Is Derrida a Transcendental Philosopher?" in *Essays on Heidegger and Others*, p. 126.

127. Rorty, "Method, Social Science, and Social Hope," in *The Consequences of Pragmatism*, p. 193.

128. Rorty, "Deconstruction and Circumvention," in *Essays on Heidegger and Others*, p. 87.

129. Rorty, "The Contingency of Community," *London Review of Books*, 24 July 1986, p. 10.

130. Rorty, in his introduction to *Essays on Heidegger and Others*, pp. 4-5.

131. Rorty, "The Contingency of Community," p. 10.

132. Rorty, "Science as Solidarity," in *Objectivity, Relativism, and Truth*, p. 39.

133. Rorty, "Is Derrida a Transcendental Philosopher?" pp. 126-27.

134. See Rorty's introduction to *Essays on Heidegger and Others*, p. 1; and *Objectivity, Relativism, and Truth*, p. 93. See also "The Contingency of Selfhood," chap. 2 of *Contingency, Irony, and Solidarity*.

135. Rorty, "Freud and Moral Reflection," in *Essays on Heidegger and Others*, p. 162.

136. Rorty, "Solidarity or Objectivity," p. 23.

137. Rorty, "Science as Solidarity," p. 11.

138. Rorty, "Pragmatism," in *The Consequences of Pragmatism*, p. 165.

139. Rorty, "Science as Solidarity," p. 38.

140. Rorty, "Freud and Moral Reflection," p. 163.

141. Rorty, "Pragmatism," p. 165.

142. Rorty, *Philosophy and the Mirror of Nature*, p. 163.

143. Rorty, *Philosophy and the Mirror of Nature*, pp. 315-17.

144. Rorty, "Pragmatism," p. 165.

145. Rorty, *Philosophy and the Mirror of Nature*, p. 377.

146. Rorty, *Philosophy and the Mirror of Nature*, pp. 315-16.

147. Rorty, *Philosophy and the Mirror of Nature*, p. 371.

148. Rorty, "Postmodernist Bourgeois Liberalism," p. 202.

149. Rorty, "De Man and the American Cultural Left," p. 133.

150. Rorty, "Science as Solidarity," pp. 16-17.

151. Rorty, "Science as Solidarity," pp. 17-18.

152. Rorty, "Pragmatism without Method," in *Objectivity, Relativism, and Truth,* p. 75.

153. Rorty, "De Man and the American Cultural Left," p. 132.

154. Rorty, "Pragmatism," p. 75.

155. Rorty, "De Man and the American Cultural Left," pp. 132-33.

Notes to Chapter 7

1. George M. Marsden, "Evangelicals, History, and Modernity," in *Evangelicalism and Modern America,* ed. George M. Marsden (Grand Rapids: William B. Eerdmans, 1984), p. 98.

2. For a discussion of evangelicalism and the future shape of evangelical theology, see my book *Revisioning Evangelical Theology* (Downers Grove, Ill.: InterVarsity Press, 1993).

3. Several evangelicals have recently expressed sympathy for postmodernism. See, e.g., Jonathan Ingleby, "Two Cheers for Postmodernism," *Third Way* 15 (May 1992): 25.

4. See Robert Bellah et al., *Habits of the Heart: Individualism and Commitment in American Life* (Berkeley and Los Angeles: University of California Press, 1985), p. 81. See also, e.g., Alasdair MacIntyre, *After Virtue,* 2d ed. (Notre Dame, Ind.: University of Notre Dame Press, 1984), p. 221.

5. E.g., George A. Lindbeck, "Confession and Community: An Israel-like View of the Church," *Christian Century,* 9 May 1990, p. 495.

6. See, e.g., Daniel A. Helminiak, "Human Solidarity and Collective Union in Christ," *Anglican Theological Review* 70 (January 1988): 37.

7. See Lindbeck, "Confession and Community," p. 495.

Works Cited

Altizer, Thomas J. J., and William Hamilton. *Radical Theology and the Death of God.* Indianapolis: Bobbs-Merrill, 1966.

Anderson, Walter Truett. *Reality Isn't What It Used to Be: Theatrical Politics, Ready-to-Wear Religion, Global Myths, Primitive Chic, and Other Wonders of the Post-modern World.* San Francisco: Harper & Row, 1990.

Arac, Jonathan (ed). *After Foucault: Humanist Knowledge, Postmodern Challenges* New Brunswick, NJ, Rutgers University Press, 1988.

Artaud, Antonin. *The Theatre and Its Double.* Trans. Victor Corti. London: Calder & Boyers, 1970.

Barber, Benjamin. "Jihad vs. McWorld." *Atlantic Monthly* (March 1992): 53-63.

Barth, John. "The Literature of Replenishment, Postmodernist Fiction." *Atlantic Monthly* (January 1980): 65-71.

Baynes, Kenneth, James Bohman, and Thomas McCarthy (eds.). *After Philosophy: End of Transformation?* Cambridge: MIT Press, 1987.

Becker, Carl L. *The Heavenly City of the Eighteenth-Century Philosophers.* New Haven: Yale University Press, 1932.

Bellah, Robert, et al. *Habits of the Heart: Individualism and Commitment in American Life.* Berkeley: University of California Press, 1985.

Benamou, Michel, and Charles Caramello (eds.). *Performance in Postmodern Culture.* Milwaukee: Center for Twentieth Century Studies, 1977.

Benjamin, Walter. *Illuminations.* Trans. Harry Zohn. Ed. Hannah Arndt. London: Fontana, 1970.

Benveniste, Emile. *Problems in General Linguistic.* Trans. Mary Elizabeth Meek. Coral Cables, FL: University of Miami Press, 1971.

Berlin, Isaiah. *The Age of Enlightenment: The Eighteenth Century Philosophers.* New York: New American Library, Mentor Books, 1956.

Burnham, Frederic B. (ed.). *Postmodern Theology: Christian Faith in a Pluralist World.* San Francisco: Harper & Row, 1989.

Clive, Geoffrey. *The Philosophy of Nietzsche.* New York: New American Library, Mentor Books, 1965.

197

Connor, Steven. *Postmodernist Culture: An Introduction to Theories of the Contemporary.* Oxford: Basil Blackwell, 1989.

Conrads, Ulrich (ed.). *Programmes and Manifestos on Twentieth-Century Architecture.* Trans. Michael Bullock. London: Lund Humphries, 1970.

Crimp, Douglas. "The Photographic Activity of Postmodernism." October 15 (Winter 1980): 91-101.

Culler, Jonathan. *On Destruction: Theory and Criticism after Structuralism.* Ithaca, NY: Cornell University Press, 1982.

Culler, Jonathan. *Structuralist Poetics: Structuralism, Linguistics, and the Study of Literature.* Ithaca, NY: Cornell University Press, 1975.

Davaney, Sheila Greeve (ed.). *Theology at the End of Modernity: Essays in Honor of Gordon D. Kaufman.* Philadelphia: Trinity Press International, 1991.

de Santillana, Giorgio. *The Age of Adventure: The Renaissance Philosophers.* New York: New American Library of World Literature, 1956.

Derrida, Jacques. *A Derrida Reader: Between the Blinds.* Ed. Peggy Kamuf. New York: Columbia University Press, 1991.

Derrida, Jacques. *Of Grammatology.* Trans. Gayatri Chakravorty Spivak. Baltimore: Johns Hopkins University Press, 1976.

Derrida, Jacques. *Margins of Philosophy.* Trans. Alan Bass. Chicago: University of Chicago Press, 1982.

Derrida, Jacques. *Positions.* Trans. Alan Bass. Chicago: University of Chicago Press, 1981.

Descartes, René. *The Philosophical Works of Descartes.* Trans. Elizabeth S. Haldane and G. R. T. Ross. New York: Dover Publications, 1931.

Dilthey, Wilhelm. *Dilthey: Selected Writings.* Ed. H. P. Rickman. Cambridge: Cambridge University Press, 1976.

Diogenes, Allen. *Christian Belief in a Postmodern World: The Full Wealth of Conviction.* Louisville: Westminster/John Knox, 1989.

Dort, Bernard. "The Liberated Performance." Trans. Barbara Kerslake. In *Modern Drama* 25 (1982).

Eagleton, Terry. *Literary Theory: An Introduction.* Minneapolis: University of Minnesota Press, 1983.

Eco, Umberto. *Postscript to "The Name of the Rose."* New York: Harcourt Brace Jovanovich, 1984.

Eribon, Didier, *Michel Foucault.* Trans. Betsy Wing. Cambridge: Harvard University Press, 1991.

Ferre, Frederick. *Hellfire and Lighting Rods: Liberating Science, Technology, and Religion.* Maryknoll. NY: Orbis Books, 1993.

Fichte, Johann. *Science of Knowledge.* Trans. Peter Heath and John Lachs. New York: Appleton-Century-Crofts, 1970.

Fiedler, Leslie A. *The Collected Essays of Leslie Fiedler.* New York: Stein & Day, 1971.

Foster, Hal (ed.). *The Anti-Aesthetic: Essays on Postmodern Culture.* Port Townsend, WA: Bay Press, 1983.

Foucault, Michel. *The Archaeology of Knowledge and the Discourse on Language.* Trans. A. M. Sheridan Smith. New York: Pantheon Books, 1972.

Foucault, Michel. *Discipline and Punish: The Birth of the Prison.* Trans. Alan Sheridan. New York: Pantheon Books, 1977.

Foucault, Michel. *The Foucault Reader.* Ed. Paul Rainbow. New York: Pantheon Books, 1984.

Foucault, Michel. *Language, Counter-Memory, and Practice: Selected Essays and Inter-*

views. Trans. Donald F. Bouchard and Sherry Simon. Ithaca, NY: Cornell University Press, 1977.

Foucault, Michel. *The Order of Things: An Archaeology of the Human Sciences.* New York: Pantheon Books, 1971.

Foucault, Michel. *Politics, Philosophy, Culture: Interview and Other Writings, 1977-1984.* Ed. Lawrence D. Kritzman. Trans. Alan Sheridan, et al. New York: Routledge, 1988.

Foucault, Michel. *Power/Knowledge: Selected Interviews and Other Writings, 1972-1977.* Ed. Colin Gordon. Trans. Colin Gordon, et al. New York: Pantheon Books, 1980.

Foucault, Michel. *The Use of Pleasure.* Volume 2 of *The History of Sexuality.* Trans. Robert Hurley. New York: Pantheon Books, 1985.

Frascina, Francis (ed.). *Pollock and After: The Critical Debate.* London: Harper & Row, 1985.

Gadamer, Hans-Georg. *Truth and Method.* Trans. Garrett Barden and John Cumming. New York: Crossroad, 1984.

Garvin, Harry R. (ed.). *Romanticism, Modernism, Post-modernism.* Lewisburg, PA: Bucknell University Press, 1980.

Gonzales, Justo L. *A History of Christian Thought.* Nashville: Abingdon Press, 1970.

Grenz, Stanley J., and Roger E. Olson. *Twentieth-Century Theology: God and the World in a Transitional Age.* Downers Grove, IL: InterVarsity, 1992.

Grenz, Stanley J. *Revisioning Evangelical Theology.* Downers Grove, IL: InterVarsity, 1992.

Griffin, David Ray. *God and Religion in the Postmodern World: Essays in Postmodern Theology.* Albany, NY: State University of New York Press, 1989.

Griffin, David Ray (ed.). *The Reenchantment of Science: Postmodern Proposals.* Albany, NY: State University of New York Press, 1988.

Grossberg, Lawrence. "The In-Difference of Television." *Screen* 28/2 (Spring 1987): 28-45.

Hampshire, Stuart. *The Age of Reason: Seventeenth Century Philosophers.* New York: New American Library, 1956.

Hassan, Ihab. *The Dismemberment of Orpheus: Toward a Postmodern Literature.* New York: Oxford University Press, 1971.

Hedwick, Klaus. "The Philosophical Presuppositions of Postmodernity." *Communio* 17/2 (Summer 1990): 167-80.

Heidegger, Martin. *Basic Writings.* Ed. David Farrell Krell. New York: Harper & Row, 1977.

Heidegger, Martin. *Being and Time.* Trans. John Macquarrie and Edward Robinson. New York: Harper & Row. 1962.

Heidegger, Martin. *Discourse on Thinking.* Trans. John M. Anderson and E. Hans Freund. New York: Harper & Row, 1966.

Heidegger, Martin. *The End of Philosophy.* Trans. Joan Stambaugh. New York: Harper & Row, 1973.

Heidegger, Martin. *An Introduction to Metaphysics.* Trans. Ralph Manheim. Garden City, NY: Doubleday/Anchor, 1961.

Heidegger, Martin. *On Time and Being.* Trans. Joan Stambaugh. New York: Harper & Row, 1972.

Heidegger, Martin. *On the Way to Language.* Trans. Peter D. Hertz. New York: Harper & Row, 1971.

Heidegger, Martin. *Poetry, Language, Thought.* Trans. Albert Hofstadter. New York: Harper & Row, 1971.

Heidegger, Martin. *The Question Concerning Technology and Other Essays.* Trans. William Lovitt. New York: Harper & Row, 1977.

Heidegger, Martin. *What Is Called Thinking?* Trans. Fred D. Wieck and J. Glenn Gray. New York: Harper & Row, 1968.

Helminiak, Daniel A. "Human Solidarity and Collective Union in Christ." *Anglican Theological Review* 70/1 (January 1988): 34-59.

Hodges, H. A. *The Philosophy of Wilhelm Dilthey.* London: Routledge & Kegan Paul, 1952. Reprint edition. Westport, CN: Greenwood, 1974.

Holdcroft, David. *Saussure: Signs, System and Arbitrariness.* Cambridge: Cambridge University Press, 1991.

Ingleby, Jonathan. "Two Cheers for Postmodernism," *Third Way* 15/4 (May 1992): 24-27.

Jencks, Charles A. *The Language of Post-Modern Architecture.* Fourth edition. London: Academy Editions, 1984.

Jencks, Charles (ed.). *The Post-Modern Reader.* New York: St. Martin's Press, 1992.

Jencks, Charles (ed.). *What is Post-Modernism?* Third edition. New York: St. Martin's Press, 1989.

Kant, Immanuel. *Fundamental Principles of the Metaphysic of Morals.* Trans. Thomas K. Abbott. Indianapolis: Bobbs-Merrill, 1949.

Kant, Immanuel. *Prolegomena to Any Future Metaphysics.* Trans. Paul Carus. Peru, IL: Open Court, 1967.

Kee, James M. "Postmodern Thinking and the Status of the Religions." *Religion and Literature* 22/2-3 (Summer-Autumn 1990): 47-60.

Kroker, Arthur, and David Cook. *The Postmodern Scene: Excremental Culture and Hyper-Aesthetics.* New York: St. Martin's Press, 1986.

Kuhn, Thomas. *The Structure of Scientific Revolutions.* Second edition. Chicago: University of Chicago Press, 1970.

Lawson, Hilary. *Reflexivity: The Post-Modern Predicament.* London: Hutchinson, 1985.

Lawson, Hilary, and Lisa Appignanesi (eds.). *Dismantling Truth: Reality in the Post-Modern World.* New York: St. Martin's Press, 1989.

Lemert, Charles C., and Garth Gillan. *Michel Foucault: Social Theory as Transgression.* New York: Columbia University Press, 1982.

Lentricchia, Frank. *After the New Criticism.* Chicago: University of Chicago Press, 1980.

Levinas, Emmanuel. *Existence and Existents.* Trans. Alphonso Lingis. The Hague: Martinus Nijhoff, 1978.

Lindbeck, George A. "Confession and Community: An Israel-like View of the Church." *Christian Century* 107/16 (May 9, 1990): 492-96.

Luecke, Richard. "The Oral, the Local and the Timely." *Christian Century* 107/27 (October 3, 1990): 875-78.

Lyotard, Jean Francois. *The Postmodern Condition: A Report on Knowledge.* Trans. Geoff Bennington and Brian Massumi. Minneapolis: University of Minnesota Press, 1984.

MacIntyre, Alasdair. *After Virtue: A Study in Moral Theory.* Second edition. Notre Dame, IN: University of Notre Dame Press, 1984.

MacIver, R. M. *The Web of Government.* New York: Macmillan, 1947.

Macksey, Richard, and Eugenio Donato (eds.). *The Structuralist Controversy: The Language of Criticism and the Sciences of Man.* Baltimore: The Johns Hopkins University Press, 1972, p. 249.

Marsden, George M. (ed.). *Evangelicalism and Modern America,* Grand Rapids, MI: Eerdmans, 1984.

Matthews, Robert. *Unravelling the Mind of God: Mysteries at the Frontier of Science.* London: Virgin Books, 1992.

McFague, Sallie. *Metaphorical Theology: Models of God in Religious Language.* Philadelphia: Fortress, 1982.

McGiffert, Arthur Cushman. *Protestant Thought before Kant.* London: Duckworth, 1911.

McHale, Brian. *Postmodernist Fiction.* New York: Methuen, 1987.

Mead, George H. *Movements of Thought in the Nineteenth Century.* Ed. Merritt H. Moore. Chicago: University of Chicago Press, 1936.

Megill, Allan. *Prophets of Extremity: Nietzsche, Heidegger, Foucault, Derrida.* Berkeley: University of California Press, 1985.

Miller, James. *The Passion of Michel Foucault.* New York: Simon & Schuster, 1993.

Nagel, Thomas. *The View from Nowhere.* New York: Oxford University Press, 1986.

Nietzsche, Friedrich. *The Complete Works of Friedrich Nietzsche.* Ed. Oscar Levy. New York: Russell & Russell, 1964.

Nietzsche, Friedrich. *The Gay Science.* Trans. Walter Kaufmann. New York: Random House, 1974.

Nietzsche, Friedrich. *The Philosophy of Nietzsche.* Trans. Thomas Common, et al. New York: Modern Library, 1937.

Nietzsche, Friedrich. *The Portable Nietzsche.* Ed. and trans. Walter Kaufmann. New York: Penguin Books, 1976.

Nietzsche, Friedrich. *The Will to Power.* Trans. Walter Kaufmann and R. J. Hollingdale. Ed. Walter Kaufmann. New York: Random House, 1967.

Norris, Christopher. *Derrida.* Cambridge: Harvard University Press, 1987.

Norris, Christopher. *What's Wrong with Postmodernism: Critical Theory and the Ends of Philosophy.* Baltimore: The Johns Hopkins University Press, 1990.

O'Hara, Daniel T. (ed.). *Why Nietzsche Now?* Bloomington, IN: Indiana University Press, 1985.

Passmore, John. *A Hundred Years of Philosophy.* London: Gerald Duckworth, 1957.

Pavis, Patrice. "The Classical Heritage of Modern Drama: The Case of Postmodern Theatre." Trans. Loren Kruger. *Modern Drama* 29/1 (March 1986): 1-22.

Pearcey, Nancey R., and Charles B. Thaxton. *The Soul of Science.* Wheaton, IL: Crossway, 1994.

Percesepe, Gary John. "The Unbearable Lightness of Being Postmodern." *Christian Scholar's Review* 20/2 (December 1990): 118-35.

Peters, Ted. "Toward Postmodern Theology." *Dialog* 24/3 (Summer 1985): 221-26.

Placher, William C. *A History of Christian Theology.* Philadelphia: Westminster, 1983.

Portoghesi, Paolo. *After Modern Architecture.* Trans. Meg Shore. New York: Rizzoli, 1982.

Postman, Neil. *Amusing Ourselves to Death: Public Discourse in the Age of Show Business.* New York: Viking Press, 1985.

Postman, Neil. *Technolopoly: The Surrender of Culture to Technology.* New York: Vintage Books, 1992.

Putnam, Hilary. *Reason, Truth and History.* Cambridge: Cambridge University Press, 1981.

Reese, Hilary. *Dictionary of Philosophy and Religion.* Atlantic Highlands, NJ: Humanities, 1980.

Risatti, Howard (ed.). *Postmodern Perspectives: Issues in Contemporary Art.* Englewood Cliffs, NJ: Prentice-Hall, 1990.

Rorty, Richard. *The Consequences of Pragmatism.* Minneapolis: University of Minnesota Press, 1982.

Rorty, Richard. "The Contingency of Community." *London Review of Books* 8/13 (24 July 1986): 10-14.

Rorty, Richard. *Essays on Heidegger and Others.* Cambridge: Cambridge University Press, 1991.

Rorty, Richard. *Objectivity, Relativism, and Truth.* Cambridge: Cambridge University Press, 1991.

Rorty, Richard. *Philosophy and the Mirror of Nature.* Princeton: Princeton University Press, 1979.

Rose, Margaret A. *The Post-Modern and the Post-Industrial: A Critical Analysis.* Cambridge: Cambridge University Press, 1991.

Ryle, Gilbert. *The Concept of Mind.* New York: Barnes & Noble, 1949.

Saussure, Ferdinand de. *Course in General Linguistics.* Ed. Charles Bally, Albert Sechehaye, and Albert Riedlinger. Trans. Wade Baskin. New York: Philosophical Library, 1959.

Sayre, Henry. "The Object of Performance: Aesthetics in the Seventies." *Georgia Review* 37/1 (1983): 169-88.

Scharlemann, Robert P. (ed.). *Theology at the End of the Century: A Dialogue on the Postmodern.* Charlottesville: University Press of Virginia, 1990.

Schleiermacher, F. D. E. *Hermeneutics: The Handwritten Manuscripts.* American Academy of Religion Texts and Translation Series #1. Ed. Heinz Kimmerle. Trans. James Duke and Jack Forstman. Atlanta: Scholars Press, 1977.

Solomon, Robert C. *Continental Philosophy since 1750: The Rise and Fall of the Self.* Oxford: Oxford University Press, 1988.

Spanos, William V. (ed.). *Martin Heidegger and the Question of Literature: Toward a Postmodern Literary Hermeneutics.* Bloomington, IN: Indiana University Press, 1979.

Spretnak, Charlene. *States of Grace: The Recovery of Meaning in the Postmodern Age.* San Francisco: Harper/San Francisco, 1991.

Taylor, Mark C. *Deconstructing Theology.* New York: Crossroad, 1982.

Tillich, Paul. *A History of Christian Thought.* New York: Simon & Schuster, 1968.

Todorov, Tzvetan. *Grammaire du Decmeron.* The Hague: Mouton, 1969.

Ulmer, Gregory L. *Applied Grammatology: Post(e)-Pedagogy from Jacques Derrida to Joseph Beuys.* Baltimore: John Hopkins University Press, 1985.

Van Gelder, Craig. "Postmodernism as an Emerging Worldview." *Calvin Theological Journal* 26/2 (1991): 412-17.

Venturi, Robert. *Learning from Las Vegas.* Revised edition. Cambridge: MIT Press, 1976.

Westphal, Merold. "The Ostrich and the Boogeyman: Placing Postmodernism." *Christian Scholar's Review* 20/2 (December 1990): 114-17.

Westphal, Merold. *Suspicion and Faith: The Religious Uses of Modern Atheism.* Grand Rapids: Eerdmans, 1993.

Wittgenstein, Ludwig. *Tractatus Logico-Philosophicus.* Trans. D. F. Pears and B. F. McGuinness. London: Routledge & Kegan Paul, 1961.

Wittgenstein, Ludwig. *Philosophical Investigations.* Trans. G. E. M. Anscombe. Oxford: Basil Blackwell, 1953.

Wolterstorff, Nicholas. *Reason Within the Bound of Religion.* Second edition. Grand Rapids: Eerdmans, 1984.

Wyschogrod, Edith. *Saints and Postmodernism: Revisioning Moral Philosophy.* Chicago: University of Chicago Press, 1990.

Young, Robert (ed.). *Untying the Text: A Post-Structuralist Reader.* London: Routledge & Kegan, Paul, 1981.

Index

203